Life in Every
Breath

Life in Every Breath

ESTER BLENDA

Reporter, Adventurer, Pioneer

FATIMA BREMMER

TRANSLATED BY GLORIA NNEOMA ONWUNEME

 AMAZON **CROSSING**

Leonard and Sally, I dedicate this book to you.

Contents

Author's Note   xi

1. Sweden's Most Famous Maid   3

2. The Terrible Child   32

3. The Boy, Elin Wägner, and the League   55

4. Bansai and the Sharp Hatpin   77

5. Peasant Uprisings and Forbidden Letters   95

6. Ester Becomes Ester Blenda   106

7. The Nomadic Teacher   129

8. With the Tent Folk of the Far North   144

9. A Summer with Elin Wägner   172

10. War Hero and Author of Girls' Books   202

11. On Muleback across the Andes   235

12. Train Hopping in America   256

13. In the Shadow of a Volcano   293

14. A Farm of One's Own   324

15. The Catastrophe   354

Epilogue   369

Acknowledgments   373

Sources   375

About the Author   431

About the Translator   433

AUTHOR'S NOTE

This book describes certain events, environments, places, and people in detail. This has been made possible thanks to a large number of articles in various magazines and books, some written by Ester Blenda Nordström herself and others found in the biographies about, and memoirs by, people in her immediate circle. A portion of the information came from letters preserved in the manuscript collections of organizations such as the National Library of Sweden, the National Resource Library for Gender Studies in Gothenburg, and the National Archives of Sweden.

However, my primary sources for these meticulous descriptions have been the extensive range of private correspondence and photographic collections. Ester Blenda Nordström had sent or received most of these letters. The relatives who now own the material generously granted me access to the letters and other documents, enabling me to create a profile that is as complete and accurate as possible, more than half a century after Ester Blenda Nordström's death. They have also contributed by sharing their personal memories, documents, and other potentially relevant information.

All direct quotes have been translated from books or news reports.

I have therefore taken few literary liberties; I simply have not needed to. I have had so much information at my disposal, except when it comes to a particular aspect of Nordström's life—her involvement with Carin Wærn Frisell (married name Dahlbeck, then Hellström). She was a central figure in Ester Blenda Nordström's life, but she lived just outside of the public eye. The information available about her private life is therefore very scarce and limited to public archives, a single newspaper article, and memories shared by relatives.

By all accounts, Ester Blenda Nordström and Carin Wærn Frisell were lovers, but at a time when homosexuality was both punishable by law and classified as a mental disorder, following one's heart was far from the obvious course of action. This is possibly, or even probably, why there is so little information about their mutual love. I have managed to gather bits and pieces over the course of several years: letters from joint trips, a short love poem, travel diaries, and letters to friends and relatives in which they wrote about each other . . . Photographs speak to the strength of these feelings just as powerfully as the written evidence does. Several photographs portray Ester Blenda Nordström and Carin Wærn Frisell together through all stages of adult life, and many of these images are poignantly tender and intimate.

This body of material has given me the opportunity to re-create moments in the book that were special to these women, as far as I have understood them. But above all, this collection of fragments has revealed the contours of a lifelong relationship that is both beautiful and deeply moving.

Stockholm, November 1948

She walks around the tiny apartment. Her legs know where to go, even though the objects and the furniture are not her own. But it is, in a way, her home too. She knows exactly how things are organized in the kitchen cabinets and drawers; she personally sorted the pile of receipts lying on the desk, held together with a large clip. She knows exactly where the favorite nightgown hangs, the pink silk one. She would know at once if the armchair were at a different angle or if someone had moved the two black antique chairs by so much as an inch. Then the scent, *that* scent that every home has, unique to itself. It's also in her own clothes.

Only the silence is new. The Swedish state-run telecommunications agency has terminated the subscription for number 31 93 93. The name on the door will soon be replaced by a new one. The owners of the building have a long list of people desperate for an apartment.

She looks at everything for the last time. The typewriter on the solid mahogany desk, the rows of books, the accordion, the violin, and the lute with the pearl-embroidered strap, the vanity that's been passed down, the beautiful glass chandelier with four lights . . . Soon, it will all be scattered among Ester Blenda's relatives.

The gold cigarette case with an engraved Lapland motif will apparently be going to a nephew. She thinks of the number of times she's seen Ester Blenda open it, place a cigarette between her lips, light it up, and hungrily take the first puff. Then let it hang there, softly, in the corner of her mouth, while digging in the dirt or reading a book. The walls and furniture still smell strongly of smoke.

She looks for the letters before she leaves. She takes back her own words and puts them in her bag. Then Carin shuts the door to Vikingagatan 34 E.

CHAPTER 1

Sweden's Most Famous Maid

Walpurgis Night 1914. Her gaze lifted from the train window and settled on her hands. The brown cotton gloves were brand new; this was the first time she'd worn them. The gold band on her ring finger gleamed under the thin fabric. She couldn't remember his name. Svensson? Andersson? It took a few seconds to come back to her. Karlsson. Bernhard Karlsson. She was still annoyed at the silly name she'd chosen, but it had already been engraved: "Your Bernhard, 12/24/12."

Ester Nordström took off her gloves. Wrung her hands, inspected her narrow fingers and palms critically. She'd deep cleaned a car engine before leaving. Deliberately let the oil and dirt seep into the pores and lines of her skin.

She had hoped that it would make more of a difference. They still looked too delicate, too much like a city girl's hands, spared from physical labor. Would they blow her cover?

Anxiety danced in her chest. She couldn't concentrate. Her thoughts raced as the rain pattered against the train window and formed long irregular channels in the dirty brown coating. Outside, several Stockholm landmarks and neighborhoods passed by her window . . . Next to her seat was a bunch of flowers from friends who had just waved her off at Stockholm Central Station. They waved their arms, laughed, and screamed as the train slowly began to roll south.

It had felt like such a fun idea at first. An adventure. And Stomberg, editor at the national daily *Svenska Dagbladet*, had been instantly intrigued when Ester told him about her unique holiday plans, having caught a whiff of a scintillating story with his experienced nose for news.

Ester was his bravest reporter. She did the unexpected, and the readers loved it. Her reports and columns, all signed "Bansai," had become topics of conversation all around the country. Among other journalists, she was known for being outspoken and bold. Ester liked it. It was a role that appealed to her.

Instant employment for
A MAID
Accustomed to performing household chores and
willing and able to milk cows.
Taninge Farm, General Delivery Nyköping

Farmer Anton Holtz's job ad for a new maid at Jogersta
North Farm; excerpt from *Ett pennskaft som piga—svar
av Bonn i Taninge* [*A Newswoman for a Maid—Response
by a Farmer in Taninge*], by Anton Holtz.

It was sheer coincidence that had brought together this particular advertisement, maid vacancy, and southbound train on which the twenty-three-year-old Ester Nordström was sitting, on her way to Sörmland County, not feeling quite as confident and excited as she would have liked. There were countless similar vacancies around the country; it had been simply a matter of choosing one of the many farmers in desperate need of female servants. Ester herself had written articles about the so-called maid problem; it was a topic that had already been hotly debated for years. In one of her interviews, she had quoted a woman saying that "it's no wonder that young women don't want to become maids nowadays. They're all basically forced to become slaves." She had also been closely following the Emigration Commission, a significant undertaking that politicians began after the Swedish exodus. Between 1851 and 1910, nearly one million Swedes had left for the other side of the Atlantic, in pursuit of happiness and a new life. Many were young women of working age. They preferred to move to America or take up jobs in city factories than work on some farm in their own home country. The commission had, among other things, established that emigration "deprives the agricultural industry of its required workforce."

According to the Swedish Master and Servant Act of 1833, farmers had the power to independently decide on what "suitable" working hours meant and could exercise the same rights over their employees as they could over their own family. They even had the legal right to use corporal punishment on servants under the age of sixteen. And yet, the commission remained unable to identify a clear cause for the dire shortage of maids. It had been blamed on everything from modern notions of equality to the socialist movement. A comparison of the treatment of maids in Swedish and American households had shown that Swedish housewives were overly strict whereas affluent US families welcomed Swedish maids with open arms.

Ester had decided to do what no other Swedish reporter had done before: dressed as a maid, she was going to take a job on a farm and see for herself why young women were fleeing these maid vacancies. She had to become one of them in order to be able to report their reality as faithfully as possible.

The train rolled along. It was the beginning of a journey that would make Ester Nordström Sweden's most famous journalist and lead her out into the world on near-impossible adventures. In time, she would go on to use her pen to help overthrow a Swedish government and save thousands from starvation in the Finnish Civil War. She would live in a Sami collective in Lapland for six months and ride a mule on the narrow, dusty mountain trails between Argentina and Chile. She would walk around the ruins left behind by a devastating earthquake in Japan and travel like the train hoppers in America, clinging to the brake rods under a rushing freight train.

She would go on to fight for women's suffrage alongside Sweden's most prominent feminists and suffrage activists and take part in an expedition lasting several years among wild bears and rumbling volcanoes in Siberia. As a pioneering motorcyclist, she would show the world that women, too, could ride and love fast vehicles. The girls' book series created by Ester Blenda Nordström would not only be widely celebrated, it would change the entire genre and serve as clear inspiration for the greatest works of world-famous children's author Astrid Lindgren. In the end, the future maid would even become a farmer running her own farm.

It all started here.

The dime novel she'd bought to pass the time on her four-hour journey remained untouched in her handbag when the train rolled into the small town of Nyköping. She sensed it was her employer as soon as she saw the man on the carriage fastened to a yellow mare. Farmer Anton Holtz gave her a firm handshake in the courtyard just outside the train station and passed her the reins. There was no room for hesitation. Ester obediently held on to the mare as he went to get her large tin suitcase filled with never-worn cotton dresses, sturdy socks, and shawls. She'd left her dresses made of exclusive fabrics back home in her apartment wardrobe, along with her beautiful hats stacked in boxes.

There was complete silence in the carriage as they rode to a small café where Holtz ceremoniously offered his new maid a welcoming cup. Ester didn't take any of the cookies on the platter until her host encouraged her to for a third time. She chose the smallest one, dunked it in her coffee, and quickly popped it in her mouth. She then noted, with relief, that Holtz seemed pleased with her conduct.

Then she went for a refill; this time, after swift deliberation, she drank the coffee from her saucer. There was no napkin. She wiped her lips off with her hands before getting ready to step out into the cool April air and back into the carriage. It was getting dark. As they left the built-up part of town behind, Ester thought of the urban festivities she would have ordinarily joined on a night like this: the sing-along at the Skansen open-air museum, the delirious cheering of students, crackling bonfires, dancing at the Hasselbacken restaurant . . . Stockholm suddenly felt infinitely far away.

Her plain brown coat was long but far too thin, and her hands had already started turning blue from the cold. Her eyes looked over the freshly plowed black fields with muddy soil and foliage that shone wet from dew. She inhaled the scents. The air smelled like childhood.

> "Taninge," he said after yet another turn as he pointed to a small farm between budding birches and fruit trees.
>
> "Ah yes, Taninge," I replied, and instantly felt that the clock was now running. It was time to get serious, and to work.
>
> From *En piga bland pigor* [*A Maid among Maids*].

Taninge was Ester's chosen pseudonym for Jogersta North Farm, the site of her experiment. It had a typical farmhouse, painted red with white trim. There were crescent windows on the gables and mullioned windows on the upstairs glass veranda facing the Kila Valley. It looked much older than the barn they had passed before reaching the foyer.

Ida, the *husmor*, or the woman of the house, greeted her on the stairs with a solid handshake and a hearty smile. She opened the door to a large room with a massive, currently lit fireplace. In complete silence, at least six farmers' wives, eight children, dogs, cats, relatives, and other visiting acquaintances from neighboring plots of land watched Ester.

Everyone wanted to see the new maid at Jogersta North Farm, the largest and most important farm in the area with its fifty-six acres of arable land, twenty cows, four or five horses, pigs, chickens, young cattle, and one bull.

Ester gripped her cheap handbag tightly. Her face and neck burned red; her heart beat even harder. She was of a slender build—probably not very impressive for a newly arrived maid. In fact, not a single part of her frame stood out as robust. Her neck was long and narrow. Her wrists were thin, as was her burning-cinder-colored hair; she repeatedly brushed back the flyaways. Freckles clustered under her light blue eyes.

The children giggled and shoved each other. Ester kept the coat and the ill-fitting hat on while she drank yet another cup of coffee and answered polite questions about her journey.

Later, in her first article, she went on to describe how the room they were sitting in had already been prepared for bedtime. How the rough, hard-scrubbed floor was covered with rag rugs in beautiful colors. One of the dogs lurched forward, and Ester gratefully welcomed him and the chance to preoccupy herself with stroking his fur.

The other maid in the house, Sigrid, had thick brown hair tied up in a topknot, and blue eyes. Her arms were rough and muscular. The two young women were briefly introduced to each other; the coffee counter awaited them. Ester dipped her hands into the warm water and got to work. The kitchen was small and dark. Traditional blood bread and dried rye bread hung on poles off the grease-blackened ceiling.

The first morning started with Ester being yelled at. She set the table for the boys' morning coffee and brought out spoons. Sigrid shook her head, calling Ester stupid for not knowing what was meant to go on the table on a regular weekday morning. Spoons were not included.

It had been only a few minutes since they'd both gotten up from the narrow pullout sofa they shared. In addition to reprimanding Ester for her table-setting choices, Sigrid had already managed to get the coffeepot going, make a bed, and reassemble the sofa by the time four pairs of boots started thundering down the attic stairs. The farmhands, all men, were on their way down. It was just before five in the morning on May 1—Ester's first real working day on the farm.

She had been given the task of handling bedding for the rest of the week while Sigrid would make the coffee. The maids were not to pour themselves anything to drink until all the farmhands had been served.

> The kitchen is filled with the sound of coffee sipped through sugar cubes. Everyone drinks from saucers, and the cups are placed next to the table where they leave wet light brown rings on the wax cloth. Two cups of coffee, with no bread, aren't exactly filling; with a lingering feeling of hunger, I tie the scarf around my head and follow Anna* to go milk cows. The air is cold and raw; the rain strikes my face, and the wind blows sharp and icy over the long plain that slowly appears like fog behind the veil of moisture. We run down the long hill to the barn; the milk pails rattle with a crystal clear, hard sound; and the heavy milk churns hit our legs with their sharp edges.

> From *En piga bland pigor* [*A Maid among Maids*].

> *The maid Sigrid was given the pseudonym Anna when Ester Blenda wrote about her experiences on the farm.

Twenty cows were waiting to be milked. Ester gulped heavily. She thought she had prepared so well for this role. She'd thought about how she would talk, behave, the chores she would be given. Now, she was seated on a milking stool in front of a huge cow and had to make every movement seem second nature. People could be deceived; cows could not. Ester knew this all too well. They were sensitive to unfamiliar hands and might refuse to let down any milk. If things got bad enough, they could even take to kicking and screaming.

Ester photographed during her time as a milkmaid in Sörmland.

The shiny, well-groomed animals impatiently stomped around their stalls on the clean-swept cement floor. Sigrid was sitting on her own stool a bit farther down, humming a polka tune to the rhythm of her hand movements. Ester took hold of the cow's teats. When she realized that she actually remembered how to make the lukewarm milk stream down from the udder, she sighed with relief. The sharp smell of manure, the stillness, and the barn's warmth caused a sense of unexpected calm to spread within her.

Two hours later, her arms felt numb and swollen. Her hands ached, and the first signs of blisters made themselves known on her fingers. They moved on to the pigsty. Now, the pigs and chickens had to be fed. Mixing up the thick mass of potatoes, wheat bran, and grits took work. Hunger pierced Ester's belly. A while later, once the farmhands had left the table, the maids had their own breakfast. Herring, potatoes, and whole-meal rye bread with margarine had never tasted so good. To wash it down, they drank the cream from separated skimmed milk. Ester's cup had a crack in it.

Ida entered the room and smiled wide. She sat down at the large folding table and poured herself a cup. She was carrying her youngest in her arms; the girl was only eight months old. The infant was fed with mash consisting of a chewed-up cookie mixed with coffee, while the new maid was asked whether the cows had been difficult to milk that morning, and whether Ester also had potatoes and herring for breakfast back home. Ester mumbled her answers, trying to speak and express herself the way she figured a maid might.

Ester's replies were her first lies of the day, and they were quickly followed by more, because Ida kept asking questions. About the division of labor on the farm where Ester claimed to have grown up; about whether she'd ever visited Stockholm or been for a ride in a real car.

Ester's motorcycle was still in Stockholm, and she could borrow her father's big car, an open-top De Dion-Bouton, whenever she liked. His livery-clad driver took them wherever they wanted to go, but Ester also loved sitting behind the wheel and cruising down the street alongside the horse-drawn carriages. She always fixed punctured tires herself and never hesitated to have a look under the hood whenever the engine suddenly ground to a halt.

> At first, you never really know what exactly you're rooting around to find in the engine, but you look so impressive to fellow passengers. When you then finally pull up on the crank after a while and it starts roaring again, you smile modestly but sagely, and you sort of mutter to yourself about how "why yes, that *would* be the problem."

> From the article "Cars I've known," published in the weekly magazine *Vecko-Journalen*, no. 41 (1928).

Ester always attracted attention, not least when she was on the motorcycle; that was where she was the happiest. Her excessive speeding had already won her several fines; once, she was stopped and penalized for "being a threat to road traffic."

A woman on a motorcycle was a rare sight. If one believes several of her friends who, much later, in various interviews and memoirs described the commotion she caused by getting herself a dark green Royal Enfield, Ester might've been the very first in Sweden. The motorcycle was launched with a powerful slogan: "Made like a gun; runs like a bullet."

On her motorcycle, a Royal Enfield, around 1914.

They were used by the Russian state, the British military, *and* the suffragettes. The women's voting rights activists attached signs with political messages to sidecars that they could buy as an add-on and rode around the streets of London. But in Sweden, the motorcycle was still only a luxury means of transportation, or simply used for sport by a limited group—usually young, well-to-do men.

When riding her bike, she always wore a leather helmet, sports trousers, leather gloves, and a sturdy black coat with a belt at the waist and wide lapels. The boots were black, knee high, and had adjustable straps that could be tightened around her narrow calves. Her waist was narrow, too, but Ester never tightened her coat belt. If it got really cold, she would change into a light brown coat with white teddy fur lining and a matching white teddy hat.

She had herself photographed in her new gear. In the pictures, she posed confidently on the motorcycle with her hands on the handlebars and a big smile on her face.

The Holtz couple had five children. The whole family slept in one of the house's five rooms; the room was dubbed "the chamber," three children and two dogs in one big bed, and Ida and Anton on their own couch. "May God protect your marital union at all times," read the ornate canvas board above it. Ester noticed that the towel hanger in there also had canvas embroidery on it, but the fine towel on the hook remained unused. No one in the household was allowed to use it—not even the master himself.

She wondered how to go about washing herself and brushing her teeth in the morning. No one in the house seemed to make any effort to cleanse themselves, neither body nor mouth. At one point, when no one was watching, she sneaked out the door and walked down the bumpy path leading to the barn where the water pump stood. The heavy clogs sank into the dirt. Sharp pebbles found their way in and immediately got stuck under the soles of her feet. Ester rinsed off with rapid movements; the water was icy cold. She froze as soon as she heard Sigrid ask whether she'd lost her mind or simply thought herself "so fancy" that she needed to wash herself on a regular Thursday. Before she could even come up with a response, Sigrid had gone back inside.

Ester exhaled. She had learned her lesson: no more washing herself before the weekend.

By 9:00 a.m., they had already served breakfast to the four resident loggers and the children. All rooms except the parlor—the family's pride and joy with its sky-blue panel sofa, desk, and walnut chest of drawers with a mirror—were thoroughly swept and dusted.

Next, Ester was urged to sit at the loom. The house needed new sheets. She carefully stepped on the squeaky treadles. On the couch behind her lay the master of the house, wearing a leather vest and stockings, and reading a copy of the weekly magazine *Vecko-Journalen*. A few years later, Ester would become one of that very same newspaper's most important and prominent writers, a nationally recognized and acclaimed star reporter traveling around the world and reporting back to Sweden. But for now, she was seated at a loom on a farm in the depths of Sörmland County, pedaling and beating with all her might, and thanking the gods for the little she already knew about weaving.

The master's snoring was soon heard between the loom's thumping. Ester noticed how tired she herself was and fantasized about what it would be like to get to sleep. She soon discovered that Anton Holtz was very comfortable on that couch and spent a lot of time lying on it, much like then. She noted that another favorite pastime of his was the drinking of *kaffekask*, a beverage with equal parts coffee and brandy.

Lunch was served at noon. Pork and potatoes filled enormous platters. Ida cooked all the food herself and watched contentedly as her four farmhands and two maids emptied the platters. The food was simple, but she did not skimp on portion sizes.

Sigrid giggled with delight at the farmhands as they pinched her arms and legs every now and then. Ester could see it all—she even caught glimpses of what went on under the table.

After the meal, the farmhands would retreat for an hour-long nap. For the maids, the work continued. The forest workers had to be fed, then the children; the dishes had to be washed, and the house needed sweeping once more. The chickens and pigs had to be fed; the milk was to be separated and measured for potential buyers; water had to be pumped into a seemingly endless number of copper buckets, then carried up to a large barrel by the house. The barrel needed daily refilling. Ester counted: filling up the tank took at least fifteen return trips, all while carrying the heavy yoke over the back of her neck.

Running the house also took an endless amount of firewood. This likewise had to be carried into the house, along with potatoes that they dug up in the field a good distance from the farm. Sigrid, who never seemed to stand still, informed her that they were to bake bread and cookies every four days. Ida said nothing, but had a disapproving look on her face when Ester stopped to catch her breath.

The afternoon coffee had to be ready for half past three. The scent from the thick slices of wheat bread that Ester cut was very tempting, and not just because the bread tasted so good. Afternoon coffee signified a deeply welcome, and sanctioned, break. There was no skimping on this occasion, either. The strong coffee was poured into cups until they overflowed and filled the saucers. Thick cream, served in a large bowl on the table, was available to all.

Ester's body ached. She ate and drank with dedication alongside the rest of the servants. The smell of wet clothes and sour boots filled the room.

With renewed strength, they took on the evening round of milking. Getting milk out of the firm udders was a bit easier this time. The girls worked quietly and efficiently before having dinner at the folding table. Ester was just as famished as she'd been before afternoon coffee.

At 9:00 p.m., the fatigue was paralyzing. The pain in her feet verged on intolerable; large water blisters stung the soles of her feet. Her shoulders ached, sore from the pressure of the yoke. Her hands burned. She fell asleep instantly.

The sofa that Sigrid and Ester shared in the maids' chamber was narrow and creaked loudly from the slightest movement. But the young women's sleep was heavy and deep. They woke up the next morning in a sea of feather bolsters, quilts, and sheepskin blankets. Duvet covers and pillowcases, which maids used to make Ester's bed back in Stockholm, were nowhere to be found here.

She didn't notice the vermin until the morning—the black dots on the bedsheet and the large lice crawling around on the couch. "But you can't get too hung up on all that" was the advice from Sigrid, who also turned out to have a head full of them. "A bedbug is no big deal, and head lice can't be helped. But fleas, yuck! They're the worst, and you never know where you have them," she said in the heavy rural dialect of the region.

She was already up and about, with her hair messily hanging down her shoulders. The small room was modestly furnished. A chest of drawers with a mirror on top, a chair, a dented tin sink with brownish, grainy soap. A set of blinds—with a motley pattern in brown, red, and various shades of blue—hung from the window.

Ester had placed a portrait of Bernhard, her sham fiancé, as prominently as she possibly could on the chest of drawers. The man in the photograph was actually an old childhood friend; she had used a spectacular frame to give the impression of tender, sincere feelings for him. This clever move was immediately successful: Sigrid was deeply impressed.

Ester looked at her hands. Barely thirty hours had passed since she'd anxiously examined them on the train. Now, they were crooked, swollen, and filled with small stinging wounds that would not heal for the entire duration of her time on the farm. She tied her scarf and put her apron back on. The cows were waiting in the barn.

He stuck a muddy boot forward, with loose laces. Impatiently instructed her to tie them. She began to seethe within, but then she clenched her jaw, got down on her knees, and silently tied the boy's shoelaces.

The Holtz children regularly put Ester's patience to the test. She generally loved children and couldn't get enough of her brother Frithiof's two kids back home—Kjell who was six, and toddler Anne-Marie who was only two. Anton and Ida's baby would usually sit on Ester's lap while they had their meals, and she enjoyed the babbling; she even enjoyed when the baby pinched her cheeks, hard. But the four older siblings were spoiled and unbearable. They screamed, shouted, commandeered, hit, kicked, and pulled. This was, at least, how Ester would subsequently describe and present them in her articles and in her hugely successful book about her time as a maid. As soon as they woke up in the morning, they would shout out orders for coffee to be served in bed, on trays. Preferably with something to dip in it. And if their orders didn't turn up quickly enough, they'd join up to chant, "Coffeecoffeecoffeecoffee!"

The tray was key; mere cups and saucers wouldn't do. If Ester or Sigrid forgot to bring a tray, with all the pressure of their work, a child's hand would emerge from the sheets and shove so hard that the hot drink would spill all over the bed. This in turn would create more work for the maids, and more laundry to join the heap of dirty baby clothes and diapers that needed to be washed a couple of times a week. The sheets on the maids' couch were usually changed only on major holiday weekends.

Ester had kept a low profile ever since Ida's cross-examination about her family, and ever since Sigrid caught her by the water pump. She focused on trying to learn all the daily routines. She had carefully copied Sigrid in everything from her dialect to her technique of scrubbing her face with soap on Saturdays without subsequently rinsing it, to make it as shiny as possible.

But at the same time, Ester tried to observe everything that was said and done on the farm, without being too intrusive or asking questions that a maid wasn't supposed to ask. She tried to memorize almost everything that she saw and heard, from the most mundane chores to

differences in how maids and farmhands were treated. She thought of herself as a camera capturing reality. And all the while, in this tiny village in Sörmland, people were completely unaware that Bansai, one of the capital city's most daring reporters, was currently paying them a visit. That pseudonym still meant nothing to them. The topics of conversation around the Jogersta North Farm table included neither world nor national news. Newspapers weren't things that people in the house spent money on, with the exception of the odd copy of *Vecko-Journalen*—or a lottery ticket whenever there was a huge jackpot out. Everyone—the farmhands, the forest workers, and the Holtz couple—would then get involved. Even Sigrid would invest some money for a quarter of a ticket. She dreamed of buying a velocipede.

During a walk, when Sigrid shared that she had used only ten kronor of her salary in the last six months to be able to buy a single ticket in the near future, Ester saw her chance to ask Sigrid what she earned. Sigrid replied, "One hundred eighty kronor a year," and went on to say that she also planned to buy a summer coat and a hat a little later. Ester was shocked to realize that this amounted to only fifteen kronor a month. Their working days were at least sixteen hours long, and they had only a few hours off each week.

Ester had discussed the issue of salary many times with her female journalist colleagues in Stockholm. They were few in number, barely a dozen, and they earned about half as much as the men. The dissatisfaction had been brewing for several years, but even they would get around 150 kronor a month. She looked at Sigrid with a mixture of pity and complete admiration.

The first weeks passed quickly with long, strenuous days that were impossible to tell apart. On Sundays, the maids would get two hours off between lunchtime cleaning and afternoon coffee preparations. Then they would walk side by side down the stream, extra tired after going to the Saturday dance, the highlight of the week. Ester instantly fell in love with the village's Saturday dances; they were fast paced, and they didn't stop until her legs started to go numb. Ester enjoyed being physically exhausted, a state she had remained in since coming to the farm. In the exhaustion, there was no room for anxiety, restlessness, and buzzing thoughts. Life on the farm was much harder than she had really appreciated before she left her comfortable Stockholm life—but the reward was that life felt simple and uncomplicated.

They'd usually kneel by the washboards down by the water. But on this Sunday in May, they simply dropped into the grass and looked up at the sky and the clouds floating past. A clear early-summer sun was blazing above. Then Ester began playing the harmonica, and Sigrid danced to the beat. In her hand, Sigrid held an embroidery project that she never completed, despite picking it up every night when they would light the lamp in the maids' chamber.

> Sometimes I go to bed, before she collapses onto the sofa, and then I wake up in the middle of the night and see her sitting with her arms on the table and her head resting in them, while the lamp burns and smokes and the doily has

long since disappeared from her consciousness. I can lie there and look at the back of her neck, where her hair lies heavy and shiny on her head that in turn lies awkwardly and uncomfortably on her red, tanned arms, and I am seized by a sense of pity, a sense of sympathy so strong that I for a moment feel I would want to do just about anything to give this dead-tired, strong, hardworking girl a day of complete rest and tranquility, just a single morning of long and sweet sleep.

From *En piga bland pigor* [*A Maid among Maids*].

The idea of women's suffrage turned out to be completely novel and entirely impossible to Sigrid. She laughed when Ester first brought it up, saying that she "might as well wish to become king."

Ester couldn't let go of the issue; she made a new attempt to explain by highlighting the injustice of how farmhands were so much better off than the maids, and also paid more. This made Sigrid stop and think. A few minutes later, Sigrid was both angry and a newly converted advocate for women's suffrage. They both got Ida on board; she was attracted to the idea of voting rights, an entirely new concept to her as well. Anton and the farmhands mocked them for believing in such an absurd idea. As Ester heard them laugh, she felt as if the outside world didn't exist in Jogersta. She had almost forgotten it herself and had begun to envision how her future life would consist of milking at dawn, then having dinner, then milking at dusk; this routine would be broken up only by Saturday dances and some Sunday rest.

In order to stay tethered to the life she once had, the impostor maid would sometimes sneak her way to the house phone and secretly call home. As soon as she thought no one could see or hear her, she talked about her escapades and adventures, about the people and the animals. She hadn't noticed that Verner, another employee at the farm, had sneaked up on her and was eavesdropping. Verner confronted her, and Ester did everything she could to persuade him not to expose her. He kept quiet. But she soon realized that she needed a plan for how to get out of working on the farm by the end of the month so that she could return to her everyday life and her real job. She was reminded of this life, and struck with a sense of intense homesickness, when a car suddenly showed up in the barnyard one day. Ester, having come straight from the pigsty with emptied pig buckets hanging off the yoke on her shoulders, was summoned to the gathering of servants and children who stood admiring the spectacular sight. The head farmhand wanted to impress and to let everyone know that the car could reach a speed of six miles an hour. He showed the start button under the glass cover. Sigrid, who had also come out onto the farm, was terrified and screamed, begging him not to press it.

Ester accidentally laughed at the thought of a car racing with the no-longer-cocky servant behind the wheel and was immediately challenged to start the vehicle with the promise of one hundred kronor should she succeed. She tied the headscarf a bit tighter under her chin, feeling everyone's bemused looks.

> I take one step toward the crank, bend forward to grab it, but release it again to see if the contact is on, turn it the right way, and mean to start it, but then I straighten myself and quietly say, with an incredible stinging within me, "You can keep your hundred bucks, Erik. You cannot expect a farm maid to know how to get one of these machines to work."
>
> I then grab my buckets and flee from the temptation, while the laughter follows me all the way to the courtyard. Once there, I thank the gods for striking down the demon of pride within me and stopping me in good time. Though

God knows it was hard to hold back with all those grinning faces around me.

From *En piga bland pigor* [*A Maid among Maids*].

Ester carefully instructed her sister in a letter. She was to call the farm's telephone, in the chamber, then ask to speak to the maid Ester to give her the terrible news that their aunt had died. She was to have died suddenly, leaving their mother faced with great difficulties managing the farm back home without Ester's help. The story was completely made up, from start to finish, and was meant to be dramatic enough to liberate Ester from her temporary employment as a maid.

In practice, the conversation turned into quite the challenge. It unfortunately coincided with a visit by Anton and Ida's neighbors; the *kaffekask* flowed generously. The mood was light. Her sister couldn't help but make fun of her. Ester struggled to appear horrified by the phone call. She threw in a few dismayed reactions and exclamations in front of Anton and his guests, who had now fallen silent and were staring at her. Later, Ester wrote about how she had been dangerously close to bursting into hysterical laughter.

Three days later, her bags were packed. It was time to say goodbye to Jogersta North Farm. Anton lay asleep in the farmhands' chamber and mumbled something while clumsily squeezing Ester's outstretched hand. She saved the farewell from Sigrid for last. The parting was harder than she'd imagined. With a choked-up voice, Ester said that Sigrid could keep anything she'd been careless enough to leave behind.

Several of her finest blouses were on Sigrid's hangers in the maids' chamber. A small brooch, which Ester had often caught her new friend glancing at jealously, was tucked away in a hidden corner, but visible enough to be spotted.

Motor vehicles were a lifelong passion for Ester. Seen here behind the wheel of her father's car, a De Dion-Bouton.

Sigrid gave Ester a photograph of herself posing in the nicest part of the house, wearing a blouse and a dark skirt, her back straight and her shiny hair neatly combed. "A picture to remember me by. For Ester Nordström from Sigrid Nilsson." Neither of them knew then that only a few months would pass before they'd be back in touch. But by that point, Ester would be facing a hurt, angry, and disappointed Sigrid.

The tears burned behind her eyelids as she left the farm and traveled back to Stockholm and her place at the editorial office. She was already gripped by doubt.

> When I came back, I had no desire to write at all [. . .] It
> was only the promise of an additional month of vacation,

as compensation for the month as a maid, that drove me to do it. Such an offer was, of course, impossible to resist.

From an interview with Ester Blenda Nordström in *Dagens Nyheter*, by the journalist signed "Clementine," May 17, 1931.

The tales that began with the article below seem to have been written under one of *Svenska Dagbladet*'s famous pseudonyms, Bansai.

A young female journalist hides behind the mask of Bansai. Instead of enjoying a traditional holiday, she has applied for employment as a maid on a farm in Sörmland. She has thus passed a month there without anyone around her knowing that her presence is nothing more than a performance.

For such a whim to strike a young lady may, at first glance, seem an instance of pure eccentricity. However, it has been steered by other motives that *Svenska Dagbladet* wishes to briefly state here. Year after year, it was becoming increasingly difficult to acquire the required female workforce for farm labor. Why was this the case? The answer may be of utmost importance to our agriculture. The answer would also likely be best offered by whosoever was personally involved and sought to have their eyes opened to the surrounding influencing factors while under the weight of such toil. The author herself will give an account of her experiences below and in the following issues. Hence, we give her the floor and invite readers to

an interesting and perhaps instructive study of how a farm
girl lives.

From an article in *Svenska Dagbladet*, June 28, 1914.

The headline couldn't be missed as it ran across four columns: "A
month as a maid on a farm in Sörmland." The article was illustrated
with two pictures of Ester at work, wearing a headscarf and apron. One
was staged on her return. The other had been borrowed from Anton
Holtz, who still had no idea that the photo he'd sent along with his
maid on her way back home had now been published in a national
newspaper—a paper in which he would personally be described in
detail in a series of articles throughout the summer.

Bansai's articles transported readers from their wicker chairs, uphol-
stered armchairs, and plush sofas to the Sörmland County farmhouse.
They sensed the smells and the flavors, heard the language, felt how the
yoke cut into their shoulders and how their hands ached. They went
back and forth between laughing and sinking into somber reflection.
The articles were personal and revealing, with a humorous edge. No
journalist in the country had done anything like this before. Swedish
investigative reporting was born.

Editor Stomberg and the rest of the editorial staff at *Svenska
Dagbladet* were prepared to receive some strong reactions. That was why
they'd decided to write the explanatory text about the publication and
talk about the reporter who was hidden behind the pseudonym Bansai.
The fact that Bansai was also a woman made the whole affair even more
scintillating; the vast majority of newspaper readers still believed that
the journalistic profession was for men only.

On June 28, 1914, the day of the publication of the first article, two
gunshots were fired in Sarajevo. Heir to the Austro-Hungarian throne
Franz Ferdinand, who had been driven around in the Bosnian capital
in an open car, was shot in the neck by Bosnian Serbian revolutionary

Gavrilo Princip. The archduke died before reaching the hospital. His wife, Sophie von Chotek, was also killed in the attack. The news quickly spread across the continent.

Although the murder and analyses of feared consequences would fill the columns of *Svenska Dagbladet* in the weeks that followed, the newspaper continued to publish Ester's articles about her laborious existence in Jogersta. The war led to a series of delays of Ester's publications, and they also didn't get as much print space as the first article. But that didn't seem to matter. Everywhere, regardless of social class and context, people couldn't stop talking about Bansai, the fearless reporter who took a job as a maid, had worked her city-girl hands to shreds, and had written about the experiment.

On July 23, Austria-Hungary declared war on Serbia, and Russia supported the Slavic countries. Germany declared war on Russia and France less than two weeks later. When the Germans also crossed the border into Belgium, England joined its allies. World War I had begun. In Sweden, the country's church bells rang as a call for mobilization of militia. The Swedish Voluntary Shooting Movement, responsible for local defense, started preparing Sweden's borders and coasts for possible invasion.

> And so the cursed war turns everything on its head. Here, the Swedish people have gone about enjoying, taking immense pleasure in the tales of your quick and animated descriptions of the hardships and joys of being a maid on a Swedish farm. But then all at once, the great powers collide, and we cannot lay hold of anything but war telegrams and the banging of cannons.

> From a reader's letter in *Svenska Dagbladet*, signed "Bajsan," September 1, 1914.

The offer of a deal with the well-established publishing house *Wahlström & Widstrand* arrived before the article series had even come to an end. In an article in *Svenska Dagbladet*, Ester promised that it would contain a lot of new material. Fifteen hundred copies would be printed in the first run.

The last of a total of nine reports in *Svenska Dagbladet* was published on September 2 and was yet another success in the shadow of the ongoing war. The very controversial issue of women's suffrage divided the whole country, and even families. In the final part, Ester wrote about how she'd managed to transform Sigrid into a voting-rights woman.

> I wonder whether that fire still burns in her soul—maybe
> I should never have ignited it, but it was difficult to resist.
>
> From *En piga bland pigor* [*A Maid among Maids*].

In her own final remarks, Ester took a clear political stance on behalf of Sweden's approximately 140,000 maids:

> And perhaps my descriptions can to some extent explain to the uninitiated *why* the difficulty in obtaining sufficient levels of female farmworkers is so great. It is not just the fact that the work is heavy and hard and monotonous; the workday is too long, the workload is too undivided and disorganized, the pay is too low, and the leave allowance far too little. There is simply no leave to speak of. Sixteen- to seventeen-hour workdays without any rest other than that which must be afforded to the maids during mealtimes, no time off, not even an occasional half-day shift on Sundays [. . .]
>
> But the workforce is needed; it is necessary for the survival of agriculture, and therefore, it should be evident

that something needs to be done to somewhat ease and improve the position of the maids.

From *En piga bland pigor* [*A Maid among Maids*].

For Ester Blenda, the whole experience had been an emotional journey back in time, back through her lineage, to the past lives of her mother and father, and to her own upbringing. It was obvious that she felt strongly about the hardworking people in the Swedish countryside. Especially the young women.

The book *En piga bland pigor* (*A Maid among Maids*) was published in November. The cover was dominated by a photograph of Ester sitting outside a barn, disguised in her headscarf and checkered skirt, milking a cow. Expectations were high. Several national newspapers ran ads announcing the book release. A copy cost 2.25 kronor, equivalent to more than four days' worth of earnings for Sigrid and other Swedish maids on standard salaries.

She has made her name with this book, and she will likely attract a lot of followers who will embark on the same path. *A Maid among Maids* will become one of the successes of the autumn deluge of books.

From a review in *Borås Dagblad*, December 2, 1914.

Of great value for society and will certainly start an extended debate. In any case, our upper-class ladies and upper-class wives have an enormous amount to learn from Miss Nordström's story, and it is in a manner of speaking, a

hymn to the hardworking peasant women who toil away
on the farms.

From a review in *Borås Tidning*, December 2, 1914.

The first print run sold out instantly. The demand for the book
on everyone's lips was enormous. *Svenska Dagbladet* reported on the
success, with an obvious sense of pride:

> Today's local news reports that the book *A Maid among
> Maids*, by *Svenska Dagbladet* employee Bansai, *has* been
> published in two editions. However, the B section had
> barely been printed before further news reached us: the
> fourth print run was published and is now sold out, and
> the fifth print run is due for publication on Monday.

Ester danced her way into the editorial office. When she heard
the latest news about the rapidly rising sales numbers, she raised her
hands in the air, thanked the heavens, and rushed to the phone. In
the newspaper published a few days later, a colleague who'd seen her
whirling around the editorial office described how the new book writer
immediately called her publisher to ask if it was true. "She reports that
she received the following answer: 'Of course it's true! It's going so
damn fast that I barely have time to turn around before a new print
run is out!'"

Once again, the "maid issue" was debated. Did it make sense that
the most common occupation among women in Sweden had almost
no working-hour regulations? That the maids were not allowed to leave
their workplaces at the end of the day without permission from the
woman of the house, and had to explain to their employer what they
meant to do in their spare time?

It took until 1933, and the voting of Social Democrats into power, before a state inquiry into paid domestic work was appointed under the auspices of the *hembiträdesutredning* (Domestic Worker Commission). But things were already starting to happen across farms all over the country. The Sörmland County paper wrote that "some small, much-needed reforms have been achieved when it comes to division of labor in the homes" out in the countryside.

Before the end of December 1914, the fifth print run also sold out. *A Maid among Maids* went on to be published in a total of fifteen print runs and thirty-five thousand copies in the years that followed. It also broke Swedish records as a play at Lilla Teatern in Gothenburg with 175 performances. Even in Stockholm and other places in the country, the book became a play and filled houses. SF Studios, formerly known as Svensk Filmindustri, turned it into a fifty-six-minute feature film that took over cinemas throughout the country. But Ester wasn't yet aware of any of this. The twenty-three-year-old company director's daughter was the Swedish sensation of the year.

At night, her hoarse laughter bounced off the walls of restaurants and beer cafés. Everyone wanted to be close to the new star, to listen to her stories, and to become part of her circle that soon grew to include people like dignitary and art collector Prince Eugen, iconic troubadour Evert Taube, and artist and fellow author Albert Engström. Another circle member was painter Anders Zorn, who had been paid astronomical sums for the commissioned portraits of the two most recent US presidents, Theodore Roosevelt and William Taft.

On the Western Front, the Race to the Sea, in which the German and Franco-British sides tried to gain the upper hand on each other, was playing out. The German army had invaded Luxembourg and Belgium and had a hold on key industrial regions in France. A 470-mile row of trenches had been dug from the North Sea to the Swiss border. As one of the most significant wars in history, it involved seventy million mobilized soldiers and led to the deaths of over eighteen million people.

In the heat of the tavern, however, Ester Nordström kicked off a sing-along with life and death as its themes. Her glass was continuously refilled by the growing crowd of admirers.

CHAPTER 2

The Terrible Child

I was a terrible child—I was not thought to be malicious, but I was terrible.

My tricks grew to be so countless in number that I remember my childhood mostly as a dizzying joy over some successful prank—and as pain from the subsequent punishment. Only joy and sorrow—and only black and white. I never walked around with a clear conscience—not for a single blessed day, and I carried a constant fear of being caught.

From an Ester Blenda Nordström autobiographical manuscript submitted to Märta Lindquist at *Svenska Dagbladet*, 1918.

It was as if her slender little girl's body itched from within. Everything moved fast—the mouth, the legs, the words. The big white bow in her hair felt too tight.

She wanted to get dirty. She didn't care about making holes in her expensive dress, or the freckles that multiplied on her face whenever she forgot to put on her sun hat. Nice girls didn't have freckles. But Ester was not interested in being sweet and proper. She was curious; she wanted to try things and explore how they worked. Portrait photographs that have been preserved from the end of the nineteenth century and the beginning of the twentieth century certainly show a petite girl in ruffled and lace-adorned dresses with a serious expression on her face. But when she looked in the mirror, all she could see was a girl with fair hair and yellow teeth.

Ester often wished she were a boy. They got to live so much more freely; to live without safety nets, constant admonishments, and finger wagging. But lectures and punishment didn't take root in the mind of the youngest Nordström child. They just rolled off her back. Her private tutor fled the scene, and her grades were poor. Soon enough, things had gone so far that she was sent away from home to learn some discipline in a rectory. The family was simply unable to cope with the rebellious, high-intensity child.

But when did it all start? Young Ester clearly had ants in her pants. Was it evident to the people around her right from when she started running around the outbuildings on Ryafors, the family farm just outside Ljungby in Småland, the farm her father, Daniel, bought with his first fortune? By the end of the nineteenth century, the family kept the old state official's farm as their second home in addition to the apartment at Kungsholmsgatan 7 in Stockholm. Her mother, Lotten, lived there for the greater part of the year with Ester, who was born several years after her other siblings. The two were almost inseparable.

Charlotta "Lotten" and Daniel Nordström already had Agda (eleven), Frithiof (nine), and Hildur (seven), but Lotten had longed to have a fourth child for several years, and had mourned many miscarriages before Ester Blenda Elisabeth's birth on March 31, 1891. A beautiful baby with even features and an intense gaze. Pale blue.

As a child, Ester was dressed in exclusive ruffles and lace-adorned dresses, but she personally wished that she were a boy.

Someone started calling her Essan, and the name stuck. The other siblings also had nicknames; some even had several. Agda was usually called Agga, and Hildur was Bissan or Biss. Frithiof sometimes went by Janne or Putte. Over time, Essan would go on to earn more nicknames as well. "The little imp" was one of them.

Only two things seemed to reduce her restlessness. One was freedom: being outdoors where she could explore nature, play dangerous games, or run and bike so fast that the wind unraveled her braids. The other was taking flight into the world of words. Ester loved to write. She could sit immersed in it for hours, without her legs twitching at all, inventing characters involved in advanced dramas and intricate intrigues.

> When I was little, everyone at home had an awful lot of fun at the expense of myself and my writings. I remember once writing something called "The Count's Daughter, or They Found Each Other"—something really thrilling, but I was not allowed to read it aloud afterward. At the time, I boasted that I would become a writer. But later, I thought that I could not possibly have come up with a more ridiculous idea.
>
> From an interview with Ester Blenda Nordström in
> *Aftonbladet*, February 16, 1925.

Apparently, no one around her could see her talent. Not just then. Her mother struggled to spell and wrote letters with difficulty. She used to work as a maid in Roslagen and was sent to Stockholm to deliver milk. There she met Daniel, the farmer's son from Småland County. He, on the other hand, should have been able to see much of himself reflected in Ester: for one, he liked writing, both diary entries and poetry. Since childhood, he had carefully recorded the results of various independently conducted technical experiments in a beautiful hardcover notebook: everything from methods for waterproofing linen and cotton fabrics to recipes for solder fluids. Daniel was extremely curious by nature—just like his youngest daughter. In his youth, he experimented with hypnosis, which led to a rumor that the farmer's son from Aramo village could cure bed wetters, alcoholics, and the infirm. People began to make pilgrimages to the small village, hoping to be anesthetized and healed by his hand.

He also drew and painted. This particular talent took him all the way to the Royal Swedish Academy of Fine Arts in Stockholm as a young man, paid for by a wealthy patron from his home region.

But Daniel, too, couldn't fully appreciate Ester's potential. As the nineteenth century turned into the twentieth, he was busy climbing the social ladder and making money. Instead of investing in his dreams of becoming an artist, he took over the painting company where he started out as a journeyman and worked his way up. Business was going well: Daniel Nordström was quick witted, enterprising, and clever. He devoted himself to his art and technical experiments in winter, the painting industry's low season. Daniel and the older Nordström children also spent most of their time at their countryside Ryafors residence, which included a workshop and a studio.

Everyone around the farm knew who Daniel Nordström was. He had painted decorations for the village church, founded a paint factory in a barn next to the farm, and painted oil portraits of townspeople. The charismatic manufacturer also hosted large dinners that often ended with dancing on the old creaky wooden floors. They spared no expense on those parties. In the letters Lotten sent to relatives from this time in their lives, she proudly described heaving smorgasbord spreads with hams and chickens; lavish main courses with potatoes and cream; with rice porridge, wine, and pastries for dessert. Guest lists of about fifty people weren't all too uncommon, often featuring some of the town's most distinguished farmers.

Daniel caused quite the sensation by introducing electricity into the pitch-black Småland forests as early as the 1890s. At that time, only twenty-odd towns in the country had their own electricity plant, most of which were lined up between Stockholm and Gothenburg. The engineering company Luth och Roséns Elektriska AB in Jönköping applied to start a plant in Småland in 1887, but the gasworks board rejected the submission.

Ester's inventive father started on a smaller scale by submitting a patent for an electric rock-drilling machine to the Swedish Patent and Registration Office. It was signed by the famous polar explorer S. A. Andrée, who shortly afterward ascended to his own death in *the Eagle*, a hydrogen balloon on its way to the North Pole. Buoyed by this successful application, Daniel then built a power plant in the rapids along the edge of the farm. It was built entirely from his own sketches of generators and electrical equipment. He attached power cords (twisted by Lotten) to large porcelain insulators in a tall birch tree.

The launch was planned down to the very last detail. One Christmas morning in the early 1890s, just as the townspeople had gotten into their sleighs and were heading down in the silence between the snow-laden spruces on the way to Christmas matins, he turned it on. The newly installed farm lighting gave rise to a dazzle never before seen in the region.

Even in Stockholm, Daniel Nordström was becoming an increasingly famous man, especially in the city's more elevated circles. His business activities were lucrative; there were plenty of painting commissions in the capital, where urbanization had plagued stressed politicians and city planners for several years. The population of the city had risen exponentially. Within just a couple of decades, the number had risen from ninety-three thousand to almost three hundred thousand, and radical measures were required to create housing for everyone while also transforming Stockholm into a big city. The demolition balls had swung mercilessly between densely built-up wooden house facades. The old and dark had been demolished to make room for the airy and light. New neighborhoods with modern stone houses began to emerge.

The councilor of justice and city planner Albert Lindhagen was the mastermind behind the new Stockholm, a concept inspired by the major imperial cities on the Continent: Vienna, Paris, Berlin, and Saint

Petersburg. Their wide and magnificent boulevards and long avenues had been re-created in Östermalm, the eastern part of the Swedish capital; this, in turn, had become the go-to part of town for the wealthy.

But Ester's father did the opposite. He moved his family to the Kungsholmen district instead, which was still more sparsely populated and had therefore—for several years—attracted industries in need of a lot of real estate. Weapon manufacturers, foundries, and velocipede factories all created jobs and the need for new residential buildings. The ongoing housing boom in the area offered plenty of painting commissions for his company, along with newly opened shops, restaurants, beer halls, and service-based businesses in need of signs. Moreover, decorative painting, like veining and marbling, was highly sought after for newly built stairwells throughout the city. The name "Daniel Nordström," known because of his artistic talent, was hot on everyone's lips.

Soon, he'd managed to earn enough money to buy the entire apartment block where the family lived; he subsequently opened Kungsholm Photography Studio at the same address. The box camera was still a novelty item, and the person with his head under the dark cloth in the studio was, of course, Daniel himself.

Ester and her siblings were dressed in expensive clothes: well-tailored sailor suits for Frithiof and delicately sewn dresses with lace, sheer tulle, and bows for the girls. Lotten was given beautiful hats and fancy jewelry, but she'd started having concerns about her family's new way of life. She continued to mend and repair their clothing. The feeling of regularly having to carry heavy milk buckets stayed with her. She was more comfortable at home in Ryafors than in the big city where grand dinner party invitations from Daniel's new acquaintances had begun to flow in. Ester was always with her. She was raised like the daughter of a maid: she learned to walk on grass and gravel; play around the animals in the barns; say her first words surrounded by farmers, farmhands, and maids.

Småland was the place that Ester would go on to describe for the rest of her life as her childhood home. This agriculturally rich region had the reputation of being home to headstrong, independent people. It was the place she returned to in her mind as she went on to write about her upbringing much later in life—both the light and the dark. Her father and siblings would buy her fancy gifts from Stockholm. Lotten would object to this and scold them, even in writing:

> You talk about saving; well, then you cannot buy gloves as expensive as three kronor. For it is a great luxury. I have never had such expensive gloves. Better, then, to spend on new lining for muffs; then it would not matter if the gloves were poorly made. I also think you spend a lot on your clothing. You should strive to be simple in all things, while still neat—I also think Ester's hat is too expensive as it is so delicate that it cannot be used for just any occasion. If she were to join you for the spring, it would be so late into the year that she could not go about wearing clothes with padded hoods—you must not tear up your red dress. I think it could be spruced up once more with suitable decoration.

> From a letter from Lotten to Agda, from Ryafors,
> November 28, 18XX (year unspecified).

But the money kept coming in. Daniel Nordström would soon have his hand in several different commercial enterprises. When the offer to become a partner in a construction company finally came along, he saw his chance to create something bigger. Daniel and his associates called themselves Marquard and Nordström and quickly became a household name.

Over time, he grew tired of the cumbersome, time-consuming, and uncomfortable journeys down the terrible, small roads between Stockholm and Ryafors. He decided to sell the farm. Ester was six years old when they moved. For the two years that followed, the family was entirely based in Stockholm. But once the railway was eventually expanded to connect the country's central and southern parts and the railway workers began to appear in Småland, Ester's father started looking for land in the area once again, all so he could commute by train to and from the business in Stockholm. He started building the family's new oasis, Villa Åbyfors, within six miles of Ljungby city, right outside the village of Berga and next to the rippling Skålån stream.

The house was majestic. A large white-painted wooden villa with a copper roof, adorned with several dormers. The entrance at the front, opposite the stream, had a large stone staircase that led up to a set of heavy wooden double doors. The spacious balcony on one end overlooked a wing building that served as the servants' quarters. Round back, facing a stretch of woodland, were several benches and outdoor table sets overlooking a fountain in a small pond, surrounded by floral plantings.

A beautiful iron railing and flagpole surrounded a towerlike roof terrace. An elegant curved wooden staircase connected the upper and lower floors within. Bows at the lamp mounts adorned the ceilings. The light streamed through four large windows into the beautiful dining room with space for a large table that could easily accommodate a dozen guests. Daniel built a new dam and a new power station, drawing electricity to their house, along with five or six other houses nearby.

Once again, the Nordström family had become the center of a small town. The electricity and Daniel's newly acquired motorcycle both stood out in the countryside. Motorcycles had just started being produced in larger numbers, and there were only a few in the country. They were used only recreationally as outriders in velodrome races, were excessively expensive, and were almost completely impossible to use on

Swedish country roads—the engine and frame couldn't withstand any vibration.

Ester looked on, wide eyed and completely spellbound as he drove around the small roads surrounding the house.

> The old man has gotten himself a motorcycle now [. . .] It weighs fifty kilos [110 pounds], and you should be so lucky to get it started after pedaling for a half hour. But then it takes off at a hellish speed.

> From a letter from Frithiof Nordström to Hildur Nordström, Åbyfors, June 1903.

Summer in Åbyfors, 1902.

Ester loved life in Åbyfors. The girl with the big white hair rosette rushed downstairs, pushed down the front door's heavy brass handle, and disappeared out of the house early in the morning. From time to time, you could catch glimpses of her during the day in forest clearings, out on the nearby stream where she rowed about in the family's small wooden boat, or in the courtyard where she rode around in the crate she'd attached to Sara the calf. It was a funny little scene, the gentle calf letting itself be led by the girl with thin reins and complete focus. At one point, Daniel took a picture of them.

Measles came and went, as did scarlet fever, diphtheria, and mumps. After several bouts of pneumonia, Ester was plagued by a persistent cough. But nothing could stop the energy within the girl's slender frame. She would jet round to the neighboring farms on her velocipede to play with the farmers' kids. Maids and male servants were interviewed with great curiosity and were almost always offered help whenever Ester stomped through with her bright red cheeks. Soon, she learned to wield the soft, firm, and even grip required to get steady streams of thick milk from a cow's teat. With time, she also learned to harness a horse to a carriage and to ride down the dusty gravel roads.

Whenever Ester returned in the evenings, she would be dirty, happy, and full of new secrets.

The older siblings, particularly Agda, tried to tame their wild younger sister. They taught her how to play their instruments. Agda had perfect pitch, but the others were also musically gifted. The house was well equipped enough for a small orchestra: piano, accordion, lute, violin, banjo, guitar, and harmonica. Soon, even Ester learned to switch freely between instruments. She became especially skilled at the violin and the accordion.

There were also several pets in the house. Frithiof collected butterflies and canaries and owned at least one turtle and a couple of owls that he kept indoors in a large cage covered with chicken wire. They went by the names "Kajsa the Elder" and "Kajsa the Younger." Sometimes, fights would break out between the farm cats and the owls, but the cages prevented the quarrels from completely devolving. Other than that, the cats were so tame that they were often found lying across Frithiof's shoulders, and the canaries had their own bathtub where they could splash around. Frithiof let Ester play with the animals. She had a natural and gentle way with them. It was as if they understood each other.

So this was the world in which young Ester Nordström grew up—among sticky paintbrushes, a considerable collection of animals, constant access to instruments, and electricity experiments. All in a family that seemed to consist of creativity and stubbornness in equal parts, and that was swiftly rising through the social ranks. They were increasingly embracing the bourgeois lifestyle. Their housekeeper, Anna Maria, cooked all the food in the house. The maid, Julia, looked after the house. A private tutor, "Aunt Wendela," provided Ester with instruction.

She didn't have it easy and was generally considered "unwilling to work." Aunt Wendela persisted and tried to use an ever more encouraging tone. Big sister Agda, Ester's senior by eleven years, helped with writing, prompted her younger sister to do her homework, and quizzed her. Pleaded with her and scolded her. But Ester's pranks simply grew in number and became increasingly dangerous. Disciplinary beatings, groundings, and bans became more frequent too. Lotten pleaded with the "apple of her eye," but nothing helped. On the contrary, her sense of rebellion was stirred. Ester earned herself new nicknames in the family, all variations on "little imp."

Then finally, her suitcases were packed in 1904. Ester was thirteen years old, and her family had run out of patience. Uncle Håkan was waiting in his Småland vicarage. Daniel's brother was the vicar of Västbo provost, a powerful and influential man in his parish; he was the chairman of the public school board and the parish governing board. He lived and worked in a small village by the stream Nissan, one and a half miles outside the Småland town of Gislaved. The pastor was described by his colleagues as a "tall, powerful figure with a patriarchal demeanor, and a winning exterior combined with an even greater sense of spiritual vigor and resilience, intelligence, and knowledge. A good preacher that the congregation gladly listens to, as well as a very affable, sociable man." But a completely different side of him emerged in his role as guardian.

After much deliberation, the family had decided that Ester's uncle Håkan was the person best suited to take her on. The hope was that a year in the High Church environment of the dark Småland County forests would cure her of her maladaptive disposition and improve her miserable grades—particularly her grades for conduct. In recent years, the question of progressing into the next school year had been far from straightforward.

The dew was still on the grass as the two girls—Ester and a friend— sneaked away from the large red-painted rectory one early morning in May. No one saw the slight figures swiftly disappearing between pines, spruces, and birches on the way to the lake. Two hours still remained until the start of the daily lesson led by the vicar, a lesson forced on the two young teens deemed too wild for their own good and the good of their families.

There was a small boat typically moored down by the beach. The girls' plan was to steal it and live like pirates for a brief moment, before lessons with tutors and catechism. They pushed the boat out; with a slight scrape against the bottom, it gave way and floated off onto the silent lake.

One hand snatched the oar from another. Then a light shove. Then a harder shove back. The fight over who would get to row the pirate ship was inevitable. The boat violently swayed from the force of the girls' furious clash. Neither of them noticed the oars coming loose from their oarlocks and bobbing away on the waves. They didn't realize that they were in trouble until the wind started to quicken and they'd wound up far from shore.

Soon after, Ester found herself lying on the priest's lap with her short skirt pulled up. It didn't hurt while the birch branch struck her.

The pain came shortly afterward, burning, stinging, and powerful all at once. She kept her lips shut tight—she'd decided that she wouldn't scream. She would go on to carry the vulnerability, frustration, and anger of this very moment for the rest of her life.

Her friend, who was lying over the other leg, desperately cried out with remorse. The louder the friend screamed, the more blows Ester received. "The punishing arm," as she later called it in her literary autobiography, would tirelessly lift and descend. The priest was a full-grown adult, and every blow was filled with a huge amount of force. The abuse didn't stop until her thirteen-year-old body let out an involuntary whimper.

The girls didn't hesitate for a second: they absolutely *would* have their revenge on the priest, and his punishment would be as physically painful as theirs was. For days, Ester remained in deep contemplation about various schemes while wandering around the yard, bitter and deliberately uncooperative. She wound up in the barn, sitting on the edge of a stall. It was quiet and empty inside; the cows had been let out for their springtime grazing. She stirred the hay with her bare legs and feet, and distractedly watched as it filled with small dark dots. Then she saw the dots jump. Fleas. And they'd been thirsting for blood ever since the cattle came out of their winter habitation. The rest was easy for an ingenious girl with a mind for rebellion and pranks to figure out. She danced with excitement once the first sufficiently devilish plan for revenge fully took shape in her head.

The boat-theft accomplice had shown up in the barn and looked at Ester with a mixture of anxiety and curiosity:

> "Well well! Oh, he's going to get his! Run back and grab an empty bottle; there's one on my desk. Hurry up!" She looked at me for a moment, then raced back out the door. When she came back with a bottle and a cork, my legs were [illegible] black as the night. I had wandered around

all the stalls and lovingly offered my skin to the starving little insects. Then we caught I don't know how many, but the bottle was crawling with baffled fleas, while our souls felt the purest joy and our hearts beat with wild delight.

From an Ester Blenda Nordström autobiographical manuscript submitted to Märta Lindquist at *Svenska Dagbladet*, 1918.

The friend had become an accomplice once again. Together, they created a precise schedule. After the priest closed his bedroom door upstairs that evening, the girls pressed their ears to it.

A night that will never be forgotten—not by us who partook of this particularly heavenly joy, nor by our poor victim who had probably never before stood so close to the pyre of insanity. Alas, our ears listening at the door caught words that could forever shatter his future as a spiritually minded man. As he lit a candle and searched his hopping bed for the hundredth time, he said things that should have made him feel embarrassed and that made our [unreadable word] ears blush with happiness.

From an Ester Blenda Nordström autobiographical manuscript submitted to Märta Lindquist at *Svenska Dagbladet*, 1918.

But she was not content with the torment-filled night during which the respected village priest swore as coarsely as a farmhand. His niece never told him that she was the one who'd planted the hundreds of starving fleas in his bed. And she wasn't done with Uncle Håkan. In time, her revenge would be public too.

Decades later, she sarcastically referred to her time at the rectory as "the happiest year" of her life even though she was rarely caught while up to her various antics, and she could roam around the hills of the sleepy, idyllic town relatively undisturbed.

Her suitcases were packed once again. Things did not get any better back home in Stockholm and at Åbyfors. Her tutor, Aunt Wendela, eventually left.

Dear Janne, please do assist us with the acquisition of a tutor for little Essan; that is to say, please do provide information by telephone or in person to those who may request it.

We have received a response from a PhD graduate named E. F. Strauss, a teacher at the girls' secondary school on Lästmakargatan. The name strikes me as familiar; could he be a former peer of yours?

He is twenty-three years old, a graduate student, and has the highest grade in languages at the PhD level. Well, that sounds wonderful [. . .] Pettson [a nickname for Ester, meaning a rascal] is as unhinged as it gets. God have mercy on this cursed little troublemaker! The poor thing who would have to read with her! She is so grimy and filthy right now. She builds tepees covered in peat on the island, and has a whole staff of kids as workers, all equally filthy and bare legged, and her commandeering shrieks are heard far and wide.

From a letter from Agda Nordström to Frithiof
Nordström, June 24, 1906.

Her grades were dropping. C in mathematics, BC in German and Latin, B in diligence . . . and Daniel had even less time to spend on his unruly daughter. He'd become part of the distinguished gentlemen's club Sällskapet, "the Society," in Stockholm, for the gathering of men with prominent positions in the worlds of business and aristocracy. Membership was highly coveted. The Society's building in central Stockholm had a banquet hall, a room for billiards and games, and a large library. Daniel saved restaurant bills in his desk drawer at home; they detailed costly orders for champagne, caviar, and oysters.

Childhood and adolescence were filled with rebellion. Ester refused to behave the way a fine young lady was supposed to.

Ragnar Östberg, one of the country's foremost architects, was now one of their family friends. He had just been commissioned to start building Stockholm City Hall, which would in time make him the first Swede to receive the Royal Institute of British Architects' gold medal.

Around the same time, the milkmaid and farmer's son moved with their daughters and servants to a large and magnificent apartment with its own service staff. Ester was sixteen years old. Frithiof no longer lived with them. By now, he'd gotten himself a dental degree, started his own practice, and was engaged to marry Gerda von Porat, a priest's daughter from Tumba, and from the same family as Uncle Håkan Nordström's wife.

Gerda was fine limbed with dark, glossy hair and narrow wrists. Her face was oval with deep-set eyes and thin lips. She was highly musical: her piano skills led to her admission to the Royal Swedish Academy of Music's piano class as an eighteen-year-old. She had since been offered further education, completely free of charge, at the highly respected Richard Andersson Piano School.

Gerda was welcomed into the music-loving Nordström family. Ester started calling her "sister" almost immediately. They would go on to remain as close as sisters throughout their lives. Gerda became the person that Ester could always confide in, be at ease with, and cry to. Gerda would go on to faithfully keep her secrets, and to repeatedly intervene to help her sister-in-law out of various tight spots and difficulties.

In 1907, wedding bells rang at the Tumba vicarage, and Gerda pulled out of her studies with Richard Andersson. Frithiof bought her a grand piano so that she could continue playing at home. The following year, her first child, Kjell, was born. Ester loved him from day one. She often walked the short distance from home to the new family's apartment just to be close to the baby.

Private tutoring had been replaced with Wallinska girls' school in Stockholm. Lotten, who still preferred to live in Småland, tried to encourage every step forward, every nonrebellious action:

Dearest little one!

Believe that I was thrilled to hear that you moved up a year. I am sure you were thrilled too? Hope you are grateful to all those who helped you along the way—now, you must work hard and be good, so that our little Essan can bring honor to our name.

From a letter from Lotten Nordström to Ester Blenda Nordström, undated.

Her grades continued to improve after another change of school: this time, it was to Palmgrenska Samskolan for both boys and girls. The hallways weren't as quiet here. An A for diligence and a couple of ABs were on the report cards shown to Lotten and Daniel. But it was still a B for conduct. Only one in every twenty-three students had such low grades for conduct. A tutor was brought on board in an attempt to salvage the situation as finals approached.

The Nordström family's fortune was growing rapidly. Daniel bought several seaside plots of land at Skurusundet on Värmdö, just outside Stockholm. The property was located right by Eknäs pier, a ferry port for the Waxholm boats that took the family to Stockholm in a little over an hour. A small rushing stream flowed through the plot. The "Ekefors" estate emerged: a magnificent twelve-room wooden villa along with a large multistory stone house on the plot where Daniel furnished a spacious painting studio for himself.

He was commissioned to paint twenty-one landscape paintings on the ceiling of the newly restored salon at Grand Restaurant National in Stockholm. The work was of such significance that it received press coverage. The newspaper *Fäderneslandet* wrote:

The large banquet hall at Grand Restaurant National has undergone a comprehensive restoration and renewal under the direction of the Marquard & Nordström company and is now called Trocadero. It is without gainsay Stockholm's most beautiful banquet and dance hall. The large mirrors between the white pillars along the walls have been gilded, and Nordström has artfully painted twenty-one truly beautiful landscape paintings up by the ceiling molding. Kungsgatan's nearby developments, along with Stockholm's continual developments on its outskirts, make the premises increasingly comfortable and central.

More than a hundred years later, dances are still being hosted under the paintings at the well-known venue that has since become known as Nalen.

One of only one thousand automobiles registered in Stockholm in 1910 belonged to Daniel Nordström. The De Dion-Bouton was the most technologically advanced and market-leading car brand in the world at the time. The car could reach the then-breathtaking speed of thirty-one miles an hour, but the family's driver cruised at the legal maximum speed of twelve miles per hour between horse-drawn carriages and other single motor vehicles on the streets. Just ten years prior, there had only been four cars in the entire city.

The driver lived in his own wing whenever the family stayed at Åbyfors Manor. On July 29, 1910, he drove the elegant high-society family about in Ljungby. Lotten was in the front seat, wrapped in a car blanket. Daniel, with a fashionable mustache and elegant sports cap, sat in the back seat with Agda, Hildur, and Ester. In the photo that remains from this day, Ester stands, wearing a graduation hat. She had received the grade "passed with distinction" for her Swedish essay writing. She was fluent in French, German, and Latin, and she excelled in English. She would go on to benefit greatly from her language skills within the year that followed, but she had no sense of this as she looked straight into the camera before the car moved along the streets of Ljungby.

She had a sunburned face after having spent the beginning of
the summer with her aunt Sofi in the coastal town of Varberg. The
Nordström siblings loved being with their aunt. Life was pleasant and
simple in the Swedish west-coast oasis, with long days on the beach and
equally long evenings and nights spent at the Society clubhouse; even
Aunt Sofi had quickly climbed through the ranks of society, through
successful business dealings. In just a few short years, she had become
one of the country's most famous juice and jam confectionery manufacturers. Like her brother Daniel, she'd started small and cooked by
herself in her kitchen to supplement the family's meager income. Now,
the brown wooden boxes from Knutson's marmalade factory were recognized all across Sweden.

The Nordström family in their car. The picture was taken in Ljungby in 1910.

In the summer of 1910, the sun blazed on. The honeysuckles bloomed twice, and the rain fell only at night. Ester had sailed and swum so much that she'd caught a cold, had remained undefeated in the many rounds of card games with Sofi, and had gained an admirer whose declarations of love she'd laughed off. In one of her letters to her sister-in-law, Gerda, in Stockholm, she wrote:

> Sven Linder is terribly boring, but terribly kind. He chases me for dear life, and Sofi claims that Mrs. Linder has said that he loves me. So there! But he loves someone new every summer, so this is nothing to cheer about.
>
> I think you should come down with Hildur and surprise me.
>
> Hope Kjell has been specially cared for today and that he is his aunt's very own little angel.
>
> My goodness, that major's wife, Flodell or Flodén, whatever her name, the one who is boy crazy and in her seventies, she lives here opposite us, and is currently singing "The Count of Luxembourg! You and I, me and you." My God, it's terrible. I've learned such lovely somewhat obscene ditties out here.

In the fall, the restlessness returned. The older siblings were all established. Frithiof was a dentist by now. Hildur landed a job as a saleswoman at Bukowski's Art Dealership, and Agda graduated as a cantor with flying colors, thanks to her perfect pitch.

Ester felt lost. Her hunger for adventure remained; her legs were still itching to move. The profession that finally aroused her interest was one that lacked a fixed framework and that called for the persistent desire and unlimited energy to throw oneself into the unknown, a great deal of courage, and an unmatched sense of curiosity.

After I finished my studies, I was unemployed and longed for something to keep me occupied. Then someone suggested that I start as a volunteer at a newspaper. I got an offer, accepted it—and that was that.

From an interview with Ester Blenda Nordström in
Aftonbladet, February 16, 1925.

Ester had just turned twenty when she started working at the daily *Stockholms Dagblad*. She was the youngest reporter among all of Stockholm's journalists.

CHAPTER 3

The Boy, Elin Wägner, and the League

May 1911. *Stockholms Dagblad* was located on Vasagatan, a bustling street in the heart of Stockholm. A walk up two, three flights of stairs, and you'd have reached the general editorial office. The corridors were narrow, and the rooms were small but cozy, with table lamps that emitted a warm glow. The city's newspaper houses were otherwise known for being dark, bare, and worn. The atmosphere was concentrated and intense while Ester was being shown around the place.

The paper had a good reputation, was moderately conservative, and had a large readership in well-to-do and well-established social circles—the world in which she herself had grown up. But its circulation had declined since the beginning of the century. The enormous influx of people from the countryside had begun to have an impact on journalism as well. The competition for readers had been won by cheap newspapers with simple, easy-to-read language and content aimed at low-skilled workers. *Stockholms-Tidningen*, established in 1889 by Anders Jeurling, was one of them. They'd also invested in a system of sales representatives in rural areas, which led to rapidly rising print numbers. At this point, they'd exceeded one hundred thousand daily copies. The free-spirited and liberal *Dagens Nyheter*, previously the publication most similar to

Stockholms-Tidningen, was struggling with its circulation of around forty thousand copies.

Stockholms Dagblad's management responded to this crisis by recruiting Carl Gustaf Tengwall from *Svenska Dagbladet* as editor in chief and responsible publisher. The man—who would go on to become very important for Ester's career going forward—was known to be a fearless, dynamic, and energetic journalist. He had the same high expectations of everyone who worked for his newspaper, regardless of rank.

People came in and out of the editor in chief's office throughout the day. It wasn't big; three people in the room at the same time was a crowd. Furnishings were purely functional—no more, no less. A large dark desk lit up by a small shoemaker's lamp, a generously sized wooden cabinet, and an armchair for visitors. Thin white cotton curtains hung by the window.

Tengwall had worked hard to bring in female employees to the editorial staff. *Svenska Dagbladet*, his former workplace, had included content specifically for women for the preceding ten years, including the column For Our Female Readers. Now, *Stockholms Dagblad* also had columns specifically for women and had even tried to publish an entire women's supplement. It was a great success, not least when it came to advertising space sales. There was a rapid rise in the appetite for consumption, and the ads were starting to take up more and more space in the otherwise traditionally text-heavy newspapers.

Despite this, the newspaper's only three female reporters—Ellen "Murre" Landquist, Agnes "Bysis" Byström Lindhagen, and Siri Thorngren—were still not invited to the big morning meetings where the agenda for the day was discussed and the most important assignments were delegated. The women sat separately in a part of the room where the men almost never went, and were rarely seen out in the general editorial office.

The new volunteer aroused their curiosity. She was very young, not very tall, slim, and radiated something different than what they were used to seeing. Something new and fresh. She seemed free. Her body language was that of a young man, as opposed to that of a woman. Yet, she was so impeccably feminine in dress and hair. And that hoarse, loud laugh—people noticed it right away.

Several people at the paper seemed to feel the same way, and all subsequently testified to her remarkable charisma. To how the unusual young woman fascinated everyone who came near her. To her enigmatic gaze.

Murre, Bysis, and Siri told Ester all about the rules of engagement that applied in the editorial office. About whom to get on good terms with, and where the cheapest lunches in the area were. About how she should watch out when bringing the building's only typewriter into the room, in order to avoid annoying the night editor, who considered it to be his.

They explained what C-scraps were and prepared her for the fact that she would have to put together a good few of these, at least for a while. They needed to be entertaining and sensational, and they were cut out from foreign newspapers such as the *Daily Mail*, *Neue Freie Presse*, and *Le Figaro*—a job that required both language skills and the lack of a need for prestige. For the first time ever, Ester made use of all the hours spent toiling away at her German, French, and English language skills.

Her first published article was a rewritten, abridged text from the newspaper the *Mexican Herald*. The notice was about the murder of the Swedish Pehr Olsson-Seffer, former Portuguese consul general and professor of botany at the Universidad Nacional Autónoma de México, who was shot by Mexican rebels on a train near El Parque.

That same week, she was sent out to the newly opened scout office on Jakobsgatan in Stockholm, and to the spring party at Skansen, a popular amusement park and open-air museum. Her coverage of these events made for one of her first newspaper articles; she cut and pasted them into her newly purchased folder, light green with blue edges. The texts were signed using her first pseudonym, "the Boy." She had chosen it with care. A pseudonym was meant to reflect the writer and was preferably a bit subtle.

The big news stories were exclusively covered by the male journalists. With some luck, Ester or one of the other women might get called out into the general editorial office to help with foreign interviews because the men rarely had a good-enough grip of foreign languages to hold longer conversations.

The Publicist Club happily received women's membership fee payments, but the club's travel scholarships, which made it possible to take on posts as foreign correspondents, were only open to male applicants. There were zero opportunities to take on weightier assignments. Although most editors had come to recognize the value of female coworkers at this point, having their pseudonym in a story's byline had less value.

> The atmosphere between us and them was friendly; no one even batted an eye at the fact that girls were entering our previously almost entirely male domain.
>
> The fact that old, incredibly conservative journalists like my roommate Axel Nihlén did not like skirts in the editorial office is to be expected, and I do not wish to deny the fact that the male journalists were, to a greater extent, deeply convinced of their own superiority!
>
> Quote by Ivar Andersson, summer volunteer at
> *Stockholms Dagblad* in 1911.

In one newspaper article, a well-known *Dagens Nyheter* writer confessed that, just a few years prior, most male journalists had dismissed female newspaper reporters as "airy little creatures" with a style and language that was "childish, sweet, and stupid, in keeping with what femininity seems to call for." An American journalism handbook had even stated that women were not cut out for journalism due to their fragile nature. The author stated that six of his female colleagues had died of overexertion; five had been sent to sanatoriums for nervous illness; seven had sunk to the bottom rungs of society due to temptations they'd been subjected to in their profession; and two went on to marry.

The women in the editorial office undoubtedly came up against a number of prejudices, but 1911 was the time of emancipation, the time of opportunity. Sitting at home and waiting for a suitable spouse to show up was no longer the only option after girls' school and perhaps a few years as a second-language teacher in a strictly run pension somewhere in Europe. A woman could even graduate from university, though the resistance to this was still significant in the academic world.

Female journalists in Stockholm at this time numbered between eight and ten. They had to work hard to be given real assignments and to be treated with respect, both within and outside the newspaper buildings. They faced completely different challenges than men, such as all the groping hands and shameful propositions they constantly had to ward off when out on assignments, especially in the evenings and nights when the dim beams of the gas lanterns were barely enough to light up streets and alleys; it all came with the territory of being a woman outdoors without a male companion.

> This nighttime hunting of women really irritated us "penholders" a lot. Some of the other girls were far pluckier and even dared to answer back, even making lengthy conversations until the woman hunter finally just stood at the gate with a long face. But I would just get scared and run like a hare.
>
> Journalist Ellen Rydelius in her memoirs, *Leva randigt* [*Living in Stripes*].

The spring that Ester spent as a reporting volunteer ended. She wrote and wrote, sharpening her newspaperspeak. She had a certain gift for the job and learned quickly. The long chain of C-scrap assignments started being broken up with report summarization work and simple reporting assignments all around Stockholm. She visited an evening event hosted by the Swedish navy for Danish seamen and reported on the atmosphere on one of the many summer boats that took Stockholm dwellers out for their weekend fun in the archipelago.

At an archery competition for kids, Ester interviewed a thirteen-year-old girl who excelled in the sport. The brazen teen struck a chord with her; she decided to write exactly what the girl said, verbatim. Capturing what a regular person had to say—and a child at that—in unedited form, with their dialect and slang expressions, was an unprecedented move in the world of newspapers. And it didn't stop there: Ester inserted herself into the text and became an active interviewer. The text captured the girl's youthful personality and the dynamics of their conversation. The result inspired the rest of the journalism corps, which soon followed her lead.

Slowly, an independent voice started to emerge. It was firm and quick, even in her news articles. One of her writing-style role models was Elin Wägner, who had worked for the Stockholm newspapers for several years and had just been appointed editor in chief of *Idun*, a weekly magazine for women. Actually, she had held the job duties of an editorial manager for several years but had only just been given the official title by the all-male managing board.

Idun was viewed as a free-spirited publication, with an eye for all current topics of conversation, both the lighthearted and the profoundly sociopolitical. It didn't shy away from radical articles. It was wary of being branded as conservative, yet it was deemed to be respectable and had managed to become one of the dominant magazines in educated households, with a circulation of fifty thousand copies.

Elin Wägner was also a recognized, and infamous, debater and author and had made a breakthrough with her third novel, *Pennskaftet* (which literally translates to *The Penholder*). In it, she portrayed a young and driven woman who did something unusual: she became a professional, working as a reporter for a newspaper.

As a leading representative in the National Association for Women's Suffrage, Elin Wägner had, of course, also made her novel's heroine get involved in the suffrage issue, one of the most controversial and burning political topics of the time. The character was also such a free spirit that she had a relationship with a young architect and lived in her own apartment.

The heroine in the book shared many similarities with Elin herself, who was newly married to journalist John Landquist and deeply influenced by the thoughts and ideas of Ellen Key, the world-famous debater, author, and feminist. Elin and John shared Key's view that mutual love and passion should be the priorities of the relationship between man and woman.

Pennskaftet had done amazingly well in sales and attracted a lot of attention. It was a provocation against the ideals, conventions, and patriarchal order of the time. Above all, it had aroused forbidden feelings in many young bourgeois women who had begun to dream of a different kind of existence, one with independence and freedom and the opportunity to get involved and to influence things. Soon enough, the title of the book became the descriptor of newswomen all around the country.

Elin Wägner had become an idol for a significant proportion of a generation of women. The job as a reporter was suddenly hotly sought after, and *pennskaft* had become far more than a nickname for young, female journalists. It had become a concept, a heavily charged symbol of the modern, independent woman and her right to free speech.

Fittingly, Ester had been nicknamed Pennskaft by a would-be suitor. His name was Kalle Ahnfeldt, and he thought she was incredibly similar to the heroine in Elin Wägner's novel with her job as a reporter and her unrestrained, outspoken ways. Kalle was hopelessly in love and desperately looking for signs that his feelings were reciprocated. They weren't, and Kalle never proposed marriage; he didn't dare.

> He just looked at me with puppy eyes, so worshipful
> and pathetic; he squeezed my hand [. . .] He was the first

perfect gentleman I had ever met in my life, possibly the last, too, as they are few in number [. . .] If he treated me a bit less gentlemanlike and with a bit less fear [. . .], I might have "become a missus by now and walked about wearing a hat and gloves."

From a letter from Ester Blenda Nordström to Frithiof and Gerda Nordström, May 7, 1920.

Elin Wägner and Ester met somewhere within Stockholm's very limited world of journalism in the early 1910s. The meeting between the two women would be of great importance to both of their lives going forward. The friendship became an intimate and lifelong one, despite being challenged by intrigue, personal crises, and occasionally enormous geographic distances between the two. They would share secrets that they shared with no one else in the course of their lifetimes, but which are revealed in posterity through their correspondence.

There was an age gap of nine years between them: Elin was twenty-nine, and Ester was twenty. Looking at them, the two women couldn't have been more different. Ester was grand, loud, bubbly, and spontaneous. Elin was quiet and buttoned up, even a bit introverted. But all of a sudden, she would break out of her silence—unexpectedly, yet naturally—and gently say something entirely decisive and powerful in the most subtle way imaginable. Later in life, this was how her friends and colleagues would come to describe what was remarkable about Elin. Her sharp sense of humor and her quick and mischievous nature were most apparent in her writing.

They also differed in appearance. Elin was petite and graceful with thick dark blond hair that she wore in voluminous updos with a side part. Her face, with its defined nose and cleft chin, already carried the gravity that came from deep life sorrows. Her eyes were somehow already those of an old woman.

Ester was also not physically imposing. On the contrary. But she exuded something completely different: a kind of rascally manner seen in young, unruly boys. Her eyes were narrower, her gaze squinting. Yet, Ester and Elin felt connected instantly. And it didn't take long before they discovered many similarities. They both lacked higher academic degrees, which was uncommon in the wider group of Swedish news-women. Both had roots in Småland County, where they were raised by domineering men of the church during parts of their childhoods, Ester Blenda with her uncle Håkan in Villstad and Elin with her uncle Alfred Ekedal, a vicar in Berg village near Lammhult.

Elin Wägner was bitter about her father, who felt she was "just a girl" and didn't need the same academic training in which he so demonstratively invested for her brothers. Her dream was to study philosophy. When Elin was denied the life of higher learning, she dropped out of high school and began helping out in her father's school principal's office instead. But her desire to think and write led her to the local newspaper, *Helsingborgs-Posten*, and then on to Stockholm. It was hardly a coincidence that she fell in love with, then married, a man who had studied philosophy at Uppsala University. John Landquist had already published several philosophical essays at that point and had spent many evenings and nights listening to his wife's expressions of disappointment over her upbringing:

> I suppose it was the legacy of generations of oppressed women within my family, the sum of their lives' resig-nations, that reappeared in me. In my family, for as far as my personal chronicle extends, the women have been submissive and thought as little about themselves as the men around them thought of them [. . .]
>
> [. . .] I think I grew up surrounded by the most pol-ished and lovable form of contempt for women imagin-able, one that was barely aware of itself. That is precisely

why it, with the infinitely natural and self-evident way in which it manifested itself, hurt so much more.

From Elin Wägner's speech to female students in
Uppsala, 1911.

John Landquist and Elin Wägner.

Ester knew exactly what it felt like to be "just a girl," and to harbor the burning longing for freedom and the same opportunities that men had. Her first newspaper pseudonym, "the Boy," was not a random selection.

The quiet Elin embraced the effusive Ester and became her mentor and confidante. She saw the talent, the courage, the curiosity, the pushing of boundaries. Ester happily took on the role of disciple. Elin had a calming effect on her.

The few female journalists in Stockholm had gotten to know each other in recent years while out on assignments or in the hustle and bustle of Klara, the newspaper district in the middle of the city. They'd started to discuss their wages and working conditions over cups of cheap coffee. All of them had to work incredibly hard to be given work that didn't simply involve completing the editorial offices' most menial tasks.

In the early 1910s, the newswomen joined up to form a network. Anyone who was able to slip away from their morning assignments would meet for coffee at Söderberg's patisserie in Hamngatsbacken. They called themselves "the League."

A will to fight had been born out of their shared frustration. They'd started hatching and implementing various schemes. Since no one was willing to financially support women journalists to move onward and upward in the hierarchy, there was nothing for them to do but take matters into their own hands.

Elin Wägner quickly concluded that Ester had everything it took to become a member. She became the proverbial baby of the group, the youngest and most inexperienced. But for the first time ever in Ester's life, she was accepted just as she was, with all sides of her being—even those that didn't fit into the template of how a young bourgeois woman was expected to behave in the early twentieth century. The League would be her first real encounter with the rapidly growing organized women's movement.

> Her charm and originality gave the circle a dramatic and invigorating element. She was the girl of the new age in a somewhat dizzying way; full of ingenuity, with an irresistible desire to do things that people did not expect her to do, and she was pampered accordingly.

> Célie Brunius, member of the League, in the magazine
> *Idun*, no. 10 (1952).

It didn't take long before Ester became a staple of their meetings at Söderberg's patisserie and at League suppers organized by members with sufficiently spacious homes. Sometimes, other friends were also invited to the so-called floor parties where everyone would sit, lie, or lounge half-sprawled on a carpet that offered protection from the drafty floors. In the center of it all was a tablecloth with food and wine.

They eventually grew in number—but it was by no means all female newspaper employees in Stockholm who were invited to the League. The inner circle was made up of Ester, Elin Wägner, Ellen "Murre" Landquist (who was also Elin's sister-in-law), and others. There was Elisabeth Krey, called Kreyan by friends, who wrote extensively and passionately about women's issues in *Svenska Dagbladet*, where she worked. She was a holder of a bachelor's degree and had studied languages at Oxford and at the Sorbonne in Paris.

The daughter of a professor, Elin Brandell was the first female journalist to be employed by *Dagens Nyheter*. There, she had worked her way to her current position and was now a highly valued all-around reporter whose pen could turn informative, cool, sarcastic, or witty—depending on needs and wants. Another professor's daughter in the society was Célie Brunius at *Svenska Dagbladet*. She was known for being highly educated and was a fencing fiend as well.

There was also Agnes "Bysis" Byström from *Stockholms Dagblad*, who was practically born with printing ink on her fingers. Her father was the well-known politician and newspaperman Jacob Byström, a reform-friendly man with roots in both nonreligious circles and the temperance movement.

Dagens Nyheter reporter Ellen Rydelius's first interview was with the famous Russian dancer Anna Pavlova. She conducted the interview in fluent Russian. During her dinner breaks and evenings, Ellen translated the works of Russian author Fyodor Dostoevsky.

When Vera von Kraemer began working at *Svenska Dagbladet* in 1900, female journalists were such an unusual phenomenon that, for a long time, she was considered more of a curiosity than a capable member of the workforce. She carried a mixture of bourgeois mannerisms and political radicalism from home. Her mother, Anna, had remarried Hjalmar Branting, party leader of the Social Democrats.

And then there was Gerda Marcus. She had recently returned to Sweden after three years as a journalist in Berlin.

Everyone at the center of the group had strong opinions about most things and had to fight to be heard in the heated conversations. The League's discussions often took place as night turned into early morning. Sometimes it was simply too late to go home at all. Ester and Ellen Rydelius were both given their very own napkin rings and sets of sheets tied up with silk ribbons to keep at Gerda Marcus's place.

The group was liberal and radical; Elin Brandell and Elin Wägner were the most influential members. Both were behind articles, debate posts, and reports on working women in different social classes, a freer view of love and sexual relations before marriage, and other social topics that had previously been far-from-expected newspaper features.

Years of perseverance and cunning had gone into getting these types of text published. Elin Wägner, for instance, made sure to become a delegate for the Peace Union of the Women of Sweden in order to attend the International Woman Suffrage Alliance Conference in London in May 1909. But that was only a formal arrangement. She'd in fact joined just so she could send minutes back home to Swedish newspapers that would otherwise hardly have bothered to invest in that kind of coverage—especially by a woman. She watched the huge opening procession, wide eyed and proud, alongside representatives of the six million working women all across England.

Once in London, she was able to cover even more activist action and delivered *Dagens Nyheter* headlines such as "In the eye of the women's movement storm—in the home of the suffragettes." Dressed in the women fighters' own colors—white, green, and purple—she sat in the middle of a jubilant Albert Hall where the previously imprisoned leaders Emmeline and Christabel Pankhurst, Annie Kenney, and Mrs. Emmeline Pethick-Lawrence were in everyone's view.

She stood outside Holloway Prison, right by Miss Emmeline Pankhurst, as nineteen pale suffragettes came rushing out to deafening cheers and were hailed as heroes after having been imprisoned for their beliefs.

By the time Ester joined the League, it had been only a few months since the group successfully raised money for a travel fund for female journalists that would enable them to work as foreign correspondents. They didn't do this work unnoticed; they hadn't meant to, either. To awaken the public and their commissioners and make everyone aware of their unfair situation, they arranged to shoot a movie, one of the first ever to take place in Sweden.

The silent film drama was about a young woman who dreamed of becoming a journalist at one of the major newspapers. Elin Wägner wrote the script herself, and Murre Landquist played the lead role. Besides the League itself, several of their male colleagues and influential editors participated. The filming was covered and reported on by several newspapers, and the premiere was at the Grand Hôtel, before all of Stockholm's establishment.

The League's members were increasingly opting to wear long pants. The conservatives viewed the latest trend of pants for women as pure provocation resulting from the ongoing liberation movement. For Ester, it was an obvious choice for several reasons, one of which being that you couldn't ride a motorcycle while wearing a skirt.

Usually, the newswomen went to work dressed in full-length promenade dresses, large hats with feathers and rosettes, and white gloves. The gloves quickly wore thin; one could often catch a glimpse of their fingertips poking through as they took notes while on assignment.

It was becoming increasingly clear that skirts were a poor fit for this job. As reporters, the women could suddenly find themselves in a muddy field or having to climb over a fence. In such moments, it was important to think fast; Elin Brandell knew this from experience. A few years earlier, when she was sent out to cover a murder in Östmark, a bucolic town in Värmland County, she lost her momentum against her male competitors who could easily navigate through the deep snow and across miserable terrains in search of information. Elin eventually tore off her tight skirt and worked in her black woolen underwear. She couldn't miss her shot on one of the few times she'd managed to escape working on C-scraps or the women's pages.

Ester's reporter assignments, on the other hand, were still not nearly as adventurous. When she was asked to write about the price of berries and fruit at the end of the summer of 1911, she chose to change the pseudonym "the Boy" to "Poulet," or "La Poulette" on occasion—the French words for "chicken" and "hen." But editor Tengwall had noticed that she was talented and decided to start giving his young reporter more-advanced assignments.

Earlier that year, the Congress of the International Women's Suffrage Alliance (IWSA) was held in Stockholm. It was the most important event for women's suffrage in 1911, with over a thousand participants. Elin Wägner was, not unexpectedly, one of the people who'd put her heart and soul into the preparations for the event. Selma Lagerlöf, who had received the Nobel Prize in Literature two years prior, spoke before the congress and openly took a stand for women for the first time.

IWSA was a splinter group from the International Council of Women (ICW); its members had grown tired of how the wider movement failed to push women's suffrage alongside the issue of women's rights to education and careers. That same autumn, the leading women of the national organizations affiliated with ICW were going to meet up. Once again, the chosen city was Stockholm. The eyes of the world would turn toward the Swedish capital, where about two hundred delegates from twenty-odd countries planned to gather. Grand invitations and festivities were in the works, alongside preparations for the meeting itself. The royal couple would be hosting a garden party for participants of the meeting, among other things.

Editor Tengwall decided to have his young volunteer cover this internationally significant event. The task was not easy; the press didn't even have access to the meeting's negotiations.

Like her friends in the League, Ester was deeply frustrated that women still had no way of influencing parliamentary elections. She threw herself into the mission, writing passionately about how the meeting rooms were being prepared for the huge influx of people, about the prominent guests who were expected to make an appearance, and the atmosphere at the head office when the first foreign visitors arrived. She managed to secure several flash interviews with stars within the movement that had just made its way to Sweden.

The negotiations, the welcome reception, excursions, and invitations—Ester filled the columns with everything having to do with the meeting. No detail was too small. Even the soft carpets in the head office were described to readers. The articles were quick and entertaining with elements of her own reflections and observations. "The Boy" was back. From this point onward, Ester readopted it as her pseudonym.

Were these the circumstances under which Ester first met Carin? Many things point to this being the case, but no one knows for sure. Carin's mother, Stina Wærn Frisell, was an important voice in Stockholm in the fight for women's suffrage. Stina's husband, Erik Frisell, was one of the country's foremost industrialists, and she was not afraid to use her position to gather votes among the conservative upper-class women. Back home, in the couple's patrician villa on Karlavägen in the high-end Östermalm district, she arranged salons on liberal politics where she called for freedom. The salons were well attended, but the space was never crowded. The house was like a small palace, recently renovated by Ferdinand Boberg, the country's most acclaimed and prominent architect.

It wouldn't be a wild guess to presume that Stina Wærn Frisell would have hosted a salon or two during the ICW congress. Was Ester one of the guests? Or was Elin Wägner the connecting link? They had mutual friends who could also have introduced them to each other. In any case, Carin entered Ester's life at about this time—and changed it forever.

Carin was very educated and very proper. She was incredibly beautiful with dark, curly hair and long, dense eyelashes. There was something graceful about her, almost sweet, and her body language was soft. It made her outspokenness and sense of humor even more refreshing. She was smart and intellectual and could be a bit sharp, almost mean, if she thought it was called for. Just like Ester.

They had a four-year age gap, but they were both sharp minds, go-getters, noisemakers. They made others laugh. But most of all, they made each other laugh. From this point onward, everything changed.

January 29, 1912, was Ester's last day at *Stockholms Dagblad*. She'd been offered a proper temporary position at *Dagens Nyheter*. Before leaving, she received a service certificate from Tengwall. On it, he'd written that she "possesses an unmistakable aptitude for the profession combined with an immense work ethic and interest."

Dagens Nyheter, spring of 1912. Ellen Rydelius and Elin Brandell shared a tiny nook on the ground floor of the *DN* building. It was called "the Maiden Tower" and had two windows facing a cement-covered courtyard. The interior was quite a hodgepodge. Acid stains from the newspaper's stereotype room, where all their photos were developed, could be seen on the ceiling; it lay on the floor just above them. It was dusty and dark, just like the rest of the editorial office. But for a while now, a new light had been shining within. In her memoirs written almost forty years later, Ellen Rydelius went on to relate how they always called on Ester when they needed to be cheered up. They never had to wait long before she would appear in the doorway with a big smile, open the accordion, and start playing a fiddler's waltz. She would lean back slightly, push and pull the bellows with even movements, and sing with gusto.

Carin poses in front of Ester Blenda's camera during a holiday in Storlien in 1923.

The atmosphere at *DN*'s editorial office was cheerful, and several joyful, festive nights followed. Ester got to know the handsome and famously talented correspondent Gustaf Hellström who had reported back from London and Paris. He was friends with both Elin Wägner and her husband, John Landquist, who were beginning to reach a prominent position in the culture section, and a place of high esteem among readers and colleagues alike.

Gustaf Hellström would remain in Ester's world for the rest of her life. He hovered in the periphery at first, seemingly quite insignificant. He wasn't mentioned in letters or other documents until the mid-1920s, when he suddenly stepped forward, entering a space in her life that was neither expected nor desirable. Gustaf Hellström would go on to cause Ester great grief, perhaps the greatest she was ever to experience in her lifetime. But the year was 1912 at this point, and Ester and Gustaf toasted merrily as they bumped into each other in the crowd and struck up a conversation whenever they met in the corridors of *Dagens Nyheter*. The newspaper was in the middle of a period of revolutionary change and renewal. The technology, form, and content had improved, and they'd started hiring female journalists here as well. The responses were exactly what management had hoped for: the readers and advertisers lost in connection with a boycott during the dissolution of the union in 1905 had returned or been replaced by new ones.

Sandwiches, goslings, turbot, apricot cake, and champagne were on the menu at the Publicist Club's annual party on Hasselbacken on March 23, 1912. One of the evening's songs was called "For the ladies," a song specially written for the newswomen.

Endlessly the penholders
Fill every page with their letters
Interviewer, oratress
Notice writress, chronicless.
[. . .] Penholder, see but do not touch
'Tis hard to do.
[. . .] our prophet dear
predicts, as we all know and fear
That our world so masculine
awaits once it is done, dead, *fin*
The day in every miniglobe
when ministers all in gowns enrobe[.]

The issue of voting rights appeared in almost all contexts and events that Ester found herself in. The fight constantly raged on at Carin Wærn Frisell's home, the large villa by Humlegården park where Ester had started to spend a lot of time. Stina Wærn Frisell had begun organizing a group that eventually became known as the Association of Liberal Women. They worked closely with the Free-Minded National Association, predecessor of the Liberal People's Party.

Ester contributed by writing verses and skits about civil rights for herself and the sisterhood, about how women were marching toward the mountains of the future and making fools of conservative men. One of them was specially written for *Föreningen för kvinnans politiska rösträtt* (FKPR), the National Association for Women's Suffrage.

Ester continued to write a lot about children and simple, ordinary people in articles belonging to the still-nascent form of reportage. There were no rules; she could direct the content and shape of her work. Her self-confidence grew as her articles took up more and more print space in the newspaper.

She had just taken up photography, and her pictures were getting published. She was already very familiar with cameras, thanks to her father, Daniel, and she seemed to have inherited his interest in new technology. Newspaper photos were still quite novel. *Dagens Nyheter* published its first reproduced photograph ever as late as the fall of 1902.

With her dual background and upbringing as the daughter of a farmer-turned-bourgeois-businessman, Ester could easily interview both workers and the Olympic Committee's secretary general as the Summer Olympics took place in Stockholm. She was as comfortable in a fine salon as she was in a working-class neighborhood, and she skillfully used her chameleonlike ways at work. And when she met young boys and girls, she took the opportunity to highlight in her writing the difference in the levels of freedom they were afforded.

How would you raise your son—if you had one? [. . .] As
soon as he got big enough, I personally would send him to
housekeeping school so that he could properly learn everything, particularly how to cook incredible food [. . .] Then
I would send him to a rectory in the country, where he
would be initiated into the art of casting candles, churn-
ing butter, and such. And when he finished and was fully
domesticated, I would press a sewing kit into his hands
and say, with complete confidence, "My son, go forth,
marry a modern woman, and be happy!"

> Ester Blenda Nordström in a fictional interview written
> by herself. Published in *Barnens dagblad*, September 18,
> 1913.

Ester stayed at *Dagens Nyheter* for just a bit over six months. When
Svenska Dagbladet finally came knocking, there was no doubt in her
mind. The daily paper offered a permanent post, and they wanted to
make Ester one of their headlining names.

CHAPTER 4

Bansai and the Sharp Hatpin

A large blue-and-yellow flag swayed outside *Svenska Dagbladet*'s editorial office in the Klara district, Stockholm. The pole was mounted just above one of the large corner house's entrances, at the intersection of two major streets. The wind flung the huge piece of fabric back and forth as passersby hurried past.

It was fall then, September, and the large treetops surrounding Klara church, just a stone's throw away, had started to change color. The pointed copper church tower overlooked all the buildings in the inner city, including the newspaper buildings in Klara.

Ester stopped outside a gate and read one of the small side signs: "Editorial Office." That was where she was meant to enter.

There were three desks with six seats along the arched windows in the upper editing room. Her friends from the League, Célie Brunius and Elisabeth Krey, sat there. A spiral cast-iron staircase wound its way up through the floor; the section below was named "the sea of thralls." There was a quiet hum from the editorial work going on down there. Now and again, someone would announce that it was high time to file stories. Another spiral staircase led down to the composing room that smelled of hot lead and newspaper ink.

The editorial secretary, Ewald Stomberg, received Ester and smiled meaningfully at her while he shouted up the stairs to her friends Célie and Gerda to come and meet "the new girl." He would go on to make Ester Nordström the country's most famous journalist. She was still only twenty-one years old, but the experienced editor knew talent when he saw it. He had hired her himself and made sure to give her assignments right from the start. News articles, reports, film reviews, columns . . . He didn't offer much by way of guidance. Stomberg always let the reporters do their assignments as they pleased—as long as they got done.

A young Ester, far right, at Svenska Dagbladet*'s editorial office in the mid-1910s. Others, from the left: Célie Brunius, Märta Lindquist, and Tora Nordström.*

He was the newspaperman of the new age. *Svenska Dagbladet*, like *Dagens Nyheter* and all the other daily newspapers, was being popularized according to the American model, and the increasingly broad-ranging papers were starting to get filled with a new type of content. *Svenska Dagbladet* decided to bet on entertaining and easy reading, social issues, and everyday life. It was no longer just a paper for the male elite.

The 1910s marked the time in which Ewald Stomberg, easily recognizable by his dark mustache and otherwise bare head, introduced the style of so-called active journalism in Sweden. Ester was to become a part of this movement, to a very high degree.

Ewald Stomberg worked hard to make way for more everyday news and wanted to make some news of his own. He believed that the press shouldn't limit itself to simply reproducing events and happenings. He wanted it to be an initiative-taking and independently active societal factor that started and drove new companies, movements, and institutions in various parts of society.

He certainly didn't lack for courage. He had already made press history as a twenty-one-year-old editorial secretary at *Göteborgs-Posten*, a major regional paper, by rallying the editorial office's strengths just before midnight on New Year's Eve 1899, thus succeeding in publishing the world's first newspaper of the new century.

During Ester's first fall at *Svenska Dagbladet*, several newspapers published reports on people who'd had their eyes gouged out in Hamburg, Berlin, and Munich. On Epiphany Day 1913, a victim was identified in Stockholm. Tram conductor Carlsson almost lost his sight, and the press wrote about him. In all previous cases, the unwitting perpetrators were women, elegantly dressed and wearing elaborate hats. The same applied to this lady in Stockholm on Epiphany.

Conductor Carlsson was a polite man who acted without thinking when he spotted what looked to be a damsel in distress. The tram had already started pulling away when she came running down the platform. The woman leaped from the platform to the tram's footsteps to get on board but lost her balance. Carlsson intervened and saved her from falling into the street.

In the chaos that ensued, her long hatpin went straight into Carlsson's eye.

There had previously only been reports of faces bleeding in Gothenburg and Malmö, all from being scratched up by sharp needle tips, but now Sweden could report its first known case of a hatpin-perforated eye.

> One can only hope that it has given our ladies something to think about in the midst of the noise of vanity. Our women have always laughed cruelly when members of the opposite sex have repeatedly proclaimed the great danger of their hatpins. The calls for caution have, of course, been exaggerated, although the number of such accidents nearly equals the number of tram journeys that take place in this city.
>
> From an article in *Svenska Dagbladet*, signed "the Dogged," January 13, 1913.

A skilled ophthalmologist managed to save the conductor's vision. Nonetheless, the incident was followed by a debate and demands for a ban on the dangerous pins that held women's hats in place. Hatpin protection started being mass produced and sold. Just over a week later, the ban proposal went through.

The very same day, Ester boarded an older tram. She had chosen it with care. The benches ran down its length, and she sat close to an older gentleman. She trembled nervously. The hatpin protruding from her headdress was only inches away from the older man's face. It was long, sharp, and unprotected.

On behalf of the newspaper, Ester was about to take the temperature of the hatpin situation in town. The method was as controversial as it was novel: she had to use public transport herself while wearing an incredibly dangerous—and now prohibited—hatpin to see what reactions she got, then write about her experience. A typical Stomberg mission.

> For when I looked up, everyone's eyes were fixed on me, and stern disapproval was apparent in all of them. With an expression of concentrated horror on his face, the choleric gentleman next to me had retreated as far away as possible, and his eyes flashed with a rage that made me stealthily look down behind my boa. I had achieved my goal; I had managed to render the public indignant and was clearly going to have an uncomfortable journey. Still, there was deathly silence; still, a swift escape could have saved me. I began to regret my boldness and had just begun considering flight from the battlefield, but then . . .
>
> "Godd—mn hussy!"
>
> "When every day, we see the papers and the accidents those things cause!"
>
> "When they can cover it for no more than five öre!"
>
> "When there's even a sign!"

> From the article "The first day. Sharp words for the hat-pin ladies," *Svenska Dagbladet*, January 21, 1913.

A lady next to Ester began to loudly tell a fellow traveler that she had personally heard about, and been involved in, several hatpin accidents. She seemed entirely satisfied with her own hat, which was firmly attached with a completely harmless string around her neck. One man was so utterly provoked by Ester's bold, seemingly unaffected disposition that he loudly voiced his astonishment. The tension in the carriage rose as the conductor started to approach Ester.

Stylish and rebellious at the same time.

Right from the moment I sat down, I noticed that his eyes inquisitively rested on my hatpin, and was therefore not surprised when he bent down and asked in hushed tones and with an embarrassed smile:

"Would the lady not like to buy a hatpin cover? That pin looks a bit dangerous!"

"Hatpin cover!" I heard my own voice sound infinitely surprised and shocked, and my expression was full of childish innocence and amazement.

"That's right, a hatpin cover!" the choleric gentleman interjected with a voice that was as sharp as a knife. "Or maybe the little miss does not think it necessary?"

"No, why in the world would I have a cover? I have never owned such a thing before—and nothing has ever come of being without!"

From the article "The first day. Sharp words for the hat-pin ladies," *Svenska Dagbladet*, January 21, 1913.

In the end, Ester allowed herself to be persuaded by the conductor to buy a cover. He helped her attach it. Her performance came to an end, and she hurried back to the editorial office. The well-executed experiment was rewarded with a lot of print space. Ester's personal experience and dramatic retelling was illustrated with drawings of her seated in the carriage with the upset passengers and the conductor who attached the cover to her hat. In the illustrations, the main character herself was sitting in the tram seat, strikingly and elegantly dressed with her hands in a fur muff.

She took on a new pseudonym: Bansai, from the Japanese *banzai*. During the previous year's Olympic Games, where Ester had spent a lot of her time, the Japanese participants' cry of victory and war echoed throughout Stockholm. The power and strength of the expression had stuck with her. Colleagues and friends had watched as she fully engaged in the fights and races while in her spot in the press box, cheering and screaming to the point that her naturally hoarse voice temporarily deepened.

In her own time, Ester skied, swam, biked, and went horseback riding. Sports and competitions were like temporary free zones: they were loud, sweaty, and dirty, and the adrenaline could freely flow in a context that allowed for it. But the only disciplines women could compete in during the 1912 Olympic Games in Stockholm were swimming and tennis.

Columns signed "Bansai" quickly became popular among the readers. In *Svenska Dagbladet*'s self-promotional ads, she was highlighted among the male star columnists in order to attract new subscribers.

Ester was photographed at the emergency rudder aboard the *William Lindberg* as it sailed toward a popular children's holiday campground in Stockholm's archipelago. They were out on a reporting assignment, and Ester was drawn into the photographer's impromptu photoshoot. She used her hand to shield her eyes from the bright sunshine as she looked out over the Åland Sea. Her skirts billowed, and the wind lifted the long black coat. One writer in the editorial office obviously was clearly as amused by the picture as the photographer was. The title of his story: "With women at the helm."

> However, in the interest of truth, we must clarify that the *William Lindberg*'s fate did not lie in the hands of a woman while this photograph was taken, for the real helmsman was still standing in the wheelhouse, not at all affected by how the young lady was moving the rudder about. "This brilliantly symbolizes how little womankind continues to mean to the vessel that is the Swedish state," is probably what was on the mind of the lady before the lens, herself a suffragette and, I might add, an equally cheerful and diligent representative of Stockholm's female journalists.

> From an article in *Svenska Dagbladet*, 1913.

At *Svenska Dagbladet*, the workday began at 10:30 a.m. and was divided into two sessions. The first lasted until 3:00 p.m., followed by a few hours' break, and then it was back to work from 7:00 to 10:00 p.m. You were expected to work overtime when required. Lunch was often eaten in town, obtained from a vending machine or at a restaurant. The newswomen had several choice spots to choose from close by.

There was almost no time for anything other than work. At this point, Carin Wærn Frisell was one of the few people outside the newspaper world whom Ester took the time to see. Carin had no profession; she didn't need one and, given her privileged background alluded to earlier, wasn't expected to secure one, either. Her mother, Stina, came from the aristocratic Wærn family, a long line of well-known mill owners in western Sweden with roots in Denmark. Her father, Erik, had also made a number of successful business deals and consolidated his place as one of the country's most successful business leaders. The family assets, already significant, quickly expanded into a fortune that Carin was to live on for the rest of her life.

Erik was often said to be dry and aloof with a penetrating, piercing stare and was known to get what he wanted. His latest success was the agreement made with the state concerning the valuable Lapland ore fields. Erik Frisell had become CEO of Grängesberg Company (currently known as Gränges), which became the country's most profitable company after it was given proprietary rights to mine and transport the ore. The nominal share value amounted to SEK 63 million, and the market value was estimated at a quarter of a billion. He was also the managing director of Luossavaara-Kiirunavaara, LKAB, which managed mining operations.

Carin's brother, Sven, had been trained to follow in his father's footsteps. Soon, he would move to London and become director of the Grängesberg Company office out there. There were no career plans for Carin. She devoted her time to charity and was occasionally called on to be a hostess. That was it. There was a slight feeling of envy as she saw Ester and listened to her stories about the unpredictable life of a reporter. She, too, had an adventurous streak deep down, and a longing for exciting journeys. She didn't think twice when Ester asked her to ride along on her motorbike.

They drove away on their own little excursions, far from the city. Packed down some food and a few pilsners, then drove straight into the greenery. On one such occasion, they found a spot right next to the water. Spread a blanket out on the sand. Took out pots, plates, and cutlery. Carin took off her white summer hat with its gilded brooch and started plating the food, opening the packed sandwiches, heating up the ready-made stew and the coffee in the saucepan. Reeds danced all around her. Gangly summer flowers swayed languidly, back and forth in the wind, almost touching her bright nautical dress with its cloth buttons.

They'd started to dress the same, often wearing sailor-inspired clothing: trousers, blouses, and dresses. Carin had celebrated midsummer at Ekefors with the entire Nordström family while wearing one of her favorite outfits: a white dress with a sailor collar and a matching white hat with blue edges. The sailor trousers that Ester often wore were a surprise gift from Carin's mother, Stina. During one of Ester's many visits to the lavish villa in Östermalm, Stina suddenly picked up one of Erik's old pairs in the closet and smiled wide at the delighted face of the recipient as she handed them over.

Ester brought out her camera, taking a whole series of pictures of Carin by the shore. Many years later, when her memories became her most welcome companions, she would bring out all the pictures from their excursions and picnics. She would remember the roaring of the motorbike as they took off, the smell of gasoline and grass in her nostrils, Carin's arms around her waist, and her warm breath on the back of her neck. The moments that were only theirs.

Ester had her own telephone at the editorial office, but no typewriter. The newspaper had only a few. The reporters wrote their manuscripts by hand on large yellow straw-paper pads. They had similar, though smaller, pads for all their assignments out on the town.

The light coming through the windows landed on the desks and their matching rattan chairs. Dark floral curtains hung by the windows. The permanent employees had their own workspaces at the double

Ester and Carin often both wore button-down shirts and ties or scarves worn like ties. From a distance, it was soon difficult to tell them apart.

desks. The writers who were paid by the line simply had to sit wherever there was room.

The preparation of C-scraps was women's work here too. Once prepared, they were then published by C. J. Engström, head of the foreign affairs department. He was a well-respected man, but he had an odd habit that usually rendered new employees briefly tongue-tied whenever they entered his room unannounced: he was typically found standing on his hands with his legs up against the wall. He then let his legs drop with a thump and got up, bright red in the face and panting, explaining that he did these gymnastic exercises to get blood to the brain and to sharpen his senses.

At this point, Ester knew exactly what to do with all the clippings from all the foreign newspapers. You were supposed to avoid agency materials or letters from any of the correspondents out in the world. Sometimes, you also received news via the high-voltage phone from Berlin. It had been a minor sensation when it arrived at *Svenska Dagbladet* a few years prior.

All the men in the editorial office were to be addressed by their titles. Ester and the other women used informal address with each other, or they might even just call each other by their surnames. But they still felt like they were equals. The newswomen had proved their professionalism and won the respect of many of their male colleagues. But it would still be years, long after many of them had passed on, before women were finally acknowledged as the actual creators of the language of the modern Swedish newspaper.

Bansai and the other penholders hadn't just gained the right to work and to enter a profession that had been previously exclusively for men. They had also gained the freedom to pick up various habits—the good and the bad. When the workday was over, a group of them would often go down to W6, the restaurant located on the ground floor of the newspaper building. A staircase ran straight down from the editorial office into W6. Toasts were made, and glasses were refilled over and over. Wine, schnapps, and beer flowed. Male and female journalists were side by side around the tables. Almost everyone smoked. Ester did too. Cigarettes, cigars, and pipes.

The newswomen were viewed as a new type of woman by their male friends, spouses, and colleagues.

> Not only was she completely unlike the emancipatresses of old with their reform dress covers, men's hats, and male physiognomies. She also had nothing whatsoever in common with the virginal mannerisms of the female university students or with the temple-enclosed incense romanticism of the Ellen Key acolytes. She was healthy and natural, something of a gentleman farmer's daughter and outdoorswoman who was handy with guns and horses, an Amazon with two breasts.
>
> From the book *Det var en tjusande idyll . . .* [*It Was an Enchanting Utopia . . .*] by Gustaf Hellström.

Gustaf Hellström's above description of Elin Wägner could have been written about almost any of the newspaperwomen. They, too, thought of themselves as more modern, and freer, than most other contemporary women. In their self-authored skits about their condition, the jargon was harsh. The profanities smoldered, and the newswomen cracked jokes about needing a drink. They showed themselves to be confident, cunning, and willing to use their femininity to achieve their goals.

> *Here cometh I*
> *Hell or waters high*
> *To do excellent reportage.*

Hither I have been dispatched
My sailboat's with spirits packed
To stimulate my matters gray
The article will sing, Wahey

[. . .] No challenge e'er did my spirit break
I daren't think of such heartache
What, then, shall we do?
With the judge rendezvous?
Tougher nuts ne'er did make me quake[.]

From *Pennskaftens spex* [*The Penholders' Spex*], found
among Ester Blenda Nordström's remaining belongings,
undated.

Ester enjoyed a festive, joyful atmosphere whenever it arose. The
strong drinks livened up her day-to-day existence. The restlessness that
had been with her since childhood still rushed through her body; an
ill-defined worry fluttered in her chest. But then, the alcohol settled
within like a soft blanket, gentle and warming. It was on such a day
that she and Elin Wägner had decided to meet after work. They both
felt uneasy and depressed.

We strolled about and wound up on the terrace of the
Opera, where we counted our cash and found it to be sufficient for one drink per person. An usher was called who
then suggested various things, but when he reached the
word "absinthe," the question was answered with an overwhelming and swift yes. We drank and grinned terribly

and felt magnificently sinful and depraved, but of course everything eventually felt smoother.

From *Minns du?* [*Do You Remember?*] by Ester Blenda Nordström for Elin Wägner's fiftieth birthday celebration.

The green herb-seasoned spirit, with 70 percent alcohol, was popular within the upper class and in intellectual and artistic circles. Names like "the Green Fairy" and "the Green Demon" had lent absinthe a reputation for causing hallucinations. It had even been banned in Switzerland ever since a man allegedly murdered his entire family and blamed it on having drunk absinthe.

Once the glasses were empty, they decided that Ester would accompany Elin home. While waiting for Linnea Johansson, the housekeeper, to finish cooking the dinner, they lay down to rest. When they told the maid that they'd just had a glass of absinthe each, she became terrified. Convinced that Elin and Ester would lose their minds any second, she decided to watch them closely to avert any disaster. She nervously sneaked around them, anxiously watching every gesture, word, and movement.

She guarded us for several hours with stealth, catlike movements and with a stiff but lovely smile on her lips the whole time, so that when the moment came, we would not lash out at her for having a displeasing countenance. Ha! It was most amusing! Nor could we deny ourselves the magnificent pleasure of speaking and behaving a bit wildly off and on to further keep the maid on her toes. We laughed until we cried that afternoon.

From *Minns du?* [*Do You Remember?*] by Ester Blenda Nordström for Elin Wägner's fiftieth birthday celebration.

The intoxication was liberating and glorious. And it happened more and more often.

In May 1913, Ester swapped out glasses of beer at W6 for drinks at the Café de la Régence in Paris. Carin and another friend of theirs, artist and sculptor Hjördis Tengbom, joined her for the combined work-and-leisure trip lasting several weeks. They entered the Victoria Palace Hotel on Rue Blaise-Desgoffe, with its red velvet walls and giant crystal chandeliers hanging from the ceilings. Hjördis Tengbom couldn't stay long; she had her family to tend to back home in Stockholm. But Carin stayed.

Summer had come early in the French capital. The sun was blazing down on them, and they took turns taking a cooling bath in the tub in the hotel room.

One day, they took a trip out to the suburb of Garches, just over a mile outside the city. They knocked on the door of a villa, overgrown with climbing roses, and were let into a cool studio filled with sketches and banding wheels. The Swedish artist Agnes de Frumerie looked surprised when the visiting journalist explained that she wanted to interview her and wouldn't take no for an answer.

Of course, it became a story. And soon, the editors at *Svenska Dagbladet* also received a sharp-tongued opinion piece written by Bansai—the writer who wrote what no one else would dare. She attacked the glamorous Parisian women, or rather the absence of them. They were accused of "prancing about" and of having ruined their often-beautiful features with poorly done makeup. The text balanced on a delicate line between entertainingly sassy and downright rude.

Ester and Carin enjoyed easy days of complete freedom, far away from the expectations of those around them, and the demands for decorum. Long nights of early summer turned to dawn as they sat at eateries all around Montmartre. They found a favorite spot, a restaurant mostly frequented by artists, who gathered around long tables lit by red kerosene lamps as dusk fell. Clinking wine bottles, glowing cigarettes, hats adorned with flowers on jet-black locks of hair. Outside, an intensely scented jasmine hedge grew against a house wall, and a little old man wearing a top hat sang melancholy sea shanties with a surprisingly youthful voice.

And then there were all the men who courted them. The most stubborn of them went to their hotel every day, hoping to catch Ester's attention. In a letter home to Hjördis, Ester confessed to all the nasty games she played with her admirers, mocked them openly, and revealed secrets about a liberated life in the city where almost anything was fair game.

> Vinding puts a flower in my letter box every day with relentless energy. I generally never look his way, and I slip away as soon as I spot his curly neck. He's just fat and girly and not fun at all. I was with Bertrand the other day up in Montmartre. It was adorable [. . .] The reception at Baron de Markel was delightful with lovely people and good food, and I met the sweetest boy I have ever been with, and we had a very nice time and were both pleased.

> From a letter from Ester Blenda Nordström to Hjördis Tengbom, May 29, 1913.

Ester made Carin laugh by mocking her admirer's awkward advances and large build.

They used paper with the hotel's letterhead as they jointly started composing another letter to their friend Hjördis, this time in rhyme. About how they ate and drank far beyond their means, how Ester swore so loudly that Carin almost fell off her chair in pure horror. They made fun of the metropolis, called it a dump, and rhymed about how they would soon travel away "as far as their coffers can bear." Seven verses, a concluding "Amen!" and then they signed with their names: "Ester Blenda Elisabeth Nordström, journalist. Carin Wærn Frisell, Miss."

But Carin wouldn't remain a miss for long. She was getting married soon. His name was Olof, and he was a pilot in the military.

Ester didn't want to get married. She wanted to write, travel more, farther away, to all the exotic countries she'd read about in books and papers. She wanted to be free.

CHAPTER 5

Peasant Uprisings and Forbidden Letters

Elin Wägner and her husband, John Landquist, moved into an apartment four floors up, on Kungsklippan in Stockholm. It took only a few minutes to walk there from Ester's apartment.

> Ester Blenda was never far away between the years 1911 and 1914.
>
> She usually swooped in, a friend to everyone, a big brisk wave. Her arrival was often announced by the sound of bickering in the kitchen, for she gladly took the kitchen route to say something spicy to Linnea or to enjoy her salty remarks about how quickly she'd swooped in, and about the world in general.
>
> John Landquist on Ester Blenda Nordström in his memoirs, *I ungdomen. Scener ur den förlorade tiden* [*In Youth. Scenes from the Lost Time*].

The League dubbed Elin and John's apartment the "Copper Corner" because there were so many beautiful copper molds in housekeeper

Linnea's kitchen. She prepared a big dinner for the whole party on the day of the Copper Corner's inauguration.

As they sat gathered round the table, John stood up. He surprised everyone with a specially written address in verse about the members of the League. Elin Brandell's dark features were presented as Spanish and proud. Ellen Rydelius, who often hosted parties, was called the general of entertainment. John was in a brilliantly good mood and turned to Ester with a smile: "But Nordström, like Cupid himself, has swung herself into a triumphant parade in the world of everyday press. Among gray veterans, she tosses a wreath of roses as a memento from her dizzying journey. What crying and lamenting our circle will generate the day she is put in a cage."

Soon, she spent more time with Elin and John than she did at the apartment she shared with her sisters in the Kungsholmen district, or in her parents' twelve-room villa. Elin and John encouraged her to be braver in her writing, to get involved, and to apply her skill to important issues that deeply affected people. Elin's third novel, *Helga Wisbeck*, was about to be completed after several years of hard work. It was about a female doctor who renounced marriage and children in order to devote herself wholeheartedly to her profession. Elin also devoted herself wholeheartedly to what she believed in. In addition to her controversial books, she tirelessly fought for women's suffrage. For one, she was arranging a huge signature petition. Almost 350,000 people had signed. Few people burned for the work the way Elin did. At home, however, the fire no longer burned as bright. Over the past year, she and John had begun to drift apart.

John and Ester had begun to meet up by themselves. They often drank, and sometimes they rode out together into the area around Stockholm. They were both skilled equestrians who loved speed and riding the horses in heated gallops around Lidingö Island. Elin never joined them; she wasn't interested in horses or riding.

Later, John wrote in his memoirs about how he had started noticing new things about Ester. Like how her cheeks turned rosy pink after their high-paced gallops, her remarkable ability to charm everyone around her, and how brightly she shone in society. He began to grow uneasy when Ester left town for reporter assignments or leisurely trips. He ruminated about whom else she might have been seeing and imagined her dancing with different men.

He sat alone on a Saturday night when he wrote the first letter. Earlier that day, he had been out riding without Ester by his side. She had traveled up to Åre ski resort and was covering their annual winter sports competition. There, she had learned to wrap the gaiters around her sports trousers just as skillfully as the men competing, so that they didn't slip down or roll up.

That was because Ester had, of course, not settled for just standing and watching. She had thrown herself into the competitions, experienced the dizzying speed and clear danger on the slopes, almost broken her nose after losing her balance and falling off a skeleton bobsleigh, and finally found herself standing on the podium in the bobsleigh and tobogganing event. She was also good at having fun; she joined bridge tournaments and danced to the gramophone or piano playing, long after the electric lights were turned off at midnight and the flickering flames of the candles took over.

Back in Stockholm, John was worried and jealous. He only got as far as a single sentence before the bitterness cut through:

> Dearest,
> Although thou hast long forgotten thine humble acquaintance here in Stockholm in dance circles and the swirling speed of the bobsleigh, I still felt moved to send you a few lines in the quiet of this Saturday night [. . .]
> Sometimes, when I think of you, I get sentimental. You are too happy; may it always be thus! Beware, do not

end your future too soon! [. . .] There are so few who are healthy and happy—become one of them! Well, I needn't have said this; I'm sure you can defend yourself and become one!

I now bid you adieu; forgive me, and do not fall in love with any of the Jews up there, I entreat you most sincerely.

Your friend, John Landquist

From a letter from John Landquist to Ester Blenda
Nordström, March 22, 1913.

At roughly the same time, a young man by the name of Adolf Hitler was sitting in a home for poor men in Vienna, painting watercolors after having failed the entrance exam to the city's Academy of Fine Arts. John Landquist would later become a great admirer of his race politics. John's inappropriate letter to Ester was just one of many to follow in the coming years, with a tone that grew increasingly jealous, desperate, and validation seeking. She saved them. Many decades later, after John Landquist had entered the history books as one of the most important cultural voices in the country in the early twentieth century, and after Ester had managed to become known to the entire Swedish population as Bansai, only to then fall back into oblivion, the letters would be unpacked from a suitcase filled with her personal effects and become the subject of in-depth research. But in the spring, summer, and fall of 1913, John still occasionally sat on the back of Ester's motorcycle, feeling the wind on his face.

Once, when we came roaring over Norrbro from the south
and had the castle behind us, the Parliament House to our
left, and Gustav Adolf's ahead, it just so happened that in

the enchantment of the speed, the city, and her, I pulled
her to me. For a moment, she pulled even closer to me.

John Landquist on Ester Blenda Nordström in his memoirs, *I ungdomen. Scener ur den förlorade tiden* [*In Youth.
Scenes from the Lost Time*].

The feeling lasted no more than a minute or so, but his memory
of that moment remained crystal clear for the rest of his life. John was
in love, and a hope that his feelings weren't unrequited had come to
life. He brought up the word "divorce" with Elin for the first time, but
nothing about the underlying cause. In February 1914, she wrote in her
combined work journal and personal diary:

> I sit alone this Sunday evening. I am full of worry, cannot
> be around anything, cannot write, cannot read, cannot
> slow down, cannot rest. I can no longer rest, for I am too
> full of anguish. Since I completed *Helga Wisbeck* this fall,
> I have not done anything . . . Moments of numbness, then
> hurricanes of pain when the ship hits, goes aground, and is
> badly damaged . . . It is a comfortless and difficult struggle
> to live, to engage, to uphold a proper countenance, when
> the will to will has all but disappeared . . . It is my firm
> belief that my life is only a hindrance, and my death would
> make him as free as he wishes to be.

On February 6 of the very same year, all three of them stood in a
crowded Gustav Adolf's Square, in the middle of the city, side by side.
Above them, the sky was a solid gray, the winds hard. Balconies and
multistory scaffolding on one of the houses were also filled with people
all the way down. People leaned out of windows or stood huddled in

doorposts, cheering and waving white handkerchiefs. In the distance, a black mass could be seen approaching.

Thirty thousand Swedish farmers had joined together in a huge protest and were resolutely marching toward the palace to protest against the liberal government's defense policy, including abandoned plans to build Swedish armored boats. The farmers—all strongly influenced by the world-famous research traveler Sven Hedin's anti-Russian polemic *Ett varningsord* (*A Word of Warning*)—feared that the decision would lead to a Russian invasion.

However, there was also a completely different agenda. Conservative forces in the country wanted to strengthen King Gustav V's position and stop the ongoing progression toward democracy. The goal was to force the resignation of the government, and Prime Minister Karl Staaf, with the king's help. It was not an easy task. Gustav V was not known for taking clear stands on controversial issues.

Flags and white cloth banners were raised by determined hands. One of them read "With God as king and law and fatherland." The farmers were dressed in their best coats, round hats, or fur caps. Storm hats had been banned from the march due to their upper-class connotations. This was meant to be the manifestation of the plain folk speaking with one united voice. But in reality, the idea for the demonstration first took shape at a manor just over two months prior.

The gentleman farmer Uno Nyberg at Långtora Farm, between Enköping and Uppsala, had invited his friend John Möllersvärd, director of the newspaper *Uppsala*, to a November hunt on his land. In the course of their conversation, he told Nyberg that the country's farmers should unite, go to the king, and announce to the king that he could trust them.

They didn't do much hunting that day, for Uno Nyberg had also hatched the idea of a peasants' march—and so a political avalanche was set in motion. Committees formed to arrange meetings; money was raised, and fiery speeches were made around the country in order to recruit participants. The actual trip to Stockholm also took planning, of course. The Swedish peasants' rallying around their king grew into a seven-week-long popular movement.

Ester followed the growth of the peasants' march with great interest, both professionally and privately. It made her Småland County heart beat fiercely. Now she was one of the farmers' most important voices in the media, a weighty tool of power for shaping public opinion.

A special peasants' march agency had been set up, and Ester had been there several times to report on behalf of her conservative news-paper ahead of the huge campaign in Stockholm. The agency worked around the clock; securing enough housing for thirty thousand peasants was no small matter. In Bansai's articles, the fighting spirit and commit-ment shone through between the lines. Her ability to write plainly and engagingly drew readers in. In an interview with a volunteer lieutenant, she highlighted the heroic efforts made by him and others:

> Lieutenant: "The most touching proof of this, I think, is five gentlemen—a doctor, a manager, and others—who come together every night and sew for all they're worth, on two regular machines and three with motors. Every night, they make fifty to sixty each, and that comes to be a whole lot after fourteen days. Their wives sit next to them, carry-ing on with their needlework, because the gentlemen do not want any help! And so we have received such invalu-able help from the garrison's regiments and corps. They received 3,915 men to be housed."
>
> Nordstrom: "You must have an incredible job here at the agency?"
>
> Lieutenant: "Oh, well, we keep going, certainly. For instance, many of us have not left here until seven thirty

in the morning for the past two days. And there is so little time to eat!"

From the article "Feverish activity at the peasants' office,"
Svenska Dagbladet, January 31, 1914.

In her very own way, Ester managed to capture the mood by choosing simple-but-telling snapshots in the middle of the ongoing political action.

There's a great deal of buzzing up there, a crowd of people, a running and a shouting, and—above all—such a great deal of telephoning that it takes a sharp brain not to get entirely dizzy and confused and to lose even the most fundamental faculties of comprehension [. . .] We stand for a moment and watch the constant stream of people pouring in through the door, admiring the endless patience of the committed people.

From the article "Feverish activity at the peasants' office,"
Svenska Dagbladet, January 31, 1914.

Schools, churches, unfurnished apartments, and halls had been made available to the protesting peasants. In a temporary department, forty-four women in two work-shift groups had labored over the making of straw mattresses and pillowcases using sewing machines donated by the manufacturers Singer and Husqvarna. They'd been helped by other volunteer women around the city. When the straw for the mattresses began to run out, a load of one hundred thousand kilos of straw was sent as a gift from peasants in Uppland, the part of the country where the uprising began.

Ester had personally offered her own apartment to five peasants from the farms around her second hometown in Småland. She also persuaded Frithiof to open up his home to Småland peasants.

In the days before the big march, both the peasants' march agency and Ester worked at a feverish pace. She filled many pages of the paper completely on her own, including a description of the atmosphere aboard the extra train that took the Halland County peasants to Stockholm where Ester was the only woman on board and was asked whether she wasn't afraid to be alone with eleven hundred men. The march of the Finnish cavalry was played continuously on a gramophone. The peasants finally walked across the last bit of Norrbro, the bridge taking them up toward the Royal Palace's courtyard, to the sound of the same music.

Ester, Elin, and John tracked how the different county groups took turns during the march. What was on their minds? Could Ester continue to simply ignore the forbidden letters she received from John, or did she want to tell Elin? Was Elin able to concentrate on the political action amid ongoing divorce discussions?

Two months after his wild idea of a peasant march, gentleman farmer Nyberg, with thirty thousand followers behind him, stepped forward in the protective courtyard railings to speak to the king.

Gustav V responded with a prepared speech, and the message was crystal clear: as king, he must have the final say in defense policy. He talked about "*his* army, *his* fleet." It was a powerful attack on Staaf's government.

The words were not his own. From a window inside the castle, speechwriter Sven Hedin looked out on the sea of protesters. At his side was the other person who pressured the king into giving this speech. She was very pleased. Queen Victoria, Gustav V's consort, was widely known as "the royal family's manliest man."

The crowd below cheered rapturously, hats raised to the sky. Everyone joined in song for the national anthem.

Afterward, Stockholm turned into one giant celebration. The farmers filled the city's finest restaurants. Those from Småland, all six hundred of them, entered the Stockholm Stock Exchange Building. The Grand Hôtel hosted a feast of colossal proportions when seven hundred Scanians poured in. Halland County's cultural legacy union footed the bill for a party for its two hundred representatives at the iconic restaurant Pelikan in south Stockholm.

Ester succeeded in the art of documenting the historic march and courtyard speech of the day and the many celebrations of the night, while also organizing an unforgettable party for her own guests. Elin and John gave a helping hand. They had arranged for supper at the Grand Royal, an annex to the Grand Hôtel on Blasieholmen. The splendor and opulence of the premises made the Småland peasants marvel with admiration.

One of them even said, "I think it's nicer here than at the king's."

Ester used the quote in one of her articles published in *Svenska Dagbladet*. Grand Royal, newly completed and called Sweden's finest restaurant, had been named in honor of the very purpose for its creation: ensuring that the royal family would have an exclusive party room when needed. But on February 6, the hall and its winter garden were filled by Ester's Småland farmers. She clearly had her father's talent for party planning. It was an evening with luxurious dishes and generously supplied drinks. Periodically during the evening, everyone stood up to sing the national anthem, "*Du gamla, du fria*," and cheered afterward.

> It was a very successful evening. No other Stockholm party could boast hostesses as entertaining, nor any as knowledgeable about Småland peasants' land, language, and way of reasoning, as Elin Wägner and Ester Blenda. The guests were well worth talking to. I have a vague recollection of seeing speakers at the front, maybe even Sven Hedin, but

we were so preoccupied with the guests and each other that it went unnoticed.

From John Landquist's memoirs, *I ungdomen. Scener ur den förlorade tiden* [*In Youth. Scenes from the Lost Time*].

The conservatives were certain they'd won. The media coverage, with sympathetic articles and reports that spoke to the heart and the gut—Ester's specialty—had been crucial in winning public opinion and putting pressure on politicians.

Three days later, on February 10, 1914, the news of the government's resignation was announced.

CHAPTER 6

Ester Becomes Ester Blenda

Stockholm, spring of 1914. The housekeeper, Linnea Johansson, couldn't help but interfere when she heard the plans that Ester and Elin were making at home over the kitchen table. The twenty-three-year-old Ester obviously thought she knew a lot about maid work after all her years spent in the family home in Småland, where she had milked cows, ridden horse-drawn carriages, and gone out onto the farmland since childhood. And now she intended to be employed for a whole holiday month by a farmer who had no idea that he would, in fact, be welcoming a nosy newspaper reporter into his home.

But Linnea knew that this was worlds apart from working on a farm *in earnest*, when you could simply choose to stop at any time and head back to your newspaper editorial office desk, or when you went to bed every night with starched, crisp sheets as you felt complete fatigue take hold of your arms, legs, and head.

Linnea liked Ester a lot and didn't want her getting into trouble. She was resolute by nature, and therefore took charge; she began to plan and instruct Ester in preparation for her month as an undercover maid.

Linnea had been a maid all her life. Even though she had been promoted to housekeeper and was given free rein to manage the

Wägner/Landquist couple's household, she still very much performed the duties of a maid.

Linnea was highly respected in the home, and it was clear for everyone to see. She was the same age as Elin; they'd been inseparable since 1906 when the then-twenty-four-year-old Elin suffered a number of misfortunes too great for her mind and body to bear. First, an unhappy relationship with a man who was engaged to marry someone else. Then half sister Ruth's disappearing into the water during a swim outing and never reemerging, despite Elin's desperate attempt to dive after her in the dark water. For weeks, she lay in bed at the home of her uncle Alfred in Berg village, Småland County, the place of the accident, and refused to eat. The family was sure she was losing her mind. The one who finally managed to get some food down the thoroughly apathetic Elin was the maid in her uncle's house. Linnea sat by Elin's side and coaxed her with spoonfuls of food, talked to her, or remained silent until the patient's trust in her caregiver was so great that she let herself be saved.

Elin wrote her way out of her grief under the pseudonym "the Laughing Water." Her writings gave her a new lease on life in Stockholm, and she barely had time to settle in the city before she wrote to send for Linnea, who in turn instantly packed her bags and came over.

Linnea was as faithful as she was difficult to impress. She stood with her feet firmly on the ground and didn't deny finding several of Elin's and John's literary Stockholm acquaintances to be odd and strange. When people like these showed up at the house, she didn't hesitate to demonstrate her skepticism; everyone who knew her knew this. Like when lecturer and poet Sigurd Agrell was invited to dinner at the Copper Corner and arrived so early that the host couple hadn't even returned home yet for the day. Linnea had heard rumors that Agrell had a weakness for performing Assyrian dances on café tables and therefore placed him squarely on a chair, before sitting down in the same room and staring suspiciously at him in complete silence until more people arrived.

But for Ester, Linnea offered as much help as she possibly could before she embarked on her mission.

Her missives from Jogersta made her friends back in Stockholm start to worry. Would Ester be able to complete her daring mission?

Neither of them had really thought about how the "sociological study," as John called it, would be received by the Holtz family, the objects of the study. Anonymization of the family in the articles was a given, but they never got beyond that point in the discussions before Ester's departure. Potential consequences were never brought up in the planning stage.

This new worry soon proved more than justified. Ester would certainly become the country's most famous maid and make journalism history—but the people she stepped on along the way didn't let her go unpunished.

Elin and John encouraged her to compile her texts in book form in order to immortalize this unique close-up of Swedish peasant life in general, and the lives of female maids in particular.

Engagement in social causes and realistic depictions were close to both their hearts, not least in Elin's writing. One of John's best friends was the journalist and author Ludvig "Lubbe" Nordström, who had already made a big name for himself as a folk painter after taking a job as a fisherman on Ulvön Island and using the experiences gained from this work in his poetry debut and a collection of short stories.

They all believed that literature should reflect reality, an attitude shared by Mark Twain, Edith Wharton, and Henry James. Within Sweden's borders, this spirit characterized the so-called 1910 Authors, a group in which John and Elin already held prominent positions. Among them was Maria Sandel, the jersey knitter who had started writing novels about working women in filthy factories. Her latest book, *Virveln* (*The Whirl*), on the life and conditions of factory workers and the Swedish general strike of 1909 received a lot of attention for its realistic depictions of the inner workings of that world and for its bold political stances. It was still highly topical by the time Ester came home to Stockholm with her torn-up hands and started writing what would become Sweden's first investigative report. In fact, very few similar articles had ever been published in the world at that point.

In the summer of 1914, the sun was shining all over Europe. The period subsequently known as La Belle Époque was a time of carefree living and a strong sense of faith in the future. The sky was brilliantly blue; the sun's rays never seemed to dim. Southern and central Sweden saw temperature highs of just over ninety degrees. The exceptional summer temperatures would still be discussed over a century later; people would remark how the time just before the outbreak of World War I was so pleasantly bright, light, and framed by the cheerful sounds of orchestras entertaining happy holidaymakers.

As the sensational maid articles signed "Bansai" were being published, Ester worked intensively to compile the texts in book form. She discussed possible titles with Elin, her friend and mentor, who suggested *A Maid among Maids*. Elin also felt that she needed to have a more artistic writer's name and suggested that she start using her middle name as it had a better ring to it.

And so, Ester became Ester Blenda Nordström. On the front cover of her scrapbook for newspaper articles, she wrote "Blenda" between her first and last name. It shone in its new blue ink.

Once that fateful shot was fired in Sarajevo, everything changed and, strangely, nothing changed. Ester Blenda continued to work on her book during the day, and she danced, toasted, and sang at night—all while the threat of a world war loomed, before finally becoming a reality. Sweden was beginning to prepare for invasion, and John Landquist was one of the men called in to dig trenches in the Uppland clay. At night, he slept in a hay-filled barn, worried about how Ester Blenda was handling her new role as the country's leading star reporter and national sensation.

> I was not sure that she really fit into the regular work life of a journalist. And I thought there was something too unrestricted about her conduct. Her sociability spread far and wide once it started blooming [. . .]
>
> This concern and interest in her peace of mind was shared by everyone in our family. Elin, Linnea, and I all agreed that she should have a significant other, a man who could give her peace and security [. . .]
>
> Moments of infatuation with her came and went within me. They went unnoticed. She cooled me down with her cheerful mood. She was a faithful companion, and it would not occur to her to do anything that would hurt her friend.
>
> From John Landquist's memoirs, *I ungdomen. Scener ur den förlorade tiden* [*In Youth. Scenes from the Lost Time*].

This seemingly brave confession of his fleeting feelings of love for her was a great understatement. In fact, both his heated emotions and jealousy increased during the summer months. He did not seem to have batted an eye about how it was Ester Blenda's loyalty to Elin, rather than his own conscience, that prevented the situation from going any further; by the time he came to write his autobiographical book about his years as a young adult, it still wasn't clear that he found it strange upon reflection.

Elin seemed completely oblivious. None of her remaining letters or diary entries suggested that she knew that her husband's infatuation with her best friend and confidante was probably a significant cause of her ongoing marital crisis.

Ester Blenda's thoughts were soon directed away from these intrigues, as the inevitable suddenly happened: the articles on everyone's lips in Sweden finally reached Jogersta. There were differing theories about how they finally got back to Ester's short-lived employers. It may have been the male servant Verner who finally spilled the beans. Ingvar Holtz, son of Anton and Ida, claimed that it was family neighbors who had discovered the articles and noted that the national media was making fun of the farm.

At first, there was complete confusion at Jogersta North Farm. Was *Svenska Dagbladet*'s star reporter Bansai really their maid Ester? Was it really their farm that had been hung out to dry in the newspaper and, in time, in a book as well?

All hopes that the whole thing could be a misunderstanding were dashed when they saw the newspaper picture where part of the farm loomed behind a smiling Ester Blenda wearing a headscarf. It was Holtz's own picture, the photo he gave to his maid before she went home.

The scale of the scandal was of unfathomable proportions for the family. In quiet, rural Jogersta, where the lukewarmth of everyday life was never disrupted and where people had largely been out of view from the rest of the country, the commotion and chaos were unstoppable.

Did *none* of them know that Ester Blenda wasn't a real maid?

> Goodness no! She was a good person and had no airs about her in the least. And she tended to her work, although milking was probably hard for her. She was just like one of us. We could never think she was anything else. On Saturdays, she was out dancing like us, and she could

dance! And play the harmonica. She was a happy girl. And what she wrote wasn't too far from the truth, either.

> Erik Karlsson, employee at Jogersta North Farm
> between approximately 1910 and 1914, in *Dagens*
> *Nyheter*, August 1, 1971.

The sense of betrayal hit them hard. Ida Holtz felt that she had been exposed and mocked before the entire Swedish people and, perhaps even worse, before the women on the parish's neighboring farms. She wrote a bitter letter to Ester Blenda. The letter has since disappeared, but Ester Blenda's reply remains.

The very same day that she received the letter from Ida, she grabbed a whole stack of letterhead that read "*Svenska Dagbladet* AB, Editorial Office" and sat down to respond to the accusations. She delivered a long and emotional written defense speech in which she tried to make Ida believe that Jogersta had not been the sole model for her articles and upcoming book.

She invoked her upbringing on the family estate in Småland County. She also assured Ida that there were several different farming families that she had come across over the years and that had been used for the personal descriptions she shared of everyone on the farm. And above all, she insisted that her intention was not at all to ridicule Swedish farmers:

> On the contrary, my whole mission was to seek to make the public understand and gain an insight into the hard-working life of the rural population, and all the silent toil and travail that women in particular have been allotted and which is so little understood and valued [. . .] I have never met a woman of the house who could even begin to come close to Ida when it comes to hard work, kindness,

and understanding, why I preferred to adopt Ida as a key model in my articles [. . .]

[. . .] Not a word of everything I have written is untrue, and a proposal to forbid a person from describing what they have seen and experienced, when it contains nothing that would offend, is out of the question. I have portrayed what I have seen in my own way, and perhaps I have made it a little too humorous seen from a different viewpoint, but there is also a lot of seriousness, and in my profession as a journalist (which I have held for three years), I must also consider how to make the written word easy to read and entertaining to the reading public.

[. . .] I would love to hear back from Jogersta, which I have grown attached to and feel connected to in some way. And then it would be wonderful to hear about whether Ida finally finds something in my articles that is not pure falsehood. And once again, I want to emphasize that it pains me deeply to think that everyone in Jogersta is hurt by anything, which you have no cause to be. I care for you all too much to wish to make you uncomfortable or aggrieved in any way. And believe me, Ida, there is no reason for you to feel this way, either.

Ida's devoted

Ester

From a letter from Ester Blenda Nordström to Ida Holtz,
July 17, 1914.

Ester Blenda was clearly shaken; she couldn't let go of Ida's letter or of thoughts about Jogersta. The very next day, she took a new stack of stationery from the editorial office and sat down to write to the maid Sigrid as well. Once again, she claimed that there were many young maids hiding behind "Anna." The tone was both appealing and flattering; her words oscillated between expressing a sense of shame and an attempt to minimize matters.

> Dear Sigrid—I believe I am permitted to write to you, too, I think, to tell you not to be angry with me. Dearest one, please do not go about believing that you are depicted in my articles. As I wrote to Ida, I have met so many who have been entirely like you, to the point that Anna might as well be one of our very own maidens down in Småland. Although you were unusually diligent and hardworking— uncommonly diligent, I believe. And I admire you greatly for your ever-cheerful mood, and for your ever-cheerful view on life even as it stretches out bumpy and wearisome before you.
>
> Please rest assured, dear child, that you will always find in me a friendly and good companion, who will gladly help you should you ever need help. I hope, Sigrid, that you do not hold a dim view of me, that you do not remember me with thoughts that are too dark.
>
> From a letter from Ester Blenda Nordström to Sigrid Nilsson, July 18, 1914.

But the Holtz couple knew that Ester Blenda had written about their farm. Everything fit, except the names. Anton Holtz, who was described as drunk and lazy, felt scandalized and lied to.

He turned to *Svenska Dagbladet* to have a response published and justified the request by saying that the newspaper let an "irresponsible female writer give the public a false idea about life in his home and of him as typical of the farmer class." Other farmers supported him in readers' letters. *Svenska Dagbladet* declined. The editorial management stubbornly pointed out that neither their names, nor that of the farm, had been used.

The reader response to the article series was overwhelming. But now, more and more critical voices were beginning to crop up among reviewers and readers of Bansai's bold reporter tricks. Could a spoiled company director's daughter from the big city really insert herself into, and faithfully present, life as a simple peasant girl in the country in just four weeks? What gave this brazen hackette the right to try to impose modern women's notions on her fellow maid and the farmer's wife? How did *Svenska Dagbladet*'s reporter know that it truly was a typical Swedish farmhouse that she had described in such detail and in such an exposing way? And did she not understand the derogatory view of Swedish farmers that could take root in the public following her description of the alcoholic master?

Ester Blenda took center stage and responded to her critics right in the columns. She explained that she had simply "photographed" the farmer in words and had not made him any better or worse than he really was. But concerns about whether her actions were wrong also seem to have seized her. The thought of fleeing altogether took hold at this point too.

Anton Holtz didn't back down. Enraged, he moved on to *Dagens Nyheter*; they seemed amused by his attempts and wrote a notice with the headline "He said, she said." They wrote that they had advised Holtz to speed up his work on his counterattack book that would set the record straight. They stated that his account of what happened "when a cigarette-smoking, harmonica-playing Stockholm lady is meant to be a peasant girl" would be a bitter pill to swallow for *Svenska Dagbladet*'s Bansai.

The columns gained renewed momentum. The news of an attack book made the story even more sensational. The fact that Åhlén & Åkerlund, the publisher behind Ester Blenda's upcoming book, would also be issuing copies of Holtz's pamphlet made the whole story even more scintillating for the scandal-thirsty public.

With all the buzz surrounding her, Ester Blenda, who was in the middle of trying to complete her book, was hardly able to work in peace. In September, she therefore traveled with John and Elin to Varberg city. Elin and John rented an apartment where the three of them sat and drank lots of coffee while proofreading.

Now and again, they took breaks from work; they fished for herring, went on day trips, and swam in the bay with the sandy beach where the record-high temperatures of the bygone summer had left the water pleasantly lukewarm. In the afternoons, they walked back over the cliffs, having had their fill of the sun. Ester Blenda had her motorbike with her and drove around the areas that she knew well through all her previous trips to Aunt Sofi.

Outwardly, they were a happy trio on vacation. But beneath the surface remained a boiling cauldron of jealousy, suspicion, darkness, and frustration. Despite Ester Blenda's obvious disinterest in John, she didn't refuse his proposal for a long riding trip, just the two of them.

Afterward, when he tried to recall what caused her horse to suddenly jerk, he claimed that it may have been Ester Blenda herself choosing to set off at an impulsive gallop. It was still early morning when he saw her lying motionless on the paving stones about forty yards away. John leaped from his saddle and pulled her off the road while her horse galloped away. By the time the ambulance arrived, she'd opened her eyes and managed to get up but had a bad headache. The doctors concluded that she has suffered a concussion and she needed to stay in the hospital for the rest of the week.

My dear little darling!
How are you? You say you are better, but is it so? I would have traveled to Varberg with Hildur, had you told me how bad things were. It is so difficult to hear unfortunate

news from afar; I would hope that you suffer no greater complications from this episode. I should like to welcome you home again with all your limbs intact. Many people long for your articles. One of Frithiof's good friends called and asked why you had not written anything [. . .]

Father was so affected that when he thought we would lose you, he was unable to fall asleep at night. I shivered as I thought about how things could have gone. So you see, your father and mother's sense of calm is not as worthy of admiration as you children might think. I send you a little summer token of love, the last rose; I believe it will make you happy.

From Mother

From a letter from Lotten Nordström to Ester Blenda Nordström, undated.

When Elin and John visited her at the hospital, she joked about the whole incident. Back in Stockholm, Ester Blenda went for an X-ray, and a crack was found in her skull. She was often exhausted and dizzy. But she didn't slow down. On the contrary. *A Maid among Maids* was due to come out soon.

Anton Holtz had received help from his more literate brother-in-law to quickly put together his attack book. It was entitled *Ett pennskaft som piga* (*A Newswoman for a Maid*). The cover was almost identical to Ester Blenda's book *En piga bland pigor* (*A Maid among Maids*), but the photograph where she was sitting and milking a cow had been replaced by an illustration. Ester Blenda was still milking a cow in the picture, but the milk was flowing down into a giant ink bottle instead of a bucket. Her dotted skirt, apron, and headscarf were replaced by elegant clothes, and she was casually smoking a cigarette. A large white feather—the symbol of Swedish newswomen at the time—was tucked behind her ear.

The covers of En piga bland pigor *[A Maid among Maids]* and the attack book *Ett pennskaft som piga *[A Newswoman for a Maid].*

Everyone must, after some consideration, realize how vile it was to sneak into a home in disguise and under false pretenses, to then, in taking advantage of the public's desire for sensationalism, scandalize its inhabitants [. . .] In response to my advertisement in search of a maiden skilled at milking, she stated that she was very big and strong, and was used to both milking and other agricultural activities in her parents' home, but was without credentials due to never having held any formal employment [. . .] As for one of her observations made in the course of the thirty days— that of "women prematurely worn out, pale and thin by the age of thirty," etc.—this is too ridiculous to be worthy of any earnest response. It ought to be common knowledge that farming women, with their healthy lifestyles, tend to maintain their ability to work longer than any other, often until sixty to seventy years of age. There are exceptions to all rules, but none such can be said to be true of anyone at my farm.

> From the book *Ett pennskaft som piga—svar av Bonn i Taninge* [*A Newswoman for a Maid—Response by a Farmer in Taninge*], by Anton Holtz.

Ester Blenda was portrayed in the book as a generally useless maid: sloppy, lazy, and careless. Holtz described her as a pale city girl with a taste for men and the good life. And a purveyor of strange ideas on women's issues.

Some of the episodes and events recounted in the attack book were so obviously distorted that they were immediately dismissed as exaggerations or pure fabrications by both critics and the public. But for those readers who knew Ester Blenda and her personality, it was clear that Holtz was an unexpectedly good judge of character. He also described her as a dreamer with a great imagination and noted that her mood could change quickly. One second, she was eager, enthusiastic, charming, and social. The next, she was absent in every sense of the word. He detected a dark streak in her, skillfully concealed by fun and games. Ester Blenda's friends from that time in her life testified to exactly the same thing.

Holtz also noted Ester Blenda's special connection with animals, and how she turned to them during her time on the farm, as they seemed to calm her down.

> He seems to believe that a book should be written under oath. Now he has responded without practicing what he

preaches in any way. The worst thing is that he comes across as boring in his attempt to avenge a supposed injustice, and the exaggerations are too obvious to be amusing. In his opinion, his maid was ignorant, lazy, and hysterical. This may well be the case, and he has the right to say so in a book, provided he can do so in literary fashion. But if he is unable to do so, then he ought not to trouble the public with a book. He should, instead, briefly state his case and not charge so much for his assessment.

From *Svenska Dagbladet*, September 18, 1915.

Everything about Ester Blenda's and Anton Holtz's conflicting books became national news. Rumors that *Farmer in Taninge* earned four thousand kronor—a staggering sum at the time—and that it was about to reach the same number of print runs as Ester Blenda's bestselling book were published together with tongue-in-cheek advice that they both continue to fight in public in order to secure even more money and fame.

For the tenth print run of *A Maid among Maids*, Ester Blenda added a few polemical lines to her book:

A book has been written against this book—the author calls it *A Newswoman for a Maid* and clearly hopes that the public will view it as a reply to *A Maid among Maids*. But it is not; there is not a line in that book—with the possible exception of part of the prologue—that can be said to constitute a reply to any of what I have written [. . .] It is beneath me to have to explain that the events and stories in that book are lies from start to finish, and I do not consider any of it worthy of denial, except perhaps the claim that I would have assumed the position under a

false name. I gave my full name, even showed them character references on arrival, and performed my duties to
such a standard that, at the point of farewell, the farmer's
wife asked me to come back and remain in her employ for
a whole year if possible.

Around the same time, a young female author in Copenhagen tried
to attract attention by hanging on to the back of a car at high speed, and
newspapers all over the country speculated whether *Svenska Dagbladet's*
Bansai had struck again. Ester Blenda was forced to publicly deny this
in writing. The story of the fake maid became a refrain in local revues.

Her life spun faster and faster. The long workdays and lavish
banquets that continuously alternated started to feel more and more
demanding. And a jealous John kept the illicit love letters coming . . .

Dear Ester,
I do apologize for not approaching you at the tavern yesterday. You stepped out with a Miss So-and-So whom I did
not wish to make conversation with. Listen, you must not
grow exceedingly weary of how anxiously I have behaved
recently, to the point of even latching on to you with my
company yesterday.

It is not always easy to instantly accept things as they are.

The affection I have begun to feel for you has, for natural reasons, not remained without being of some torment
to me, and my life was already sufficiently complicated
before this.

From a letter from John Landquist to Ester Blenda
Nordström, November 1, 1914.

He was not the only one to cast longing eyes on her. She personally often joked ironically about her appearance, and clearly still didn't see herself as attractive or comprehend how powerfully attractive she was to others; this would be talked about by many men both during and beyond her lifetime:

> Who hasn't their share of dream girls? One of mine was Ester Blenda Nordström [. . .] There was something dizzying about that writer girl. She was pretty, freckled, reckless, quick, and plucky and simply had this essence that drew all the boys' eyes her way.
>
> Ethnographer and Sami researcher Ernst Manker in his book *På Tredje botten. Minnesbilder* [*On the Third Floor, Vivid Memories*].

> The bold journalist Ester Blenda Nordström, with a boy's cut and bright eyes [. . .] masculine angular movements, trim and tall.
>
> The painter and sculptor Göran Brunius in *Komiska konturer tecknade ur minnet* [*Comic Contours Drawn from Memory*].

Ester Blenda began to withdraw from Stockholm. Lost the desire to work. Was overcome with self-doubt. She spent time with her mother at Åbyfors and with Aunt Sofi on the west coast, all to get far away from the attention, celebrity, published lies, the tavern on Kungsklippan with Elin's sad eyes and John's double dealings. She deliberately let her visits turn sparse throughout the fall. Elin and Linnea, the housekeeper, were disappointed and began to wonder why. John joined in with their lamentations.

Other friendships, both old and new, blossomed and took up more space instead. There were many trips out with Carin. They both loved to run away from it all, to take in freedom together. They drove along winding country roads, past red-painted farms, and stopped wherever they thought it looked nice, not heading back to town till dark. Ester Blenda dropped Carin off outside her new home in Södermalm, in the southern part of Stockholm. An enchanting view over the eastern bay of Lake Mälaren opened up just a few steps from the gate; apart from this, the new district and the apartment were far from the grandeur that Carin was accustomed to.

Her husband, Olof, waited inside. He was both handsome and famous. In 1912, Lieutenant Olof Dahlbeck performed the Swedish navy's first flight over Stockholm. At a temperature of fourteen degrees, he took off from the ice on a tiny island at Värtahamnen and landed on roughly the same spot a moment later in a Nyrop No. 3 plane, modeled after a French plane. But to the public, it was simply known as the Aeroplane; it was the only Nyrop that existed in Sweden at the time.

Olof, or Olle as he was usually called, had a private plane as well. He completed the first delivery flight with newspapers using this plane: two thousand copies of *Dagens Nyheter* from Stockholm to Uppsala, a city just over forty miles away.

There was no information about how Carin and the notable pilot met and found each other, but a web search of his name revealed a photograph from 1911 where he was sitting in his plane with a woman who looked incredibly similar to Carin Wærn Frisell in the passenger seat. She had dark hair, was wearing a light hat and black coat, and had her eyes turned to the photographer. Five men were lying on the ground, using their full weight and every muscle in their bodies, to stop the heavily smoking plane from taking off before the photo was taken.

Carin and Ester Blenda photographed during a forest outing.

Things didn't always go smoothly up in the air. From time to time, Olof crashed into a hill and had to be helped out of a smoking wreckage, or he had to pull himself out. One time, on his way to Copenhagen, he crash-landed behind a barn on the Näs farm in a tiny village in Småland County. Two children rushed out into the November cold to see what had happened and could not hide their delight when they realized that

Sweden's first (and only) aviation hero was sitting in the grass in front of them, firing off one profanity after another.

Long afterward, the girl wrote about the spectacular event:

> A nationally known aviation pioneer came crashing down from the sky just then [. . .] Having him fall just behind our farm—it was more than any child could have hoped for. My brother and I were the first to come running to the scene of the accident and to hear his wild oaths and curses, issued while he was seated next to his broken machine.
>
> From Astrid Lindgren's book *Madicken på Junibacken* (*Meg of June Hill*).

The girl with the thin braid went by the name of Astrid Lindgren; in time, she would become far more famous than the pilot himself.

Carin and Olof were young, beautiful, high profile, wealthy. It should have been a happy marriage, and yet, their marriage would come to an end within a few years.

Hjalmar Lundbohm, Ester's senior by thirty-five years, became one of her newly made friends. Was Carin the one to bring them together? Lundbohm was a geologist and chemist and the first manager to be employed at the ore company LKAB, where Carin's father, Erik Frisell, was CEO. Lundbohm received the position after mapping the iron ore at the mountains Kiirunavaara and Luossavaara in Lapland on behalf of the company and discovering the large deposits. He worked closely with Erik Frisell, and Hjalmar Lundbohm had become close with all members of the family—including Stina and Carin.

He obviously had both a keen geologist's eye and great business sense. When Lundbohm began his major survey shortly after the turn of the century, Lapland was still unexploited by European colonization. The potential was enormous—and Hjalmar Lundbohm could see it.

By the time he met Ester Blenda just over ten years later, he had already made a fortune building up the city of Kiruna and introducing both industrialism and tourism to the region.

The "King of Kiruna" was short, rotund, red blond, and had a peculiar habit of always leaning his head back when listening to someone else talk. As a result, his bushy chin beard often jutted straight ahead. He was known for his great cultural interests and lovable manner and was widely regarded as a bit of a genius. His circle of friends included some of the most significant and influential artists and cultural stars in Sweden: Prince Eugen, the author August Strindberg, and the artists Albert Engström, Anders Zorn, and Carl Larsson.

Hjalmar asked his friend Anders Zorn to paint Ester Blenda. He immortalized her lying in a black silk dress and heels on the leather sofa in his studio in Stockholm. In her hands, she held a lute. Her gaze was comically absent. Afterward, she received the painting as a gift from Hjalmar. His friends soon became Ester Blenda's friends as well.

They discovered that they had a lot in common: they were both driven, restless, and constantly in search of their next projects. The age difference of thirty-five years seemed insignificant. They went to dinners and shows together. When the famous French nude dancer Adorée Villany, who had previously shocked all of Europe with her erotic show, took the stage at the Oscar Theater in Stockholm, they sat side by side in the salon.

> Today, Lundbohm and I are going out to become spectators of indecency = Adorée Villany, who dances naked. By the way, it is unlikely to be all that inspiring, as she is so terribly thin.

> From a letter from Ester Blenda Nordström to her friend
> Hjördis Tengbom, January 7, 1915.

Hjördis Tengbom, the friend who was with Ester Blenda and Carin in Paris, had attended both the art department at the Technical School and the Royal Swedish Academy of Fine Arts. She had also studied in France, England, Germany, Denmark, and Norway. She and Ester Blenda had known each other for a long time and had many mutual friends, including Elin Wägner.

During the late fall of 1914, Ester Blenda and her friend Hjördis became very close. Both had weary hearts. Hjördis was married to the prominent architect Ivar Tengbom and had put her own career aside to bear, birth, and raise four children in recent years. Their marriage was not a happy one; Hjördis was depressed.

They started to meet up often, either along with Carin and Elin, alone, or with Hjördis's children. Sometimes, Ester Blenda babysat for them. She also regularly looked after Kjell and Anne-Marie, the children of Frithiof, and always took the job very seriously.

On occasion, she took all the children at once to various events; if there was nothing to do, she created her own adventures. Everything was much easier in the world of children; here, she could escape all the demands placed on her, as well as her increasingly claustrophobic social life. Everyone wanted to be right next to the new star. At the lavish Christmas do of 1914 with colleagues and friends, Ester Blenda's stunning breakthrough was honored with a unique composition of ten verses that were specially printed so everyone could join in song. Her portrait was on the front, and a picture of a maid milking a cow on the back:

> *As maid among maids you were dressed*
> *As maid among maids, you impressed*
> *[. . .]*
> *Green tablets you got 'stead of liquid detergent*
> *To rub your assuredly beauteous integument.*

Beneath yokes of water your back did crook
You certainly toiled for your book!
[. . .]
You raced on your motorcycle, quickest bar none
On streets, over bridges—your duty you've done.
Right across Sweden you thunderously blow
Always with someone in tow
[. . .]
Then you posed for Zorn when your muse did sing
And heading to Lapland seemed, to you, just the thing
The express you boarded, and northward you went—

The trips to her mother in Småland and Aunt Sofi in Varberg were no longer enough in the end. Her search for her lost sense of harmony took her 760 miles away from Stockholm's sticky beer glasses, stressful deadlines, and the anxiety of being stuck at a desk. Ester Blenda fled to Hjalmar's Lapland.

CHAPTER 7

The Nomadic Teacher

The white reindeer didn't accept the hands holding the reins. They were not as determined and powerful as what he was accustomed to. He raced and violently flung his body side to side until the driver fell out of her sledge and was dragged through the dry snow, behind the carriage. The Sami guide, Tjoggi, intervened. He shook his head when the reporter Bansai from Stockholm quickly brushed off the snow and sat back down in the sledge.

Many more attempts were required before the animal was finally tamed. The new driver didn't hold back; she steered the reindeer out over the plains at a furious speed, straight toward the desolation and silence. Tjoggi drove after her, in the direction of his encampment.

In the eyes of many at the time, the Sami were regarded as a primitive, lesser people with unhygienic and uncivilized lives. In *Nordisk familjebok* (*Nordic Family Book*), for example, the Sami people, derogatorily referred to as "Lapps," were described as hunchbacked and smelly.

The condescending fascination with the Indigenous people extended far beyond Nordic borders. As early as 1822, a living Sami was exhibited in

London. Since then, they had been paraded in front of stunned crowds at exhibitions all around the world.

Although it was later to be completely discredited and labeled as pseudoscience, the study of eugenics was already a strongly established scientific discipline throughout Europe at large. Human races were compared and defined by identifying and classifying bodily character-istics that were deemed to be hereditary. At this point in Ester's life, it had gained a foothold in Sweden as well; Sweden would soon become a world leader in the field. And the support for the research was both immense and widespread. Parliamentary politicians and academicians in zoology, psychiatry, and botany established the Swedish Society for Racial Hygiene and were actively lobbying for a eugenics institute in Sweden, echoing similar proponents across Europe whose influence would have devastating effects.

Dr. Herman Lundborg, a professor and leading eugenicist of the time, who defended his dissertation on the subject of hereditary dis-ease in the Blekinge region, was the loudest and strongest voice on the matter. He combined medical studies with forays into genealogy; in his seven-kilo dissertation, he had concluded that hereditary disease was the root cause of the ongoing cultural and economic degeneration.

Lundborg frightened Sweden with the threat of endangerment to the whole nation if people with substandard aptitudes were allowed to continue to reproduce. He eagerly oversaw racial hygiene work in the belief that it would save the country's future.

Since 1913, he had been stationed in Torne Lappmark to investi-gate the Sami people and the Tornedalians. Highly esteemed Swedish politicians and scholars described them as inferior individuals. In his extensive field inventories, the doctor and his team of assistants worked and interpreted their way through encampments and villages. The work was state sanctioned.

Residents were told that they'd receive free medical checkups. They were asked to undress, and precise measurements were made of head dimensions, face height, nose width, jaws, legs, feet, hands, arms, and body height. Cold metal instruments met warm human skin. Surprised and often embarrassed and furtive glances flickered around for something to fixate on while the mystifying activity proceeded. No explanations were given. Hair color; beard growth; pubic hair; and eyes, irises, and pupils—everything was thoroughly examined and documented in data forms. Disabilities were noted. An elaborate color scale was used to determine each individual's skin color.

You couldn't turn down a free medical checkup when times were hard. The Nordic Sami had started experiencing major problems concerning their livelihoods. LKAB had become the country's most successful company with an almost unimaginably lucrative business. The plant accounted for almost 85 percent of Sweden's total ore exports. The newfangled city of Kiruna had expanded rapidly. Hjalmar Lundbohm, the mine's manager and the city's leading figure, had a clear goal in mind: to make the town "the world's best community." Modern communication systems had been built up, and settlers were allocated land by the state in order to establish themselves in the region. They received plots of land that had previously belonged to Tornedalians and Sami settlements for several generations. The Sami, who depended on reindeer husbandry, were threatened with fines should their animals cross the new cultivation boundaries to graze.

They had already been living under strenuous conditions. The 1905 dissolution of Sweden's union with Norway, which led to a closed national border, had caused major problems in the migrations with herds in northern Lapland, which had previously included Norway, Sweden, and Finland. Many Sami had already been forced to give up reindeer herding or move south.

At this point, there was a lively debate about living conditions in Lapland, the designated "Land of the Future," where mining, forestry, and hydropower development paved the way ahead. The state had partially financed the railway construction in order to have control over how the iron ore assets were transported. It was a powerfully protectionist marking of territory. Northern Sweden, with its large stores of natural resources, was viewed as Sweden's Klondike.

The interest in the Sami had never been greater. *Svenska Dagbladet's* star reporter Bansai was on site in Lapland to, once again, report straight from the heart of the matter. But this time, Ester Blenda wasn't concealing her intentions, or her identity. She was going to talk about the Sami, their everyday life, customs, and traditions. She wrote her reports in her typical style with vivid environmental descriptions, and in personal form / first person. Five articles emerged from this work, with plenty of print space, several photos, and long exposés about a Sami fair in Jukkasjärvi and the Sami encampment out in the wilderness, and tales of wild sledges over the deserted, snowy expanses. Bansai didn't hesitate to highlight what she found exotic or the humorous elements to entertain the readership, but she also described a hardworking, quiet, welcoming people with proud traditions.

It was as far away from the salons of Stockholm as one could get. She felt at peace and at home among the people who had lived in and off nature in the exact same way for many thousands of years. Lapland's seclusion from the outer world was healing. The anxiety in her chest began to settle.

> Do you understand how wonderful it is to sit crouched in a half-dark hut, for instance, where only the fire in the middle of the floor and the stars peeking in through the tent opening shine, where the coffee smells lovely and strong in the kettle that hangs in a hook over the fire, and you eat salted trout and bread baked over the fire [. . .]

I feel like a god, and would prefer to stay here among the Lapps and the northern lights forever.

From a letter from Ester Blenda Nordström to her sister-in-law, Gerda Nordström, Kiruna, December 3, 1914.

She meant every word. Ester Blenda really wanted to stay. The plan gradually took shape during the monthlong reporting trip. She had figured out how she could get away from Stockholm for an extended period of time and spend it in Lapland. And it would all result in a new reportage book.

It was a bold idea, a new adventure, and would soon make her one of the most important voices for the Sami cause in the early twentieth century—and the object of admiration by Sweden's most influential eugenicist of all time. But it was all about to go wrong right from the start. The newspapers found out about her plans and started writing.

To the Nomadic Life as a Lapp Catechist
Bansai Turns North Once Again

Svenska Dagbladet's employee Miss Ester Nordström (Bansai) has applied for employment as a "wandering nomadic teacher" up in Lapland. This has already been mentioned in several newspapers, with or without further comments, but as the matter had not yet been fully decided, we have not addressed it, until now.

On the order of Jukkasjärvi school council, the cathedral chapter in Luleå will employ Miss Nordström in the aforementioned capacity for eighteen weeks next summer, where she is to be stationed in Saarivouma as soon as she certifies that she is sufficiently fluent in the Finnish language. And since Miss N. has been taking lessons in this language for some time and currently intends to travel up to a Finn village to perfect her knowledge of Finnish for a couple of months, one can, with prior knowledge of Miss N.'s immense energy, be certain that the Lapp children in Saarivouma will not be without a teacher this summer.

From an article in *Svenska Dagbladet*, February 27, 1915.

The vacant teaching position was with the Finnish-speaking Saarivouma Sami people in Övre Soppero town. Their children needed teachers as they migrated up along Torne Marsh to their summer encampment by Lake Altevand in the Norwegian mountains.

The news that *Svenska Dagbladet*'s Bansai had applied for a position as a nomadic teacher was cause for concern all over Norrbotten County. Two camps formed, one for and one against. She was described in local newspapers and the national press as an "adventurous Stockholm missy," and critics questioned whether children should be left in the care of such a person. They said it was reprehensible, and some suspected that her purpose was not at all to teach the Sami children; rather, she was only in it to write about "yet another feat of hers."

But Ester Blenda didn't retract her job application; her curiosity and desire to tell stories had returned. Besides, a teacher was sorely needed; she knew this from her reportage trip. The vacancies for one permanent nomadic teacher in Övre Soppero and three migratory teachers had been advertised for a long time. Only two applications had been received by the school council, none of which were for the wandering teacher positions.

The school council faced a difficult decision. Either they hire a scandal-ridden Stockholm journalist, albeit with a high school diploma and good language skills, or they would have to stop educating the Sami children—completely contrary to the new legislation on education for the Sami people.

Ester Blenda reluctantly left Lapland to await the outcome of the protracted decision-making process.

Then finally, it came: the cathedral chapter offered her the post. Hjalmar Lundbohm, the council member with the most power, was likely to have pushed the issue hard and gotten his way. But despite having her influential rich friend in her corner, Ester Blenda was worried that her fame and reputation would ruin her plans.

> Lagan, January 28, 1915
> Dear sweet little Hjördis, you are truly incredibly adorable, and your letter made me so happy. It was so good and like you, and it has helped me along. Because I have had quite the time—I'm still having quite the time, by the way—but it's starting to somewhat settle. I was so saddened by the town and the gentry that I was seized by an endless longing for Småland and the peasant farmers—and so I have come here to the home of my childhood, and here I have had a great and wonderful peace, and how I only wish I could stay here for all eternity. On February 1, I will be pulling my socks up again. Let's see how it goes with the Lapland story! I see in the newspapers that they have certainly started arguing and writing about it now, and it seems the cathedral chapter refuses to not take me. It would really make me very sad if the whole delightful plan went awry. I have put so much effort into getting almost a whole year alone up in the wilderness and have longed so for it—longing is, of course, exactly what one must never do, as that is when things go to pot one way or another—but I know that this year will be awful if I do not escape from all of mankind. It's a terrible profession

I have—people get so close to you, and you always have so many around you. "Life is wonderful," you write. Yes, of course it is, but sometimes it is quite complicated and difficult, and you do not have enough strength to bear all the consequences of your own folly. This is what makes one feel so infinitely contemptible at times.

Alas, little Hjördis, how sad it is sometimes to live!

From a letter from Ester Blenda Nordström to her friend
Hjördis Tengbom, January 28, 1915.

Svenska Dagbladet approved the yearlong sabbatical. Throughout the spring, Ester Blenda studied Finnish in Kiruna while living in Hjalmar's home. Prince Eugen was also visiting, and they apparently had so much fun together that he stayed in the house for three months with Ester Blenda and the "King of Kiruna." They skied every day and stopped on the slopes to drink hot tea out of a thermos. When the prince fell in the snow, Ester Blenda handed him her arm, muscular from all her hours on the motorbike, and pulled him up. In the evenings, they played poker; in a letter written much later, as she reminisced about the early days of her time in Norrbotten, Ester Blenda disclosed, with some embarrassment, how she "beat the kind man, winning over two hundred freshly embossed shiny one-krona coins that he had brought with him in a chamois-leather bag."

They spent time with more of Hjalmar's friends. One of them was Dr. Herman Lundborg; Hjalmar and his extensive local network helped the doctor get in contact with the local population for his ongoing field studies. He was thrilled to be joined by a bestselling author and showed great interest in her upcoming book. At Hjalmar's grand sixty-second birthday festivities in April, she also met several of Herman Lundborg's closest associates. She promised the whole party to make dinner should they visit the Saarivouma Sami.

Ester Blenda was most likely both well versed in the matter of state-supported eugenics research and positively oriented toward it. There were many strong proponents of the work in her circle of acquaintances. The high-profile figures and influential politicians of the time—people like Ellen Key, Anders Zorn, Sven Hedin, and the Social Democratic Party leader Hjalmar Branting—wholeheartedly supported the new science. The critical voices were few and lacking in influence.

Even her now very close friend Hjalmar Lundbohm was greatly interested in eugenics but torn when it came to Dr. Lundborg's work. He himself had taken the initiative and financed many different scientific studies in the field, but his and Lundborg's agendas and attitudes differed significantly.

They agreed that the races should be kept apart. But in Hjalmar Lundbohm's case, it was from a place of wanting to distinguish the Sami culture from the Swedish one in order to safeguard the former, a culture he found to be unique—not from a place of seeking out defects and evidence of a lower-status race.

Lundbohm believed that the Sami should be kept away from the comfortable, modern civilization so as not to be tempted to abandon their own natural nomadic existence, an existence that rendered them a sensible and harmonious people. Part of his vision of the ideal society he wanted to create involved a reality where the Sami would live and work as they had always done. It included prosperous, healthy Sami who could earn a living and raise strong children to take over both reindeer cultivation and the traditions.

Hjalmar Lundbohm was tormented by the fact that the industrialization that he'd introduced to the area now posed a great threat to the future of the Sami. As early as 1907, he wrote in a memorandum to the head of the Ministry of Civil Affairs that several governing laws and ordinances in place at the time of the ongoing industrial expansion in Lapland overlooked the fact that the Sami were Lapland's Indigenous people and therefore held the oldest rights to the land.

In a letter to his friend Albert Engström, an artist, author, and member of the Swedish Academy, he expressed his concern with even greater emotion: "This noble and good race is currently subject to us white people who represent the culture, to the point that we are violent to the Lapps because they disregard property boundaries and political boundaries that we have raised more or less arbitrarily throughout their land. It makes one ashamed to be the bearers of culture when one bears witness to this misery."

The Sami's social situation and social hygiene were other issues close to his heart. Both settled and nomadic Sami were included in a large study he had carried out on all schoolchildren in Kiruna due to the spread of tuberculosis in the area. The results showed that the Sami children were just as severely affected as the country's wider population, and thus in need of the same amount and degree of medicine, care, and other assistance.

The manager made personal home visits to camps and villages; when the need became too great in individual families, he contributed his own money. Over the years, he had become a personal friend to many Sami people in the area. But he also increased their dependency and sense of the white man's obvious superiority. They viewed Lundbohm as their protector and gave their *tisponentti* (i.e., manager) the loving nickname "Locköga" ("Heavy-Lidded Eye").

Hjalmar Lundbohm was a skillful lobbyist and used all his influence to spread his view of the Sami to the public, and to influence the laws that affected them. Parliamentary politicians, academy members, merchants, district chiefs, and visiting high-ranking clergymen were invited to the exotic mountain world where the manager hosted grand dinners with reindeer. He took his guests to encampments and proudly showed the wonderful views of nature that he himself had come to love and perpetually long for.

It was no coincidence that he had a hand in the game in the new school system that had just been introduced for the Sami. Hjalmar

Lundbohm had been appointed as an expert in the state commission that led to the reform. In the past, many of the children of reindeer-herding Sami received inadequate education, or none at all. Now they had the right to basic education, but it had to be delivered in special nomadic schools, and the subjects had to be relevant to their future lifestyle and primary means of earning a living.

Many Sami people were critical of the reform. They wanted to create a school that was adapted to the rapid developments of society and where students could attend in real school buildings. But no one listened to them.

Hjalmar Lundbohm's own scientific research had turned into a whole series of studies that he had published under the name *Lapparna och deras land* (*The Lapps and Their Land*). The next volume would be Ester Blenda's planned reportage book about her time as a nomadic teacher.

She began to prepare for the move to the Saarivouma Sami people, for the work of joining the collective and forming her own interpretation of the people in it. The national newspapers interviewed Bansai about her upcoming assignment. Reports were written about her progress in gaining knowledge about Lapland, and a minister by the name of Bergfors in Vittangi village confirmed in the media that her knowledge of the Finnish language would soon be sufficient. The newspaper *Norrbottens-Kuriren* asked the substitute teacher whether she was truly up to par.

> "Miss Nordström possesses a high level of intelligence and a rare vigor, which overcomes all difficulties, and to this is added another good quality that makes her very well suited for her calling: namely her ability of getting on good terms with the Lapps to such an extent that she is a real favorite of the Saarivouma Samis whom she will serve as

a teacher. We are fortunate that the Lapland education system has been given such a capacity as Miss Ester Blenda Nordström," says the newspaper's interlocutor.

The criticism quieted down. In a letter to Hjördis, Ester Blenda wrote that she was "not yet really whole of soul, but the whiteness and stillness and real people ought to help." Judging by the letter, she was still in a fragile state, but there was also a cautious expression of hope. She seemed to be on her way out of the long and heavy period of self-doubt, unwillingness to write, and longing looks that she sought to escape.

But Ester's woes were far from over. John Landquist's feelings for her did not abate. His fervor only seemed to grow.

> Her decision to take a job as a wandering teacher, then write a book about the life of the Lapps greatly increased my esteem for her. Not only did she undertake a new difficult job, which must be trying enough for a spoiled Stockholm girl, but she abandoned the Stockholm parties, gallantry, flattery, praise around her person, without the slightest sign of perceived deprivation, as if they had never existed.

> From John Landquist's memoirs, *I ungdomen. Scener ur den förlorade tiden* [*In Youth. Scenes from the Lost Time*].

Hjalmar also showed signs of infatuation. It was becoming clear to everyone around them that the manager hoped for more than just friendship. When he was away in Stockholm on his frequent business trips, he wrote many long letters, sometimes several each week. Questions about business, personal thoughts, and his longing to return to the wilderness were committed to lined paper or Grand Hôtel stationery with a dark blue printed illustration of the elegant hotel by the sparkling water of the nearby bay.

He called Ester Blenda "dear" and "little girl." In her replies, she revealed her depression and how tired she was of her exhausting reporter job. But she gave no sign that his feelings were reciprocated.

In March, Ester Blenda traveled to a local Sami fair and school meeting in Vittangi to meet her prospective students and their families. She had had only Lapland clothes and gear available to her for a while now, with the exception of a small case sent to her by Frithiof, Gerda, and their little Kjell. She had written to them and thanked them for the present that she called "the best gift imaginable."

Her family was worried. They'd all sensed that something was wrong ever since Ester Blenda had returned from her undercover mission. They always jokingly described their "Essan" as "a goddamn ray of sunshine." But lately, it had been as if the bright, light, warm part of her had been obscured. At the same time, no one had failed to notice the continued rise in the number of evenings she spent at the pub, and at champagne-soaked events.

Big brother Frithiof had expressed his deep concern in a letter. Now that the ground under her feet was starting to feel more solid again, and she was at a safe distance from Stockholm's temptations, Ester Blenda wrote a sincere reply:

> I was so moved when I read it and shed a tear into my morning tea. You are so right, beloved brother, in everything you say, and I know so well how little I really am worth once all the scattered pieces are added together. If I were to tell you that it was fear of myself, of my own so-called immortal soul, that made me decide on this time of hermitage, spent as close to God as possible—then you might not believe me, and would instead smile your

[illegible] smile that I know so well [. . .] You, precious brother, are a grand exception, and truly you are, I tell you, because men are real asses. But now I will try to examine for myself why that is—when I walk on the white plains and sleep in the dark huts, I am lonely and alone. This is probably good for someone like me, I think. And maybe you can be more satisfied and happier with me when I return—it's so nice to know that you exist in this world, you and all the children.

From a letter from Ester Blenda Nordström to Frithiof
Nordström, Kiruna, April 8, 1915.

She confirmed their worries and suspicions that her habits had begun to grow excessive. The observation that men in general were "real asses" was most likely a fitting description of John Landquist with his double dealings and plotting and scheming.

But it is still partly why I left—I say partly because there is another part that is much more serious and heavier, but I will still keep it to myself for the time being.

From a letter from Ester Blenda Nordström to Frithiof
Nordström, Kiruna, April 8, 1915.

For the first time, she revealed that there was something else going on as well, something even darker. A secret she was not ready to share yet. Could she have been referring to her forbidden feelings for Carin? Feelings that were no longer just friendly? Although Ester Blenda's relationship with her brother was both close and open, she was obviously hesitant to share the thing that troubled her the most. Frithiof also had conservative leanings, as surviving relatives have attested to. Maybe she suspected that the secret she was carrying wouldn't be received with open arms. And the risk of that happening seemed to be more than she could handle in her already fragile state.

CHAPTER 8

With the Tent Folk of the Far North

On May 1, Ester Blenda took up her temporary employment as a nomadic teacher, exactly one year after her first day of work as a maid at Jogersta North Farm. This, too, was no walk in the park. The move up to their summer stay was taking place as the spring's heaviest storm raged on. A long row of people, dogs, and reindeer—moving slowly forward in the deep snow on the desolate plains. Crouching in the whipping, swirling, icy cold. The reindeer bowed their heads toward the ground, mouths open, tongues hanging down. Each animal was tied to a heavily loaded sledge with short leather reins. Ester Blenda barely saw the reindeer behind her in her raid of eight to ten animals.

After eight hours with no break, the reindeer began to drop. Sometimes she didn't even notice it, just falling over exhausted, right over the sledge in front of her, which had suddenly come to a standstill while a panting animal was forced to get back on its feet by the raid leader. Wet snow ran down her chest and back, the leather clothes turned stiff and became covered in ice. The deathly silent march never seemed to end.

My eyes are blind and aching from snow and storm; my feet are like lumps of lead; my hands are sore from cold even though they are stuck in fur mittens stuffed with hay; my face is like ice and no longer senses the wind; and as I run my hand across my cheek, where I feel a slight dampness, the white mitten turns red with blood. My face must have brushed past some sharp object without my noticing— perhaps a reindeer horn during an attempt to get a fallen animal back on its legs—I have a deep wound just below the eye. I wish I could be like the reindeer, simply sink into the snow for just a few minutes and drill my face down toward my chest so I could breathe a few deep warm breaths and not constantly inhale this wet icy air that makes my lungs feel like they will burst into pieces. It would probably mean death, but perhaps a sweet death.

From *Kåtornas folk* [*Tent Folk of the Far North*].

One of the raid leaders was named Elli; she was eighty-two years old and married to the district's most influential and wealthy Sami. Physically, she was as slight as a young girl, but her hands were more like claws than human hands, and her face was deeply furrowed. Elli was wearing a black coat with a belt tightened at the waist, reindeer-hide leggings wrapped around her legs, and white fur shoes on her small feet. On her head was a colorful hat with embroidered ribbons.

They walked all night, without interruption. When they finally stopped, Ester Blenda approached Elli, legs wobbling.

"You must be tired now, Elle?"*

"Tired!" She looks at me with her clear eyes that blink at the flurry of snow, forcefully blows her nose into her lit-tle bird's claw of a hand, and looks again. Then she laughs with her toothless mouth and looks so amusingly child-like at the same time—and then she contemptuously says, "Surely I am not that old!"

With a sense of horror mixed with reverence, I watch her traipse up to the hut, lift the door aside, and briskly step over the high threshold.

From *Kåtornas folk* [*Tent Folk of the Far North*].

*Elli was named Elle in the book.

Wet shawls were hung to dry; shoes filled with wet hay were placed in front of the fire. The coffee simmered. Outside, the storm still roared; the goahti rocked; and the canvas clattered gruffly against the poles. Sometimes, the door couldn't withstand the violent forces of nature and was thrown aside, causing smoke and sparks to dance around within the large covering.

While the men and women quietly talked about the journey, Ester Blenda fell asleep with her stinging cheek against a wet dog's back. She woke up half an hour later—the break was over, the group had to move on. They would have to walk another half mile before setting up camp.

No one demanded that Ester Blenda help build huts or chop wood just yet. In time, she would learn—but right now, she was sitting on a sledge and watching as the encampment took shape. She saw how wooden frames were covered with goahti sheets, equipped with iron chains and copper kettles for coffee making. As she started to regain energy, she walked around and took photos with her camera.

The goahti she randomly wound up in belonged to the young couple Lasse and Margi Sikku and their four children: the oldest was ten, and the youngest was only an infant. Lasse was Ester Blenda's height. He was muscular with strong, sinewy hands, and his brown hair stood up in tufts under the colorful brimmed hat with a large tassel on top.

Well-defined, high cheekbones; a tanned face with narrow lips; a pointed chin and friendly eyes. He always had a twined rope hanging across his soft leather clothes. A large knife, attached to a wide leather belt, hung over one hip.

Margi was four inches shorter and wore layer upon layer of skirts and shawls. Her lips were full and often smiling; her face was much rounder than her husband's.

The household's two coffee cups were passed around, round after round with steaming hot contents. After four cups, Ester Blenda fell asleep again. Margi carefully placed a pillow under her head and spread a fleece over her.

The encampment was in a low birch forest. When the young teacher from Stockholm woke up more than twelve hours later, the sun shone in a bright blue sky. Sara Nutti, her maid-to-be, came skiing down a slope with a bunch of branches under one arm. Both Sara and Margi laughed when Ester Blenda confusedly asked how long she had been asleep.

Everyone gathered around the large food pot where meat and marrow bones were boiling.

Ester Blenda listened to conversations about pastures, the weather, reindeer that calved during the night, and upcoming migrations.

No one was talking about women's suffrage or about the ongoing world war. These issues hadn't affected their everyday life any more than the raised prices of coffee and flour had. In this encampment, the things to fear most of all were the wrath of God and the devil himself. Their own gods, and their pantheistic worship of earth and water, had been subject to the Swedish colonialism and attempted eradication for hundreds of years. The sacred places of the Sami had been desecrated, drums had been burned, the traditional Sami costume decorations had been condemned as a form of excess by the powers that be in Sweden, and the songs of the shamans had been replaced by the words of the traveling Laestadian preachers, all in the name of God. A joik was no

One of the Sami residents, Lasse Sikku, and Ester Blenda, 1915.

longer a tribute to the sun's rays and the clear blue color of the sky; it was the song of the devil.

The conversion work had been successful; most of the Swedish Sami were about to become ascetic Christians as envisioned by Lars Levi Laestadius, Swedish Sami preacher and missionary.

The newcomer in the group also observed evening rituals, so that she could write about them later. Like how men took off their hats in the stillness of the fire and placed their heads in their women's laps. How nimble fingers picked apart tangled locks in search of vermin that were then immediately extinguished between a thumb and the side of a knife. Afterward, the blades were wiped off against birch bark and placed back in their sheaths, ready to be used to cut meat and bread.

They walked at night, as the road ahead was the clearest and the upper snow crust was solid. But the fresh overlying snow made the marches, extending several miles through the deep slopes between arboreal boundaries, heavy and slow. Twelve hours at a time. The option of dividing the walk into shorter legs was practically nonexistent; they had to get across the bare high fells, the region's moors, to get fresh firewood.

Ester Blenda continued to take photos: sunsets, the raid up on the high fells, a break at sunrise, the erection of goahtis, the drinking of coffee, her first grouse trap, a reindeer that had fallen into the snow from exhaustion and was kicked back up by its owner.

They got caught in a new storm. Four days, in the middle of the high fells. The wood had to be rationed for cooking. The rest of the time, the cold was so severe that they could barely hold their cups of lukewarm coffee.

Once the weather cleared up, they were able to see all the way to the settler village of Soppero and to hear the explosions from Hjalmar Lundbohm's mines in Kiruna.

> How strange it feels to perceive the noise of the world and the work of men while out here in the quiet and dead wilderness where one has already forgotten that there is any other life beyond the wreath of fells that surrounds the horizon and shuts out all thoughts, all consciousness of life that is not this [. . .] When the sun goes down at night, you put on your skis, hang your ax in your belt, take the forked branches in your hand and the snares around your neck, and run up the cliff to set the traps. A knife dangles at each hip, the ski pole crunches against the snow as if it were steel, the sky is full of rosy clouds that slowly travel east, the cold and clear spring air surrounds one, and the grouse coo with infatuation in the thickets. Could life be any more beautiful, full, than it gets on such a night? What

would you care about people and noise and all the vanity
of the world? How would you dare to think about what
lies beyond the solemn edge of the fells?

From *Kåtornas folk* [*Tent Folk of the Far North*].

She captured two grouse and brought them back to the hut. Lasse
laughed contentedly and declared Ester Blenda to be a real hunter.
Shortly afterward, she also became the camp's field doctor when a six-
month-old baby became seriously ill from inflammation in one cheek,
which was red, hard, and hot. Ester Blenda was the group's most well-
read person, and her knowledge was greatly respected. A quick glance
at the girl was enough: it looked like a boil. She ordered the anxious
mother to put on warm porridge wraps and when the abscess changed
color to greenish yellow, Ester Blenda took her small medicine box with
simple dressings and sterilizing liquid to the family's goahti. She did
everything in her power to relieve the pain felt by the small body as it
lay pale from cold and disease.

A few days later, the baby was well, and the new teacher's status in
the camp rose further. A large piece of dry meat served as a token of
gratitude from the relieved parents. The meat was an important addition to Lasse and Margi's household, which was to accommodate the
new teacher until they reached their stop for the summer, where Ester
Blenda would have her own goahti—the school goahti—and her own
household.

The other villagers were already in place when they finally reached
their destination, at five o'clock one clear morning. The Saarivouma
Sami, a total of four clans, were the last ones to reach the expansive
grounds. The goahtis, with their ring pillars of smoke, were already
densely packed down the birch slope that descended toward the blue-
green Lake Tarfallajauri by the mountain Rokkomborre. They were
received with open arms and boiling kettles.

"So, you're the teacher!" she says, and laughs, facing me with irresistibly friendly eyes as I meet her gaze drunk from sleep. "You've had a hard time during this move [. . .] Now you can rest, and you're welcome here too! [. . .] But we'll be nice to you; do not be afraid. We'll try to make it so you don't wish you were somewhere far, far away from us!"

She smiles so kindly to me, and her voice has the sound of a mother who seeks to calm and to comfort. And everyone nods at me and laughs and looks at me so gently that I almost get something of a lump in my throat, and struggle to see them clearly. The finest lady on earth, the finest and best of all those living in the civilized world, could not have received a stranger into their circle in a nobler and more beautiful way than Sanna and these Lapps received me.

From *Kåtornas folk* [*Tent Folk of the Far North*].

One by one, the children were called into the hut where the new teacher was offered a welcoming coffee. Choked giggles, ruddy cheeks, self-introductions delivered with voices so low and murmuring that it was almost impossible to make out the names. A few hours later, most of them stood and watched as Ester Blenda and her maid, Sara, finished preparing the teacher's residence and school that had just been erected with Lasse's help.

They climbed up and down ladders and lay straight across the wooden frames and covered them with heavy cloths. The floor was filled with branches that they'd chopped out in the strong wind. Pots, trays, and *koksir* (wooden spoons with long handles) were hung up, and other household utensils were unpacked and arranged around the space. Sheepskin fleeces for sleeping on were rolled out. Ester Blenda set up a boxy coffee grinder of a classic farmer's model with a shelf at

Ester Blenda during the construction of the school goahti and teacher's residence by Lake Tarfallajauri.

the bottom, and a huge wooden tobacco pipe. The last two items were a farewell gift from Prince Eugen, which he himself went to Kiruna to buy before her departure. His adjutant and chamberlain stayed with Hjalmar in the meantime. From Hjalmar, she received a portrait of the prince, who had also written a greeting on it.

They would need to place their food supply in Lasse and Margi's *luvvin*, a type of above-ground storage unit consisting of two crossed birch trunks tied together with a rope and a simple floor made of narrow bars. There, dogs and predators wouldn't be able to access the limited rations.

When everything was ready, Ester Blenda instructed Sara to take a picture with the camera. She stood up outside the goahti with Lasse, put her thumbs in the belt that held together the reindeer fur she was wearing, and smiled broadly. Lasse looked into the camera with a questioning, almost mystified look. Then they made their first pot of coffee.

Ester Blenda stood completely still outside her new home, a small black tent, in a valley as deep as it was wide, with glistening lakes and rivers. She looked in astonishment, with a tightness in her chest from the wilderness that surrounded her, and marveled at the daylight that never ended.

The next day, the goahti teemed with people. Everyone wanted to say hello and enroll their children. Those who'd gone to school before submitted grade books from the previous semester. Anxious beginners burrowed themselves into their mothers' *gáktis* while all the formalities were settled. There would be a total of fourteen students; the youngest had just turned seven, and the oldest was fifteen. They were divided into three different classes, based on age and prior schooling.

The day went fast; it was soon noon. Ester Blenda stood by the pots while Sara chopped wood. The rest of the evening was spent making preparations with books and lesson plans. Before the last ember died out, Ester Blenda worked on her upcoming reports for *Svenska Dagbladet*.

Lessons were meant to start at nine o'clock, but the first tiny steps were heard outside the hut as early as eight in the morning. There was light rain and a cold wind, so Ester Blenda let the children into the warmth. Half an hour later, everyone had arrived, and she started the first day of school. They prayed together and sang hymns. All the songs were new to the children; the agenda was to turn them into good, Christian citizens with the help of the new school system.

Hearing the children read out loud for the first time scared Ester Blenda; she realized that she had her work cut out for her. The textbooks were in Swedish, and their knowledge of the language was basically nonexistent. She had two blackboards sent over in a school-supplies box, but they were missing chalk. The youngest children received lead pencils for learning how to write the simplest letters of the alphabet. Pieces of graphite flew in all directions in the goahti as their clumsy fingers struggled to apply the right amount of pressure to write their first letters.

The slightly older ones got to practice writing in exercise books. The books were the same as those used in the Swedish primary school and were filled with preprinted prompts: "Sit up straight! Keep your feet level with the floorboards! Rest your hand gently against the table!" The Sami children struggled with great concentration as they sat on the branches of the goahti floor with their knees pulled up. The next challenge, for teacher and students alike, was math. None of the children had ever heard of addition, subtraction, multiplication, or division. Those who could count at all did so using simple lines that they added or removed, depending on the task in front of them.

And so, the days passed in the camp's school goahti. Frustrated sighs, tired moans, laughter, drumming fingers, and eyes staring at new mysteries. Catechism, biblical history, reading, math . . . There were identical school goahtis all over Lapland's fell grounds, filled with Sami children to be educated. And researched. Because whenever Herman Lundborg arrived in a new village or camp, he used the school goahti as a temporary reception hall. Calipers and other measuring tools were brought out of large leather bags. The children were stripped naked and photographed. They never sought consent from their parents. All this photography was also completely in opposition to many people's new Laestadian beliefs. Herman Lundborg often brought young female assistants with him. They were Sami themselves or spoke Finnish. Some of them were also his mistresses. In time, several became pregnant and gave birth to his children.

Of all the Sami children examined in the area, one would gather courage much later in life to write a testimony about how that "research" looked. Eleven-year-old Sara Ranta-Rönnlund and her schoolmates had heard rumors about Professor Lundborg and were terrified at the prospect of his visit:

Much fear arose in the Lapp encampment, when word spread of how Lundborg was especially interested in investigating whether the blood of the Lapps would run down into their heads if they were hung upside down from a tree. It was also said that he drilled holes from temple to temple in his victims' heads, draining their knowledge, thereby making himself more clever. He pressed down on upturned noses and bent straight noses, because that's what eugenicists do. He felt that the Lapps should have wide mouths, and so, in a very simple way, he would make the mouths fit this standard configuration. First of all, he would start by remolding the schoolchildren. Knowing their facial features would be changed, the Lapp children who stood for hours looking down onto the lake's reflective surface to firmly retain the memory of their original appearance were many in number [. . .] The door was opened by Professor Lundborg, who, with all his height, crouched out through the goahti door. He exchanged a few words with our teacher, and we hesitantly stepped into the school goahti. The professor first demonstrated what he was going to do on his son. Many of the children were scared, but, when the teacher made it through the measurements, they calmed down, unscathed and with an unaltered appearance. The professor's son wrote on a piece of paper while the father half dictated incomprehensible numbers and strange words.

From Sara Ranta-Rönnlund's book *Nådevalpar* [*Grace Puppies*], quoted as written in Maja Hagerman's *Käraste Herman* [*Dearest Herman*].

Sara Ranta-Rönnlund first published her story in 1971. By then, the State Institute for Racial Biology in Sweden had changed its name to the Institute of Medical Genetics. But before that—under many years of leadership by Herman Lundborg—it had been built up and had conducted extensive research in close collaboration with Germany's race institutes set up by the Nazis. Their boss, Hans F. K. Günther, had worked at the sister institute in Uppsala for a time. Photographs were shared between the countries in the course of the formulation of Nazi racial policy and the creation of racial legislation.

In the summer of 1915, investigations proceeded in Lapland. Hesitant hands took off gáktis; freezing naked bodies were photographed in nine recurring positions, then numbered in thick albums. They were categorized as "imbecile," "raw," and "of mixed breed."

Lundborg's research team had not yet reached the Norwegian border where Ester Blenda and her students were, and the substitute teacher had not yet had to fulfill her promise to make him dinner as mentioned during Hjalmar's sixty-second birthday celebrations.

In the articles she sent to *Svenska Dagbladet*, she never mentioned the ongoing research that would eventually go down in history as a collective abuse of the Sami population. The first and only time that Ester Blenda directly touched on racial segregation in her writing was when she herself was exposed to it during a short visit to Kiruna. She and her maid had skied over forty miles across the mountains to get to the nearest post office at Torne Marsh station. There, they had the idea of taking the ore train to Kiruna, so that Sara could experience a real city for the first time and Ester Blenda could buy a few things.

It was Pentecost when they arrived in the city, grimy, sweaty, and uncombed with their fur coats and heavy backpacks. The bare ground, chirping of birds, budding trees, and summer-clad Kiruna residents made them feel ill at ease.

So we went to the railway hotel to get a room and clean ourselves up. But had to leave with unsettled business—people did not rent rooms out to Lapps!

"Poor Lapps!" I said to the harsh lady who drove us out. "Poor Lapps, what have they done to hurt us?"

"Nothing!" was her answer. "But they are not allowed to take up space meant for other people. Where are you from since you speak Swedish so well?"

"From Stockholm. But you don't need to give me a room for that reason. My hope is that you go somewhere while you're tired one day, and that you get driven out for the simple fact that you are of a different race, while you simply long for rest. Consider this, and maybe you will show more kindness the next time a Lapp comes by. Their money is probably the same as that of other people!"

I don't know how she looked after that speech, because I threw the *lauko** over my shoulder and left with Ellekare** in tow. But she cried out to us that maybe there was a room, now that she'd thought about it. This went unanswered.

From *Kåtornas folk* [*Tent Folk of the Far North*].

*The origin of the *lauko* term is unclear; it is presumably a Sami word for an article of clothing. **The maid Sara was given the fictitious name Ellekare in the book.

Her feelings for the encampment's residents deepened, not least for the children. She even struggled to send them to the naughty corner for not doing their homework. At one point, she discovered that one of the older students had cheated and was reminded of how she herself used the same methods as a child when she, too, lacked the will to learn.

She stubbornly pressed on, teaching students to read books with illustrations of animals and objects they had never seen and would probably never see. They labored through God's commandments in poor Swedish. The pronunciations, and the hard and soft consonants, were difficult to master and distorted the commandments when read aloud. "Live" became "lice." "Basket" became "casket." Ester Blenda sometimes had to make an effort to not simply laugh out loud. But it worked out; they soon moved on to writing their own sentences and doing column addition.

Under the clear influence of Hjalmar Lundbohm's ideas, the temporary teacher criticized what she dubbed an "outdated teaching system" in the articles she submitted to *Svenska Dagbladet*.

Teaching in the school goahti.

In a headline, she concluded that these were "inappropriate methods, which must be changed." She wrote about how much better it would be if the children could learn based on their own environment; about how book illustrations of sledges, reindeer, and wolves would stimulate faster learning. She wrote that the stories about shoemakers and sailors that always ended with a "moral of the story" would be far more successfully edifying if they were about Sami people, reindeer husbandry, and Lapland instead.

Her articles added to the continued debate about the Sami schools and their teaching materials.

Even though the Bansai persona otherwise focused on the mundane, and her love of the hospitable people and their lifestyle was obvious, many of her texts strengthened the position of the adherents of the dominant doctrine that "Lapps should be Lapps." Hjalmar Lundbohm's view of the Sami had now become Ester Blenda's too. The reporter's relief over living isolated from civilization and the big city, of which she had grown tired, shone through in her writing. She lyrically and vividly described to her large readership how the young voices of sin-defying Sami girls rose over the mountains in glorious *joik*; she described in detail the weeklong visit by the Laestadian preacher with a large gray beard whose roaring voice made the encampment dwellers throw themselves straight onto the floor and ground and stretch out their arms toward the mighty man. Ancient medicine, superstition, and magic were recurring themes.

Line after line of tender romanticizing of the peculiar lifestyle made the curious public grow more sympathetic toward the Sami. Their hospitality, caring ways, and other favorable aspects were highlighted. Ester Blenda consistently showed solidarity and connection with the northern native people, but the image of a deviant people was strengthened rather than made more nuanced.

The report became the basis for political proposals for continued segregation and a closed-off school system. This was just the way Hjalmar Lundbohm wanted it—and contrary to many Sami people's own wishes. And it played right into the hands of Herman Lundborg and other leading eugenicists.

The snow on the fells slowly melted and gave way to the late Arctic spring. The birch buds grew large before they finally burst into a bright green. The forest was filled with new life; the smell of all the greenery was intoxicating. The encampment's goats were retrieved from their winter stay, and a coffee party ensued when everyone was able to get real milk in their cups for the first time in many months. Ester drank thirty-two cups; Sara had close to forty.

The children thrived with their teacher. They often stayed and played outside her goahti when the four-hour school day ended. Ester Blenda happily joined them, sometimes for several hours. She sent them down the slope once it was time for dinner or another visiting patient. It always got so quiet and empty when they left.

She had plenty of patients, often two or three a night. They arrived as soon as school was over and sat patiently around the fire in the goahti until they could present their complaint. Sometimes the would-be doctor had no idea what to do, but no one listened when she tried to explain that she didn't know.

At one point, a little old woman from Vuoskojaure, slightly more than fifteen miles away, visited to get her hearing restored. For lack of other options, Ester Blenda dropped some hot oil into the ear canal. By the next day, the old woman managed to get rid of her wax plug and returned to the teacher to thank her.

The school goahti had become the encampment's new gathering point. It was always filled with visitors, both men and women, who discussed, drank coffee, and scared each other with horrific stories of evil spirits and curses. The women always kept busy with handiwork. Margi, who was often there, wove beautiful shoelaces while they talked. Sara knitted colorful gloves, and Ester Blenda herself worked on a new gákti with her puppy, Tsappe, in her lap.

The only reminders of life outside the encampment came in the form of letters from Gerda, Frithiof, or one of her friends from back home. She replied in long, lyrical letters.

> Now I am so unashamedly happy and healthy and new and strong and feel that every breath is happiness and joy and all the glory of life. One becomes like this—one has to become like this—even if one were as miserable as could be at the point of starting to live between the fells and the birches up here. You must come to me . . . [. . .] Just that, to not have to think of any of the world's cares, other than lying on your back on the fells and watching the clouds pass by across the little piece of sky you can discern through the rooftop opening.

> From a letter from Ester Blenda Nordström to Hjördis
> Tengbom, July 20, 1915.

There would never be a visit from Hjördis. But Carin came to visit her on several occasions. They spent time with Hjalmar and his prominent friends who often traveled up from Stockholm to stay in his large villa. Hjalmar arranged dinner parties and planned excursions in the area. Together with Prince Eugen and his friend Baron Leuhusen, they traveled to Puoltsa, an old agricultural village a few miles west of Kiruna.

It was so beautiful that they decided to stay a whole day. The snowbanks reached high above the windowpanes of the graying mid-nineteenth-century log cabins that had become a historical tourist attraction.

Ester Blenda stood by one of the huge mounds, brought out her camera, and pointed it toward the house where the others were gathered. Hjalmar and Carin looked at her as she pressed the button, but

Prince Eugen missed the moment. He turned to Baron Leuhusen to say something and was only caught in profile.

They left small trampled paths behind and between the houses where there were untouched snow-covered tufts of grass, creeping juniper bushes, and herbs. The Kebnekaise massif rose toward the west, and the view reaching down to the Kalix River was wide open. By the water lay small crooked boathouses, smoke goahtis abandoned in winter, and fishnet hangers with rusty hooks.

The mood was light. Baron Leuhusen sat straight down in a snowdrift, and Carin leaned against his back, smiling, putting her long, shiny fur around his shoulders, as if to warm him. She was in a great mood. Playing in front of the camera that seemed to wander between everyone's hands, she pushed her face so close to the lens that it was impossible to focus the shot. She threw herself right into the snow, laughing out loud, and landed in Ester Blenda's arms.

Ester Blenda caught her and let her stay as the photo was taken. They remained like that for a while, in a snowdrift in the middle of Lapland's high fells. She and Carin returned many times to the vast whiteness that was its own closed world. Could they already sense that their secret was safe here?

Did the men around them suspect any of it? Hjalmar, who knew them both well and couldn't seem to get any of his feelings acknowledged by Ester Blenda. Or Prince Eugen, whose painting studio was filled with canvases of naked men. Could they see it in Ester Blenda's and Carin's eyes, their obvious closeness? Did Ester Blenda and Carin even fully understand it themselves? Had they put into words how they felt?

Carin's Lapland stays were only briefly mentioned in letters to Gerda and Frithiof. Brief notes about how "Carin D. [Dahlbeck] is coming on Friday," but nothing more about what they'd done or experienced together. Ester Blenda kept this to herself.

Carin in Ester Blenda's embrace during the visit to Puoltsa.

Once spring transitioned into summer, Ester Blenda's sister Hildur also got on the train going north, joined by Elin Wägner. It had become fashionable for tourists to visit the fell grounds and to have their pictures taken by well-known photographer Borg Mesch in Kiruna. Hildur and Elin wore hats and practical sportswear: sturdy trousers, heavy jackets, and shoes. In her Sami costume, Ester Blenda stood between them, laughing proudly and straight into the camera.

She arranged for a bearer and guide to help them traverse the seven miles from the train station at Torne Marsh over the mountains to the lakeside stay. He took off his clothes and carried both guests and their baggage over the waterways. As they lay in the half-naked man's arms, their shocked faces forced Ester Blenda to burst out laughing.

The newly arrived women attracted a lot of attention. Curious eyes watched their every action, quietly observing how they did their best to survive camp life. They watched how they washed in the morning, surrounded by mosquitoes outside the goahtis, got dressed, tried to cook over an open fire . . .

Elin Wägner, Ester Blenda, and her sister Hildur photographed in Kiruna in 1915.

Elin and Hildur sat with Ester Blenda while she taught during the day. In the midst of the crowding of schoolbooks, pots, goats, and children, Elin sat and wove shoelaces with a special technique that the Sami girls had shown her. Ester Blenda looked at her friend, noting that her cheeks were starting to take on a beautiful red hue. She also appeared to be doing better far away from Stockholm, and from John. They enjoyed their reunion in a shared silence.

You found your bearings almost instantly—your warm smile and the quiet kindness in your eyes made you their friend faster than is usually the case with strangers, and it was not long before their gentle "*Boris boris*" and their greetings with Laestadian half embraces were extended as willingly to you as they were to me, their longtime friend.

From *Minns du?* [*Do You Remember?*] by Ester Blenda Nordström for Elin Wägner's fiftieth birthday celebration.

The harmony came to an abrupt end. John Landquist followed Elin and Hildur up to Lapland, under the pretext of wanting to be able to escort his wife home safely once the holiday was over. After a day and a half of marching over the mountains, he knocked the goahti sheet aside and stepped right into their stillness. But Ester Blenda was relaxed and happy and welcomed him. He even got to sit in during a lesson.

On seeing the joy in the goahti, the children's eager and devoted eyes facing their teacher, he started to believe that she had enchanted them too.

During a short school break, Ester Blenda suggested that she and her guests take a walk to a port over on the Norwegian side. They would do a four-day hike through pure wilderness, with the exception of an empty tourist cabin. Then they would go on to a nearby city where Hjalmar Lundbohm was temporarily staying. She wanted to introduce her friends to each other. Elin and Hildur refused to go hiking. John accepted.

It was decided that Elin and Hildur would return to the station at Torne Marsh. From there, Hildur would travel back to Stockholm, and Elin would travel to rejoin the others.

John hardly dared believe that Elin would let him go on a long hike all alone with Ester Blenda. The first night, he was tormented by a guilty conscience about having left his wife; by the third night, all was forgotten. Then temptation coursed through his body. They slept on a mountain slope out in the open, unprotected, in the biting cold. Eventually, the cold became unbearable.

> There was the possibility of us warming each other up. Ester Blenda called to me from her sleeping bag, telling me to crawl into hers. But the virtuous little missy was stern: "Now, you must make sure to not touch me in any way!" Me: "By all means, is that all, nothing could be easier." This last statement proved to be an exaggeration, given the spatial conditions. I lay raging at her side in the sleeping bag.

> From John Landquist's memoirs, *I ungdomen. Scener ur den förlorade tiden* [*In Youth. Scenes from the Lost Time*].

He never touched her. Just lay close by, listening to her breath as he tried to muffle the rhythm of his own. Ten years would go by before Ester Blenda commented on the night again. In a letter, she then described to John how she had experienced similar situations later in life, but with men who did not behave quite as honorably.

> And so, these matters from Altevand and the fells had, for ten whole years of our youth, occasionally gnawed at the mind of the lovely, bold girl who was worshipped by several, and had traveled through two continents. It was lovely to the point of being unreasonably so.
> I read the letter a number of times. Then I burned it. It was in violent conflict with my feelings and my goal at this time.

> From John Landquist's memoirs, *I ungdomen. Scener ur den förlorade tiden* [*In Youth. Scenes from the Lost Time*].

The letter he sent to Ester Blenda after returning to Stockholm affirmed that the emotions still raged in his body. But he realized that he would never win her heart and had finally given up:

Ester:
You are probably sitting in a goahti once again, high above, between fells and the sea with Sara and your Sappe.

I have still not returned to the order of things following this journey. When the unfamiliar darkness of night comes down here, it clothes me. How I then long to return to the clear days of your nights, the rosy clouds of your skies, and your silent, snow-capped mountains! Now a new journey awaits: I seem to be going into a dark tunnel, to work, the battles, the brooding . . . [. . .] The fact that I owe you a lot of thanks, Ester, for this journey, is so obvious that it cannot be put into words. But if I may add one thing: I want to silently thank you for my having gotten to know you myself. There has always been a disharmony in our acquaintanceship that emanated from me. It had been rising recently [. . .] You had, without knowing it, challenged the most difficult forces I hold within me: the lust for power, the vengeance, the jealousy, and yet another.

But once I got to know you as you were, understood your purity, saw your youth, then these forces, which had naught to conquer here, fell away. May it go, and be, well with you.

John

From a letter from John Landquist to Ester Blenda
Nordström, August 7, 1915.

Once everyone had gone home, the fever came. Her head throbbed; her body shook with chills. People tiptoed around the teacher's goahti. Whispered questions. Anxious heads peered in through the tent opening several times a day. Some whispered that the teacher would not make it. The teacher herself said, with as much firmness as she could muster in her feverish delirium, that she certainly had no plans to die.

A week went by, and Ester Blenda's condition didn't improve at all. The Sami did not trust her assurances. The elder woman, Old-Inka, was summoned. It was Sunday, and she was wearing a new dark blue calfskin gákti with red-and-yellow cloth stripes along the edges and seams. Her apron was red. She had a thick silk bib around her neck, held together by a simple pin capped with a blue stone. Fatigued from the fever, Ester Blenda looked up from her fleece at the pattern of roses and leaves. Old-Inka brought out an apparatus. She was going to perform a bloodletting.

The goahti was filled; a ring of people formed around the ailing woman. A large pot with lukewarm water was presented. The old woman brought out one of Ester Blenda's feet, moved it up and down in the water while her mouth quivered with whispers so low that they were inaudible.

She blew as she stroked Ester's leg, with her eyes staring straight ahead into nothing. Ester Blenda's foot was rotated in specific movements before it was finally fixed, and Old-Inka found a spot above the ankle. A hard grip around the ankle caused the vein to swell; she wrapped a shoelace several times around the leg and prepared the sharp instrument.

> She read and mumbled and conjured and blew and struck veins until the blood splattered, and my blood was so black and ugly and sick that all the Lapp men and women surrounding me (eight to ten of them sitting in a circle) swayed and moaned—and when the blood was

done flowing, the wound was treated with spit and spells and blowing, and the sweat flowed like a thousand small streams down the old woman's thousand wrinkles, and her toothless mouth gaped open and closed shut. She alternately blew her nose into her hand, then spat generously into it and stroked my long leg (she punched a hole in the vein just above her left shoulder); then she finally placed a piece of paper wholly in her mouth and applied it like a plaster, secured a rag around it, and tied a black thread around that (white wouldn't do), and the leg was done.

[. . .] In the end, she spat heavily into my fine, freshly washed hair, rubbed it around—and that was that.

From a letter from Ester Blenda Nordström to Frithiof
Nordström, August 23, 1915.

Ester Blenda vomited. A spoonful of lyptol, an antiseptic used as a cure-all in the encampment, was forced down her throat while Old-Inka placed her gnarled hand over her stomach and chanted new spells.

After the bloody ritual, Ester Blenda fell asleep. Fifteen hours later, she woke up. The fever was gone. She wrote to Frithiof to tell him that she was eating and drinking, and she "feels wonderful" again; she concluded that the whole thing was "damn strange."

Many more strange things came to pass as Ester Blenda's time as a nomadic teacher came to an end. Fall had arrived. Clear air and morning frost. The moon hung big and red in the evening sky that had begun to darken for the first time in months.

One day, after school was out, she heard church bells. She stopped; that sound didn't belong in the wilderness. Was it possible that the wind was traveling in a particular direction, making her hear sounds from civilization? The women she asked fell silent and began to tell her about the carillon that was a sign of impending death. They solemnly asked where she heard the bells ringing from and were obviously relieved that it was from the north; this meant that it was not Ester Blenda herself who would die.

Barely three weeks later, a telegram arrived. Her father, Daniel, had died from a brief struggle with stomach cancer. Her grief was heavy. Anxiety took hold in her chest again. How would her mother, Lotten, cope? How could she bear to spend her first Christmas in forty years alone, without Daniel? For the first time, the distance from home felt burdensome.

Her last weeks spent in the encampment were tinged with melancholy. During the organized chaos of reindeer-calf marking—with whooshing lassos, furiously galloping animals, and swaying antlers—Ester Blenda stopped. Took mental pictures of everything she saw, the scents, the sounds, the beauty of nature that surrounded her. Margi put an arm around her shoulder and asked whether she was pleased to be able to go home again soon. It was only then that she realized the depth of her sadness over the parting that awaited her.

On the last day of school, the students arrived in their best Sunday gáktis, freshly washed and combed. Everyone had done their homework. Ester Blenda handed out the grade books and offered coffee and sugar cubes. They asked if she was going to leave them, if she would come back next year, promising that they would remember everything she'd taught them. She replied vaguely, vacillating between laughter and tears all day.

Afterward, she would go on to describe the separation anxiety that overwhelmed her after the last lesson. The unwelcome silence. How she wanted to scream at her new little friends, to tell them that they should stay a little while longer and sit down with her. While she heard them disappear off among the trees, she slowly packed up the books, put them in the school box, and put the key away.

A pair of tiny eyes in the goahti's opening. One of the students returned. Red in the face, he walked up to his teacher and extended one hand. In it lay a finely carved sheath knife. Before Ester Blenda was able to thank him, he was gone.

The last night on the fells, she took out her reindeer fleeces, spread them on the ground, and attached a mosquito net between two trees. She lay on her back, wrapped in reindeer furs, and stared straight up into the sky for a long time. The moment was immortalized with the help of the camera's self-timer.

CHAPTER 9

A Summer with Elin Wägner

She knew it even before she'd stepped back into the newsroom. The demands, the stress, the pressure. There was an instant gaping void in the wake of the harmony she'd experienced in Lapland. The anxiety swooped back in; that crawling sensation in her body returned.

Things weren't much better outside of work. Her friend Hjördis Tengbom arranged to talk about reading clubs in her home, but Ester Blenda was not among the list of invited friends; you can tell by going through Hjördis Tengbom's diary entries about the events and the people who were present. Murre Landquist had become seriously ill with pernicious anemia. And the rest of the old friends from the League weren't all that interested in going out at night anymore. No one had the time. Ellen, Célie, and Agnes all had to return home to spouses, or children, or both.

They fought bravely to maintain their careers while often having sole responsibility for child-rearing, while their husbands continued to work as usual. Célie, for instance, stubbornly continued to work between childbirth and breastfeeding. The others in the League usually laughed and said that she made sure to have her children while on vacation; she'd gotten so used to this that even she had this to say, "When

I'm about to have a child, I start boiling water in a saucepan." Elin Wägner also laughed, but her heart ached with the desire to become a mother herself. John didn't want children, and their marriage remained frosty.

Everyone in Stockholm was busy with their own lives in the fall of 1915. But Ester Blenda didn't have to be alone. The twenty-five-year-old star was a highly desirable presence in high society, with its many events offering superficial acquaintanceships and raised glasses. The tavern windows had a welcoming glow, warmth, and good company. Soon, life ran at full speed again.

Frithiof's concerns about his youngest sister returned. Anything she did, she did in high gear. Ester Blenda moved into her sister Hildur's apartment. It was a beautiful place, filled with art and antiques. The fact that Hildur was a successful saleswoman at Bukowski's, one of Sweden's most important art stores, was starting to benefit the rest of the Nordström family. She was able to offer them great prices on paintings, elegant furniture, sculptures, and antique glass.

The youngest Nordström sisters had many similarities. They both had infectious laughs, were unmarried, and loved partying. They were, of course, brilliant hostesses, Hildur with her sparkling red hair, and Ester Blenda who loudly entertained the guests with singing and playing the harmonica, lute, accordion, or violin.

Artists, writers, politicians, and industry leaders were drawn to their apartment in the Kungsholmen district. Anders Zorn, who had become so internationally renowned that he had now been given the epithet "the Master of Masters," wanted to paint Hildur. She was flattered, until he told her that it needed to be a nude study. He was stopped in his tracks.

The Nordström siblings had grown even closer since the death of their father, Daniel. Ester Blenda often spent her days off with Hildur, back home with Agda and their mother at the Ekefors mansion, or with Frithiof and his family. There, she played wild games with the kids, who loved her energy and ingenuity.

The children's favorite aunt took them on bike trips, built Sami huts in the state room by hanging blankets from the ceiling lamp over chair backs and spreading out the reindeer fleeces she brought back from Lapland on the floor. A flashlight covered in red silk paper became a fireplace.

When it was time to take family photos, one of Frithiof's children would almost invariably crawl into the arms of Aunt Essan and sit close while the pictures were taken.

Carin was the same way. Her six nephews would also hold on to lifelong memories of how Auntie or Cajsa, as they sometimes called her, let them ride on her shoulders and didn't care in the least whether her exclusive clothes got dirty from crawling on the floor or taking them on outdoor trips.

The Nordström family together. Ester Blenda with her niece Birgitta on the far left. Nephew, Kjell; sister Agda; brother, Frithiof, at the back in the middle; sister-in-law, Gerda, with daughters, Anne-Marie and Gunilla, below. Sister Hildur and mother, Lotten, on the far right.

She usually called them her grandchildren. One of them, Eva, was often with her. She sat next to her and watched as Auntie dug in the garden, wearing some seriously flared sailor pants. Carin owned a villa on Utö island in the Stockholm archipelago, and a huge summer villa named Backudden along the west coast of Sweden. Sometimes Eva also got to join Carin and Ester Blenda on weekend or day trips. Ester Blenda's preserved album holds several photos of the trio with accompanying captions from various destinations and sights.

Their love for the little ones around them was immense. Ester Blenda's desire to have children was about to grow strong and painfully obvious to everyone around her. John Landquist even wrote about it in his memoirs, about how she more than once "talked about the joy of having children around one as a mother." But she knew that family life was not for her.

As for Carin and her husband, Olof, everything they needed to start a family was in place. But it would never come to be. Within a couple more years, the marriage came to an end. After going through Carin's personal data in public archives, it was unclear when exactly the divorce went through. In the Stockholm City Archives, there's no reference to it until 1918, in a note about how she had "moved to another property in the area" and that she was a divorced captain's wife with the status "single without children." The reason for the divorce was also unknown.

In late 1915, Ester Blenda started compiling and developing her Lapland material for the book to be published by Hjalmar Lundbohm. Her acclaimed article series about her semester with the Sami people continued to be published in *Svenska Dagbladet*, and it fed into the debate about their conditions, schooling, and future.

The issue of nomadic education and teaching materials for Sami children was the focus of particularly high levels of attention and was now being raised at the highest political level. A new royal charter that regulated nomadic teaching was created, intending to make it comparable to public primary school teaching.

The new school plan included ambulatory summer schools, permanent town-based schools while in their winter stays, and a nomadic school inspector. The decision was also made to develop new teaching materials. Politicians realized that a single ABC book in Northern Sami for the younger kids and a history textbook weren't enough.

The assignment went to Karl Bernhard Wiklund, professor of Finno-Ugric languages at Uppsala University. But manager Hjalmar Lundbohm was behind the scenes, with clear opinions and a strong will. Among other things, he believed that subjects such as history and geography should be limited. According to him, any knowledge of Swedish culture and industry, for instance, was completely unnecessary, and might even be harmful.

The two men frequently exchanged letters as the new three-part textbook was in development; it contained facts about reindeer biology and zoology, the societal position of the Sami, and the laws that affected them.

The diocese, which was responsible for the project, discussed whether each separate part should be written by a unique person with a specialist area. Hjalmar Lundbohm was one of the proposed authors. Ester Blenda Nordström was another.

In a letter to Ester Blenda, Hjalmar questioned Professor Wiklund's limited knowledge of the Sami, but was obviously pleased that Ester Blenda, as a key figure in this major project, was brought up in the discussions:

> The good man does not understand the soul of the Lapps. But he does, as it happens, say many sensible words, including the statement regarding how this work requires an intelligent person with personal experience as a Lapp catechist

to draw up the goahti schools' teaching curriculum, and there is only one such, a lioness: Ester Blenda Nordström.

From a private letter from Hjalmar Lundbohm to Ester Blenda Nordström, December 28, 1915.

His subsequent marriage proposal hardly came as a surprise. Ester Blenda told Elin, who quickly announced the news to her husband, John. He asked Elin to convince her to say yes to Hjalmar. He wasn't just a man of importance; their marriage would make for a calmer life for her, as a wife. They worried about Ester Blenda's increasingly extravagant lifestyle and all the alcohol-filled nights of partying, as did her family.

Hjalmar had become a very dear friend, but she didn't want to marry him. "Too old" was the reason she cited to everyone witnessing the crossroads she was facing. But could another reason be the very secret she hinted about to Frithiof while in Lapland, the one she seemed to constantly carry with her, like a dark shadow in her heart?

Her rejection was emotional and painful for both of them. Hjalmar had come to Stockholm; they were sitting on a sofa in Hildur's home when Ester Blenda told him. Neither of them noticed that Frithiof's now eight-year-old son, Kjell, was visiting. He sneaked up to the doorway and saw them. Though a child, he was clearly affected by what he saw and was able to recount the scene later in life, in the family chronicle:

Ester Blenda and Hjalmar Lundbohm sat there, completely silent, and the old man quietly cried. Tears streamed down his tired eyes over his cheeks into his gray beard. It was awful—I had never seen an adult man cry, and I understood nothing. I have since come to understand that it was probably the final farewell between Essan and a dear friend but rejected suitor.

From *Målarmästare Daniel Johan Nordström och hans släkt* [*Master Painter Daniel Johan Nordström and His Family*], by Kjell Nordström.

Breaking Hjalmar's heart became one more thing to deal with in an already troubled time. Work on the book ceased. Ester Blenda couldn't concentrate; the words wouldn't flow. Her sister Agda helped her organize her extensive material, but it was not enough. She needed another break from Stockholm.

She hoped that a few months away, spent on a farm in central Sweden, would give her the peace she needed to write. Once again, Bansai requested extended leave from her job at *Svenska Dagbladet*, and Agda and Lotten decided to join her. Lotten had been experiencing issues with her health since Daniel's death, and Agda needed a break from the residential sewing school that she ran back at the spacious family home; business wasn't great.

Ester Blenda:
[. . .] I will probably not write to you in Bäcka, although I know now that you are the only one I write to. When I sit and think about the whole long period of time between December 1914 and January 6, 1916, the most difficult and best time of my life—I almost believe it to comprise half my life—when I remember that you have not been away from my thoughts for a single day, and when I remember what you have said at times, and what you have truly meant at times—well, then I cannot write an ordinary friendly letter to you. I would, without willing it, touch upon matters that are dangerous, and I know, or I almost

hope that it would sadden you, or even deeply sadden you, if I know you well, and I do.

I am careful about you in ways I cannot explain, and therefore I would prefer that you live in peace in your faith. This may not be right, as you say, but this is, in any case, my religion when it comes to you. And it is better than the usual primitive doctrine of doom; you will understand this once you turn thirty, or maybe sooner.

Do not be saddened by what I have written.

[. . .] As I now read through my words, I am enraged; I long for a letter from you. You may do as you please with this.

Farewell to you, little girl.

Your friend,

Hjalmar L.

From a private letter from Hjalmar Lundbohm to Ester Blenda Nordström, January 8, 1916.

The room was small, in a house next to the main building. She shut herself in, tried to find her way back to the words and her voice in the slow, bucolic milieu.

Day after day of radiant sun made the thick snow cover on trees, shrubs, and rooftops out there glisten and crackle. But the impressive display of nature didn't have the same calming, cathartic effect as usual. Writing was still a slow process. Instead, it was bridge with Lotten and Agda, needlework, and long stretches of time spent at the house piano. Ester Blenda was tired, uninspired, and stressed about her finances. Without a steady income, resources were quickly running low; she had no savings.

Was she too proud to ask for aid from Daniel's great fortune? Or was she denied funding by Frithiof, who had taken over the management of the Nordström family's finances since Daniel's death? There was no explanation to be found for the acute lack, neither in old documents nor other personal effects.

When the sleeplessness set in at night, Ester Blenda took out her violin and played. Hour after hour, she replaced one song with the next.

Carin during a visit to Bäcka.

Carin came to visit. Ester Blenda briefly mentioned this in a letter to her brother. A single tiny sentence out of her otherwise wordy letters. That she would be coming to share in her loneliness for a bit. That was all she said, even though Carin quite obviously stayed for a long time. But slowly, she seemed to be finding her place in the Nordström family;

in the next letter to her brother, dated a month later, Ester mentioned how Carin Dahlbeck had offered to take care of Lotten on the way back to Stockholm. Carin had also started sending her own birthday cards to members of the Nordström family. Tiny gestures like these made it impossible for them not to like her.

The pressure in her head let up as Ester Blenda slowly but surely realized this: she could not return to the paper ever again. Not to the long, late evenings at the editorial office, or the relentlessly feverish hours between work shifts, hours filled with parties and pure intoxication.

The reporter job no longer felt adventurous and exciting. And the writing itself, the only thing that had been able to capture her full concentration over the years, now only gave pleasure when she was allowed to control it and make decisions for herself.

She was not taking a huge leap here. She had already applied for membership in the Swedish Writers' Association, and Hjalmar believed that the upcoming book would bring in a good deal of income.

> Bäcka, February 17, 1916
>
> Beloved Frithiof, beloved kind big brother—you are probably the sweetest and best of what there is on this earth by way of men. Your letter was so infinitely nice and kind, so full of sense and thoughtfulness that both Lotten and I wept as we read it. You are right about everything, of course—my sloppiness and my laziness and my carelessness—and I want so terribly to get better. But things look dark, I think, and believe me when I say I am tired too, even though I do not show it through the very action of altering my poor living. Maybe it should be possible now that I have to take out this eternal loan, which makes me sigh deeply just thinking about it. It's so infinitely kind of you to want to be a guarantor—beloved little brother. You know, of course, that I will take care of

this misery and not let you and Hildur get into trouble for my sake. As long as I can complete my book, it should be a good deal of money, and it will in any case be done before the end of 1916. If it were not for the fact that I promised Lundbohm to have the book published by his publisher in his series, I would not hesitate for a moment to sell the publishing rights to Wahlström & W even now, and they would gladly pay me a solid sum in advance. But now that I—at least for the next six months—have completely broken things off with L., I do not wish to go behind his back and sign a contract with W & W.

[. . .] I do not think this loan will have to last too long. Rejoining the paper, as you suggest, is something that I will not do. Firstly, throwing oneself back into night shifts and all that hustle and bustle is an absolute pain— secondly (and I should think this would make you smile), any remnant of style one does have is entirely destroyed through its application to these lazy advertorials that one is forced to spew out, minute by minute. I note in myself the amount of grease I have yet to rid myself of from my four years as a journalist. And as long as I have other options, I will not walk back into that editorial mess ever again.

From a letter from Ester Blenda Nordström to Frithiof
Nordström, February 17, 1916.

Her plan for staying financially afloat until she started making money from her upcoming book? A bank loan of two thousand kronor. She persuaded Frithiof and Hildur to cosign. In the rest of the letter, Ester Blenda stated that she would not waste money; she would record her expenses; and she would not be careless with bank repayments.

She ensured that no one outside the family knew about this desperate solution and had stubbornly refused to accept the financial help previously offered by Hjalmar Lundbohm.

> I do not wish to ask any outsider for help, if I can help it. It's not nice to take advantage of one's wealthy friends, and I would rather abstain from eating entirely than ask them for help.

> From a letter from Ester Blenda Nordström to Frithiof Nordström, February 17, 1916.

The last two Lapland articles were published in February and March 1916. The pseudonym Bansai fell away from the columns, but the general public's interest in her did not diminish. Throughout the summer and fall, all the papers had been writing about farmer Holtz's success with his attack book. Print run after print run sold out. And it turned out that the maid story was far from over yet.

While Ester Blenda was away working on her new book, news broke that Jogersta North Farm was being put up for sale. Anton Holtz's book success was apparently a tiny bandage over the wounds sustained by the family in the wake of the fake-maid scandal. They decided to leave the home in which they'd lived for generations.

> Father and Mother took it very badly. They felt that their private lives had been exposed in a disgraceful way. My father tried to gain redress in several ways, but the press overpowered him—in several ways. My siblings and I believe that my father and mother felt so strongly scandalized that this became the decisive, catalytic factor for leaving the ancestral farm and taking up the lease at Brunn.

[. . .] As the very last child, born in 1924, I am unfortunately the only one of his six children who has not been figuratively hit, dropped, or beaten by the maid EBN.

From a letter from Ingvar Holtz to Carl Olof Josephson,
September 25, 1993.

Anton Holtz was going to take up a lease somewhere in the archipelago, far away from their village, and their house and everything in it were going to be sold. The auction became national news when people from all over the country traveled to Jogersta North Farm in Tuna parish to see the farm where Sweden's most famous maid served and try to buy something from it. The house was full of people right from the early hours of the morning, and everything that could be connected to Ester Blenda was feverishly purchased.

A litter borne of the sow that Miss Nordström scrubbed with solid powder was purchased at a fantastic price, as well as the bed in which the maid fought her nocturnal battles with the bloodthirsty pets. After the auction, the farmer held a small audience, recapitulating the whole ordeal. He said that when *Dagens Nyheter* announced that he would write a book about the maid, he received no less than seventy letters from various sources: from newspapers and magazines that wanted his portrait, and from people who expressed their sympathies for his endeavors—there was also no lack of those who scolded him. He even received a very favorable offer to perform in front of crowds, for money, but his ambition did not extend that far.

From an article in *Dagens Nyheter*, February 7, 1916.

Those were big words, and a pleased-looking Anton Holtz counted the income from the auction, but the farmer's heart ached within as the moving load left.

> For the rest of his life, he spoke about longing to return and said that if he were to win the lottery, he would buy back Jogersta.
>
> Sören Holtz, grandson of Anton and Ida Holtz, interview by Fatima Bremmer, January 2016.

In the spring of 1916, Ester Blenda and her friend Elin Wägner decided to travel and write together over the summer. Travels could not extend beyond Sweden's borders; the war was still raging in Europe.

Elin's pacifist convictions had started to take up more and more space in her life alongside her fight for female suffrage. She had recently participated in Women at the Hague, the first international women's peace conference, as correspondent for the magazine *Idun*; the conference subsequently gave rise to the Women's International League for Peace and Freedom.

Elin's journey to neutral Holland had coursed through a wounded Europe with bloody battles. It had been far from risk-free. Deeply affected by all the misery, death, and human suffering, Elin had decided to fight for peace together with almost twelve hundred other women from different countries represented in The Hague. The meeting had convinced her that women could counteract or even prevent future wars, if they were given political power through the right to vote. She had now begun a new career as an envoy in service of peace, and as a peace activist.

Ester Blenda's interest in women's rights and opportunities seemed to have cooled in the frozen terrains of northern Sweden. She preferred to devote herself to picturesque depictions of nature and folk realism.

Her goal for the summer was to complete her book and start making money again. She hoped that Elin's calm personality and strong work discipline would rub off on her; she wanted to travel as soon as possible.

Carin returned to Bäcka for the midsummer weekend. A few days later, Ester Blenda wrote to Frithiof about a "lively celebration" with dancing in the village that lasted until half past four in the morning the first night, and till half past three the next.

Wherever Ester Blenda was in Sweden, Carin seemed to follow. It's clear from all the letters, even though they sometimes reported nothing more than "Carin" or "C." having arrived or being on her way. The two obviously wanted to be together as much and as often as Ester's reporter job and book writing allowed.

It would be high summer before Ester Blenda moved on to Värmland County with Elin Wägner. They found lodgings on a farm in the small village of Bön, just over a half mile from the Norwegian border. The house shone dazzlingly white in the sun when they arrived with their typewriters and opened the gate to the equally bright white fence. Gorgeous hedges met splendid carpentry. The farm, with a large round gravel field in front of an open porch, was right next to a lake and was surrounded by hills covered in forests. Gnarled fruit trees were everywhere in the garden, and the sash windows were framed by light curtains. It was an idyll that was almost overwhelming.

Ester Blenda immediately became friends with the strict farmer's wife, Eva, who ran the large farm with her husband and two adult daughters. The family leased an entire floor to Ester Blenda and Elin. They shared a bedroom filled with proper duvets and cool linen sheets. There was also a large hall filled with white-painted old furniture covered in home-woven red woolen fabric, and a view of the wide lake where the Norwegian mountains rested along the horizon. Ester Blenda brought out her violin; her blue-and-white sailor suit; and the portraits of Frithiof's children, Kjell, Anne-Marie, and Birgitta, who was just over a year old. She wanted them close all the time.

The hall turned into a study. After breakfast, the two authors sat back to back, each at their own windows, ready to start work. Elin eagerly typed away. Ester Blenda stared at blank or half-written sheets in the machine. The writer's block was relentless.

> Nordström has a hard time staying put in front of the typewriter. Today she started to work on the Lapp book, but she did not last many minutes. She plays the violin sometimes when I lie down to sleep, so I fall asleep to the notes. She is now returning from the lake with the old woman and her beautiful Gordon setter in tow.
>
> From a letter from Elin Wägner to Ellen "Murre" Landquist, July 7, 1916.

Elin Wägner during haymaking season in Bön. Ester Blenda is holding the camera.

While she waited for inspiration, she took long writing breaks to help out with farm chores. Expertly put a headscarf on and relieved Karin, the maid, of her work tasks, fed the animals in the barn, and rowed out on the lake with Eva to spread or gather nets.

At first, Elin chose not to comment on her friend's escapist behavior; after a while, she realized that she had to intervene if this book was ever to be written. She set rigid schedules regulating the number and duration of breaks Ester Blenda was allowed outside the room.

"I have my dark moments [. . .] Nordström has hers, when she insists that she will never write again. I then assure her of the contempt I will have for her if she does not finish the book. And then she gets so scared that she immediately sits down. What she is doing is good, so I cannot complain, but lesser things than having to describe the wonderful Lapland might make you lose your nerve," wrote Elin in a letter to Murre Landquist, her sister-in-law and their mutual friend in the League.

Slowly, a manuscript for what would become *Tent Folk of the Far North* took shape. Solitary floating pieces were joined together into comprehensive wholes. In the concentrated silence of the study, Ester Blenda was transported back to Lapland, to the smell of wet calfskin, the taste of scaldingly hot coffee freshly brewed over the fire, the sound of playful laughter in the school goahti . . .

The reader was walked straight into whipping snowstorms, the struggle between man and animal over the fells, the lead-gray light of night, and the feeling of deathly cold air in one's throat. To bloodred sunsets and the smell of resin-laden birch buds, to the powerlessness that paralyzes the encampment when they have to pay six thousand kronor in damages because their reindeer left footprints in the snow on settler land.

Chapter by chapter, the book emerged—the one that would become Ester Blenda's international breakthrough and be translated into both English and German.

They took turns writing to their friend Murre Landquist, occasionally several times a week. She had now become so ill that she was forced to move to her parents' home, where she was being cared for intensively.

They wrote long reports about how many pike they had caught in their nets, and how they skipped writing when the weather was irresistibly beautiful: instead, they went down to the lake where they sunbathed naked and became increasingly freckled while lying on their towels and taking turns reading the philosophy book sent for by Ester Blenda.

Elin gossiped that Ester Blenda went to barn dances on weekend nights and was thrown high up into the air by strong peasant farmers and came home only once it was bright outside.

It was soon difficult to distinguish one day from the next. Breakfast at nine; work at their desks with a break for coffee at 11:00 a.m. sharp, carried up on a tray by the farmer's wife, Eva; another work session; dinner at three o'clock; and then work again for a couple of hours before breaking up for the day.

They read each other's texts, offered praise, and asked questions. Comforted each other when things went slowly. From time to time, they discussed the titles of their upcoming books.

Twice a week, the mail arrived. Ester Blenda often received letters from her siblings and Frithiof's children. She usually replied immediately.

> Bön, July 24, 1916
> Precious siblings—you have indeed rendered me both surprised and moved, but I suppose this is nothing compared to what I have done to you, so, so be it. In any case, you have written some incredibly funny letters, and I have read them several times already and laughed out loud in my well-known, artful way. If you do not write more soon, you risk having me know these ones by heart by the fall

[. . .] I have not had the strength to look at typewriter or
pen, when I have been able to help it. When you write a
lot, you see, you end up growing tired of it. And I write a
lot now—truly. Elin and I are racing each other to type our
little darlings, and when evening comes, one gets very tired
indeed, I have to say. Sometimes we take time to rest, of
course—especially now with the mowers when hay is to be
driven in. We are truly happy here, almost despicably so.

From a letter from Ester Blenda Nordström to the
Nordström siblings, July 24, 1916.

At eight o'clock every night, supper was served on warm plates in
the house's large hall. Wartime rationing was not felt here. Fat milk,
butter, bread, eggs, leg of lamb, sausages, and vegetables were served
on the breakfast table. Steaks were served for dinner. The farm's eldest
daughter had learned cookery at a major hotel and wanted to impress
the famous women writers from Stockholm.

Rumors of their presence had begun to spread in the village. Every
now and then, a curious local resident came up the stairs to watch Elin
and Ester Blenda sit and work. The women themselves, and the modern
typewriters, attracted a lot of attention.

One day, as they walked down to the great hall, Ester Blenda's book
A Maid among Maids was found lying on the table. No one remarked
on it, neither the host family nor Ester Blenda herself.

The time spent in Bön with Elin was a calm and happy one. Ester
Blenda would look back on the summer of 1916 as one of her best ever.

When dusk came, I would always go out angling off the
headland, and you always joined me. You did not care for
angling, but you would sit a little bit off to the side and

Ester Blenda loved animals. Seen here with a dog on the farm in Bön.

crochet a lace for some sheets, which you'd received the
pattern for from Eva. It would still be bright when we got
home, and then we would gather on the porch—coated in
creepers, and open—and the guitar was played and there
was singing, sometimes by me, sometimes by Eva herself,
who knew the strangest ditties and was not shy once she
became well acquainted with us. Alas, what evenings those
were, Elin! The deepening shadows under the huge linden
trees in the farmyard, the smell of freshly cut hay and the
splashing of the lake, a cowbell tinkling in the silence. I do

not remember it having rained at all that summer, but it may well have done; I remember only sun-drenched days in stillness and indescribable peace.

From *Minns du?* [*Do You Remember?*] by Ester Blenda Nordström for Elin Wägner's fiftieth birthday celebration.

They both enjoyed the hard physical labor of haymaking in August. They drank coffee from a thermos out in the fields and traveled for miles in carts loaded with sweet sun-dried hay. Ester Blenda livened up the atmosphere by playing the gramophone at the lodge.

They photographed each other with Ester Blenda's camera. She sent the negatives to Stockholm and received copies back in the mail. They sent letters with photos of haymaking, going out skinny-dipping, the farm, the animals, and the view over the lake to their families and friends.

At the beginning of August, only finishing touches remained for Elin's manuscript. She traveled back to John in Stockholm. Ester Blenda stayed put.

Bön, August 24
Thank you, dear friend, for the piano; it was kind of you to lend it to me—it's like a bit of company now that one is completely alone. It's as beautiful as ever here, but it is a little strange to walk about here just like a hermit, staring about. I cannot claim that working here is all that productive, either. I have really emptied my skull, to the point that I cannot bear to extract more from it. But it is going well, albeit slowly. I am up early in the morning now, believe you me. At least every other day at five o'clock, I go out and chase butterflies and shoot black

grouse or capercaillies to the heartfelt delight and pride of our beloved Eva.

From a letter from Ester Blenda Nordström to Gerda Nordström, August 24, 1916.

In September, she reluctantly traveled home. The manuscript had to be submitted and proofread. But her next plan had already taken root in her mind. Ester Blenda wanted to become a farmer—for real. That meant going to agricultural school, and she had decided that she would enroll as soon as the book came out. Karin, the maid, had promised to come and work for Ester once she bought her own farm. This had also been decided. She still had no money, but she intended to sell the portrait painted by the great Anders Zorn if there was no other way out. She never liked the painting anyway.

There were a lot of practical things to sort out before the book got published. Ester Blenda and Hjalmar Lundbohm had to start speaking to each other again. On reading their letter correspondence from this time in their lives, you can see how they tentatively tried to strike a tone that balanced friendship and the business surrounding the book. Ester Blenda raised the issue of also publishing the book at Wahlström & Widstrand, which had also published *A Maid among Maids*. She needed the income. Hjalmar seemed to agree with the idea and told her in writing that he had personally spoken to Wahlström, who would like to see the manuscript. Eventually, they agreed on dual publication of her book.

The cover, depicting three goahtis and a snow-covered mountain slope, had been specially commissioned by ethnologist and artist Ossian Elgström. He was a friend of Hjalmar Lundbohm and personally very interested in the Indigenous Sami population. Ossian Elgström had made his own inventories of the Sami from an artistic, but also ethnological and overtly eugenics-centered, perspective.

Hjalmar was obviously thrilled to have Ester Blenda back in his life; he quickly turned familiar in tone and started calling her his "dear" and described how empty his life was without her laughter, her songs, and her playing of the violin and accordion. Maybe a new hope rose in his heart? He prepared a surprise for his chain-smoking friend: an exquisite small gold cigarette case that he'd had the artist engrave with a miniature version of the book's cover image.

She received it as a book-release gift and loved it at first sight. The gold case would remain with her for the rest of her life.

Kåtornas folk [*Tent Folk of the Far North*] was published in the fall of 1916, both in Hjalmar Lundbohm's series and by Wahlström & Widstrand. There was a dedication on the first page:

TO
HJALMAR LUNDBOHM
CONFIDANT AND FRIEND OF THE LAPPS

Critics loved it. Readers did too—print run after print run sold out. The reviews concluded that the author has seen with "sensitive eyes" and highlighted how the book's personal nature made it different from previous travelogues that had been without meaning. In retrospect, however, it was worth noting that several of the reviewers knew the author personally. *Svenska Dagbladet* had given the assignment to Karl Bernhard Wiklund, the Uppsala University professor who had been commissioned to investigate new teaching materials for Sami children. He decided to write all three new textbooks for the Sami children himself, but he was still a big supporter of Ester Blenda.

Dagens Nyheter had Elin Wägner write a review of the book. She was—unsurprisingly—very positive about it and wrote that the Sami had now been taken out of their isolation and "won a place in our hearts."

Eugenicists were also cheering. Because despite the fact that there was no doubt that Ester Blenda's heart and solidarity were with the Sami, her view of the already-vulnerable people in the North was strongly colonialist. And she was so involved with the men who had been given power to push the issues of the Sami people that she had been unable to see how their opinions and her own background and social status had affected her perspective.

Hjalmar Lundbohm was both proud and concerned that Herman Lundborg, only a couple of years away from establishing the State Institute for Racial Biology at this point, embraced Ester Blenda's work. He had begun to worry about the consequences of Lundborg's ongoing investigations—which he had personally supported with financial contributions. In a letter to her, he wrote:

> Dr. Lundborg was here yesterday, and he, too, waxed lyrical about your excellent work. He also told me that the Lapp liaison Holm is delighted by you on account of the book. But Lundborg takes a dim view of the future of the Lapps, as does Kronlund, I believe.
>
> He has not shared his views in public and forms much of his opinion based on the condition of the half-dilapidated, bad Lapps. He is also deeply affected by the fact that he encounters so few "pure" Lapps. Miscegenation is to him an incurable evil, or at least an incurable evil for many hundreds of years.
>
> And he does not think it possible to establish sensible laws in such instances unless these are based on race-biological research.

Six hundred kronor is attached; it is a good deal less
than the incredible profit you will gain.

From a letter from Hjalmar Lundbohm to Ester Blenda
Nordström, August 5, 1917.

Sami teacher Karin Stenberg was sitting in Arvidsjaur village, boiling with rage. She viewed Ester Blenda as yet another "tourist writer"
with a "foreign gaze" who painted her people as ignorant and childish,
albeit with tender brushstrokes.

The frustration over how these outside travelers' voices grew so
powerful that legislators allowed themselves to be influenced by them
reached a fever pitch when she read *Tent Folk of the Far North*. In her
opinion, it only fed the prejudices already held by the Swedes.

Karin Stenberg was one of the people behind the newly formed
Sami association in Arvidsjaur. The desire to fight was kindled in many;
the Sami organizational movement was taking shape, with Karin as
one of its pioneers. She would go on to be both known and praised for
her tireless fight for the Sami cause over the course of several decades,
through her work of courting members of parliament, initiators of
the Sami folk high school, and the Sami national organization, Same
Ätnam. She would also save culturally important environments from
demolition.

At this point, she had begun writing the battle manifesto *Dat läh
mijen situd: En vädjan till Svenska Nationen från samefolket* (*It Is Our
Will: An Appeal to the Swedish Nation from the Sami People*). In it, she
rebelled against the depiction of "poor ignorant Lapps," against her
people being described as children who were dependent and completely
lacking in the ability to understand what was best for them, and against
the prevailing view that the Sami had uncritically allowed themselves to
be shaped by the Swedes' actions and legislations.

She raised the question of why they had paid taxes to Sweden since the thirteenth century without receiving the same civil rights as other citizens, and highlighted the abuses of her people, like those inflicted by eugenicists.

The manifesto also stated a clear wish: they wanted to get rid of goahti schools and replace them with new state primary schools for Sami children where they would be able to access the same breadth of knowledge offered in other Swedish primary schools.

> The many knowledgeable and well-meaning men and women who have also portrayed the life of the Sami people have generally, even in instances when the best of intentions were held, only portrayed it from the Swedes' point of view, made the main issue a minor issue, and vice versa. It is not the *Sami people* who have been portrayed; rather, it is the *lives of Swedes as tourists in an exotic land* with quite an interesting population, to be sure, that has been portrayed. As the Sami are characterized less like other human beings and more like animals, however, these works gain more and more interest [. . .] Not to harm the Sami people—after all, we do not wish to believe this to be the case—but to make their own little ridiculous *egos* interesting. But what is dangerous for us, the Sami, about similar "truths about the Lapp"—as they appear in the works of Ester Blenda Nordström or Ossian Elgström, for instance—is that the Swedish public who read these books are given the same distorted and uncomprehending view of the Sami as the one held by the author, viewing us as ethnographic objects belonging to a time that is already

past, which is why we should not even venture to suggest that we desire any development.

From *Dat läh mijen situd: En vädjan till Svenska Nationen från samefolket* (*It Is Our Will: An Appeal to the Swedish Nation from the Sami People*)

Karin Stenberg was clever. To ensure that the document was taken seriously, she joined forces with an established male writer outside the Sami collective, Valdemar Lindholm, who had previously written incredibly critically about deforestation in northern Sweden. But right from the manifesto's introduction, she made it clear that she was the responsible publisher, and that she and a few other Arvidsjaur Samis had conceived the idea for the work.

The introduction also confirmed that the Arjeplog Sami association unanimously gave its full support to all statements and views at a meeting, and that the publication represented how the Sami nation thought and felt as a whole.

Hjalmar Lundbohm found out what was going on through acquaintances and wrote about it in a letter to Ester Blenda; in it, he called Valdemar Lindholm a troublemaker and asked whether Ester Blenda even cared about the whole thing.

The Sami teacher's voice never broke through quite as powerfully as those of Ester Blenda and the other "travelers." After the triumph of *Kåtornas folk* (*Tent Folk of the Far North*) in Sweden, publishing rights talks began with both English and German agents who had opened their eyes to the acclaimed female reporter who was breaking new ground with her reportage books of personal experiences, and her highly unique writing style. And when the book went on to be republished almost a hundred years later by the publisher Bakhåll, it was, once again, widely praised by critics.

In November 1916, Murre Landquist died. Members of the League traveled straight to her parish home in Stockholm. Murre was still sitting upright in bed when they entered the room to say goodbye.

It was a heavy end to the year for all the female journalist pioneers in Stockholm who were finally starting to gain the status and respect for which they'd been fighting for so long.

Elin Brandell at *Dagens Nyheter* had started being sent out as a correspondent for major legal trials. Gerda Marcus was considered a leading name among the country's critics and had also served as *DN* Berlin correspondent for a while. Vera von Kraemer made a career as an editor and had written a reportage book about Japan, which she had journeyed through using a journalist's lens. But the unmistakable star of the group was its "baby":

> There are two Misses Nordström at *Svenska Dagbladet*, and one of them is probably the most widely known of all female journalists. Ester Blenda Nordström (Bansai) has achieved as much fame through her literary activities as she has through her plucky personal performance. First, she took a job as a maid employed by the "Farmer in Taninge" and wrote *A Maid among Maids*, which has become a folk book like no other, and then she became a nomadic teacher for the Lapp children on the snowy fells, living among the people of the goahtis as one of them. She knows how to plow a perfectly straight furrow in Swedish soil as skillfully as she can coax a Spanish song out of a manzonetta [*sic*]. It's no wonder that this talented and versatile young lady is popular wherever she goes.

> From the article "Our female journalists in the daily press," *Idun*, no. 48 (November 26, 1916).

She was in demand everywhere; personally, she just wanted to get away from it all—again. Her claustrophobia was back, and it was eating her up from the inside. Alcohol numbed her. Her friends could see the imbalance but couldn't seem to get through to her. She suddenly broke things off with Hjördis Tengbom after Hjördis joked about how Ester taunted a couple of guys they met on an outing. "So our friendship came to an end. Bien trieste [*sic*]," wrote Hjördis in her diary.

When *Svenska Dagbladet* held its annual Christmas fundraiser at the grand cinema Svarta Katten (the Black Cat) on Vattugatan in Stockholm, and their usual conferencier fell ill, it was Bansai they called upon to be the hostess for the evening.

She let herself get talked into it. She stood behind the stage, wearing a jet-black silk dress and shaking while holding the hand of child actress Kerstin Bergman from the Oscar Theater. When it was time for the evening's first act to be introduced, she hesitated, then stepped cautiously onto the stage, still holding the little girl's hand, and saying quite frankly, "We are both so scared, we could die."

No sassy jokes, no outspokenness, none of the expected jargon.

> If you expected the evening's conférencière to deliver a causerie, you were fooled by the facade. The subsequent acts were also presented in a similarly plain manner, but all it takes is looking presentable and having a key that can unlock even the most rigidly walled-off, unscrupulous heart. She rightly received a bouquet of flowers. We have not seen Mr. Balder, but we wouldn't mind if he suffered a toothache on a few more such evenings in future.

> From an article in *Svenska Dagbladet*,
> December 20, 1916.

The illustration for the review in the newspaper was a picture in profile of a clearly terrified Bansai who stuck her head out from between the stage curtains with narrowed eyes and pursed lips. But no matter what Ester Blenda did, she seemed to get praised to the skies.

In the spring of 1917, she wrote four long texts in *Svenska Dagbladet*, all about Sami-related issues. She interviewed the new nomadic school inspector Vitalis Karnell, who believed that the Sami people's tendencies to want to settle had to be stopped. With Sami legislation under review at this time, she wrote a debate article arguing that settled Sami people should not be allowed to engage in reindeer husbandry; rather, they should live according to their traditional ways. And when Professor Wiklund's new reading book for nomadic schools was presented, Ester Blenda applauded the text's and images' clear connection to the Sami's own world—exactly what she had personally pushed for in her articles and book.

On the last day of June 1917, *Svenska Dagbladet* received a notice of resignation from its most famous and acclaimed writer. The pseudonym Bansai went to its grave. Ester Blenda was going to make her dream to train as a farmer come true.

CHAPTER 10

War Hero and Author of Girls' Books

Bansai, who thought it would be fun to be a maid at Taninge and who therefore attracted fame (and money) for herself and the Farmer (both of whom are currently rural Sweden's most widely read writers), intends to become a farmer herself. She has been admitted as an extra student at Ultuna Agricultural Institute outside Uppsala. She is currently increasing her practical experience in this desired field, though not in Taninge, which she has rendered so terribly infamous; rather, she is on an Uppland farm. Next fall, she will begin her higher education in agriculture.

When can we expect her book about the agronomists?

From an article in *Dagens Nyheter*, October 19, 1917.

The Barony of Adelswärd

Åtvidaberg

It is a real pleasure for me to be able to confirm that Miss Ester Blända [*sic*] Nordström participated in all manner of agricultural work during the summer here, thereby showing herself to be a woman with an unusually high level of ability to work. It need not be remarked that there is no lack of energy and goodwill, as one takes Miss Nordström's hitherto practiced multifaceted activities into account.

Adelsnäs, Åtvidaberg, Sept. 3, 1917

L. L. Westlund

Inspector at the Barony of Adelswärd

Recommendation letter written by L. L. Westlund, September 3, 1917.

In 1917, Ester Blenda resigned from Svenska Dagbladet to train as a farmer. Here, she is seen driving a horse-drawn mower during a summer internship.

She was several steps closer to realizing her dream of owning a farm. A summer and fall of agricultural internships with hard physical labor had only made her even more confident but also humble. Running your own farm requires a lot of knowledge, both practical and theoretical. It would take time and even more training—and money, for her new free existence was, unfortunately, also a much poorer one.

A production company said it wanted to turn *Tent Folk of the Far North* into a movie, but nothing was set in stone just yet. Meanwhile, Ester Blenda looked for longer and more advanced education programs that would be open to admitting a woman. It was not an easy task; a woman's place on a farm was still as the wife of a farmer, or a maid. Women could take individual courses at a few agricultural schools, but only with a focus on household management. There was a real chance that Ester Blenda would even be openly ridiculed on sending her application letters to the agricultural schools. This didn't stop her, of course. On the contrary.

She moved back home with her mother at Ekefors mansion. Back to her safe space, to her "honey flower and ray of sunshine" as she usually called her mother. There, her room was always ready for her.

Carin often went there, not just for Ester Blenda's sake. She was also good friends with Agda. It's unclear whether the friendship developed as a result of Ester Blenda and Carin's close relationship or if Carin and Agda had a completely separate relationship the whole time.

Life at Ekefors was, as always, lived within a protected bubble. There was perpetually food on the table in the large twelve-room villa, despite the fact that the ongoing war had stopped the import of many foods and had forced the rationing of basic goods such as sugar, milk, bread, meat, fish, and eggs. But even here, everyone longed for a cup of real coffee. Coffee, like a lot of other things, was being rationed, and the shortage hit all Swedes, regardless of class. Plans were slowly being hatched at Ekefors. Agda, who had inherited her father's business sense, got an idea. She wanted to enter the coffee-substitute industry. There was definitely money to be made from catering to the needs of the caffeine-dependent people as their patience began to wear thin. Coffee cards had become hard currency, and businessmen were trying to bring coffee into Sweden by any means possible.

The inventiveness of coffee manufacturers was almost limitless, and there was no legislation that insisted that substitutes or additives must contain caffeine. Figs, among other things, were roasted and then pulverized and mixed with real coffee. It was less bitter than chicory coffee manufactured by roasting, grinding, and steaming dried chicory root. The color and fullness were reminiscent of the longed-for drink, but the taste certainly wasn't.

Ester Blenda had no time, desire, or money to invest in the project. But Carin did and was not scared off by Agda's unconventional manufacturing plans. They planned to try acorns as an alternative. There were several large oaks that graced the lawns of Ekefors, and when their leaves changed color from green to a golden red-yellow hue, the huge lawn was filled with thousands of acorns. They read about roasting processes and grinding methods. Kjell, Frithiof's son, who was temporarily staying at the house, cared for by Agda, watched as she and Carin energetically gathered the acorns in the garden.

The famine in Sweden was becoming increasingly difficult at this time. Trade blockades caused prices to rise. The bad harvest also led to a shortage of grains. The Stockholm City Food Committee, which had been appointed by the city council to help the capital's hungry families and its elderly population, was on its knees. Mass caterers distributed food to the people in most need. Public green areas had been turned into giant potato and vegetable farms. Karlaplan's famously beautiful flower beds were dug up and replaced by long, dense rows of cabbage. A rabbit-breeding committee was formed with the aim of starting rabbit farms in the city. They bred a Belgian giant that, weighing up to about twenty-six pounds, produced a lot of meat.

Hunger strikes against the prevailing politics descended into bloody riots on several occasions; each time, tens of thousands of protesting Stockholmers were surrounded by machine-gun outposts and attacked by mounted police with sabers and whips.

In Finland, the situation was even worse. Entire parishes were literally starving to death. One of them was the Kolari district in Lapland. Mass unemployment and the dire shortage of food had led to social problems. Furthermore, difficult political standoffs were about to devolve into a full-blown civil war.

Finland had been subject to Russia as a grand duchy ever since Sweden lost it to Russia in 1809. When the Bolsheviks carried out a coup in Russia in November 1917, Finnish socialists were inspired to do the same with the support of the newly established Bolshevik regime. Bourgeois forces in the country were, instead, taking action to proclaim their independence.

Despite the great famine in Sweden itself, a committee for "starving Finland" was appointed in Stockholm in the late fall of the very same year. Both Elin Wägner and John Landquist got involved; he was appointed secretary. In order to quickly get a sense of how severe the situation in the neighboring country was, the committee needed to send an investigative expedition there. It would take a fearless, enterprising Finnish speaker who had local knowledge of Lapland and could quickly get an overview of the extent of the famine as well as the interventions required. John discussed this challenge with his wife. Whom could the committee send? There was no hesitation in her reply.

The mission came at the right time. The income from *Tent Folk of the Far North* was no longer enough. Hildur seemed to have cosigned yet another temporary loan. Ester Blenda wrote to Hjalmar, who was in Washington, DC; among other things, he was there to try to strengthen trade relations with the United States on behalf of the

Swedish government. Pride prevented her from asking for help, but judging by the reply, her letter seemed to have contained descriptions of a rather lousy financial situation.

Hjalmar Lundbohm replied that he didn't believe her finances to be quite as terrible as she made out; after all, the book brought in a considerable sum. He also commented, with some concern, on Carin and Agda's start-up business—not least because he himself was a competitor. During his time in Washington, Lundbohm tried to come away with twenty-five hundred tons of coffee that he planned to sell back home in Sweden. He wrote that he was thrilled that Carin had finally found something to keep her occupied and that might help people, but hoped that he wouldn't destroy her business too badly.

But no suggestions of a loan. No offering more money for the book. The truth was that he had none. World War I had drastically reduced Swedish ore exports and had a major impact on Lundbohm's personal finances.

Before the Finnish Emergency Relief Committee dared to make the decision to hire the journalist who was as famous as she was scandalous, she had to meet with its chairman, national archivist Sam Clason, who was known for being picky and difficult to charm. John Landquist attended the meeting, but immediately felt that his presence was completely superfluous.

> She was standing there in the gray room filled with papers: blond, with a fine complexion, eager, and wise. She soon proved to be eminently knowledgeable about relevant matters. She stated what she should be given to take along if she is sent there, food of various kinds that fit the environment, medicines, children's clothes, I cannot remember it all. During the course of the conversation, she sat with her legs crossed on one edge of the national archivist's desk, with her right hand gently pushing a brown folio aside. I

watched with pleasure how the doubled superciliousness of the right-wing leader and senior official quickly melted away right before our eyes. His cheeks took on a slight blush; his eyes shone; he smiled; he looked younger. Ester Blenda was appointed our representative on the spot. She got everything she wanted [. . .] I thought to myself, "That girl is not unaware of her power."

From John Landquist's memoirs, *I ungdomen. Scener ur den förlorade tiden* [*In Youth. Scenes from the Lost Time*].

On December 6, 1917, the bourgeois government of Finland declared independence. Barely two months later, on the evening of January 27, socialists hoisted a red lantern in the tower of the Helsinki Workers' House, as the starting signal for revolution in the newly formed republic.

The Finnish bourgeoisie mobilized a resistance army with an unexpected swiftness. Conservative and socialist societal groups armed themselves to settle matters in a bloody class struggle. The Reds against the Whites. People from all walks of life—peasants, noblemen, and industrialists—joined in the fight. Even the women.

In just a few short months, almost forty thousand people had died in the so-called civil war; the majority fell in battle or were executed as prisoners. The dead were shoveled into mass graves. Children were placed in detention camps and brought before the court for "crimes against the state." Entire cities were under attack, and railways were blown up when White and Red Guards met in violent battles with machine guns and bombs. Civilians suffered at the hands of soldiers and were hard-hit when famine and plagues wreaked havoc in the wake of the war.

Back in Stockholm, Ester Blenda made final preparations for her journey straight into the inferno. Through the conservative *Svenska*

Dagbladet, she was able to follow developments in headlines such as "Kirkkonummi has fallen into the hands of the Reds," "Railway track south of Vilppula blown up by the Whites," "The Red Terror in Helsinki culminates—merely a small part of all the horrors hitherto known or unknown in Sweden."

Sweden was very much involved in the neighboring country's civil war. Many Swedes still lived in Finland, and large parts of the population spoke Swedish. Some prisoners of war were placed under Swedish protection, and Swedish Social Democrats tried to mediate between the parties. And England sent three ships with a total of fifty-five hundred tons of food to Swedish ports, for onward rail freight to the Finnish border.

Newspaper ads also urged Swedes to travel to Finland to fight in battles for "the salvation of the social order and the culture that Swedes established there in times past."

Visa no. 1000 was stamped by the Finnish embassy in Stockholm, on behalf of the government of Finland. It was valid for travel from Sweden to Finland for "survey of the shortage of food in Finnish Lapland" and residency in Finland between March 3, 1918, through June 1, 1918. An accompanying document adorned with a royal stamp certified that Miss Ester Blenda Elisabeth Nordström was protected and aided by the king of Sweden and the Royal Ministry for Foreign Affairs for the unrestricted crossing of the border to Finland.

The Swedish commissioner's report was described in French next to a photograph of her wearing a black hat and a white mink stole around her neck. Her gaze was steady, her lips somewhat pinched.

All types of humanitarian aid were required in the neighboring country. Frithiof was also involved in the work of the Famine Relief Committee; judging by everything, he seemed to have been engaged by Ester Blenda herself. She had great respect for her older brother's pragmatic disposition and, as a dentist, he could make great contributions.

It was decided that Frithiof would travel ahead to Finland on a short trip to generate an initial quick situation report. He set out immediately, with some travel cash that Ester Blenda redeemed for him from the committee. She received two letters he'd written to her before it was time for her to start her mission. His letters were filled with concrete proposals for possible modes of transportation and pointers to people who could help her once she was on the ground.

On the train to Kolari and the assignment as emergency commissioner during the Finnish Civil War, 1917–1918.

On March 8, the famine commissioner crossed the border into Finland via northern Pajala, where she was accommodated in an inn. She had an interpreter with her for assistance; she was otherwise completely alone. When Ester Blenda woke up in the ice-cold room, the sheets were covered with a layer of frost. She packed skins, hay, provisions, and her camera, wrapped herself in a large wolfskin fur, and fastened her skis. The journey to the first farms ran through dense coniferous forest, over snow-covered bogs, and across streams frozen right through to their bottoms. Within a few short miles, she came face-to-face with the country's great famine in a little black cottage.

> He flung out a pile of black blood that did not smell too good; he pointed to a sack of straw. The two ingredients combined were what they had to eat for bread—a mixture of horse blood and straw. The horse had died from hunger in the stall; the feed had run out. The cows could not produce a single drop of milk anymore, and the milk pails lay on the floor, no longer needed. The grain had run out a long time ago—every single grain, the seed too.

> From an article in *Svenska Dagbladet*, March 15, 1918.

Visions of starvation appeared one after the other throughout the day. Empty eyes, swollen bellies under prominent ribs. Some had already given up; they simply lay waiting for death. Several of them were children. Fresh graves showed that the worst had already hit several families.

The reindeer population, usually large in northern Finland, had been shot down along with most of the local cows by Russian border guards in Kolari; according to eyewitnesses in the population, the guards had also stolen large quantities of grain.

Ester Blenda realized that there was a need for huge amounts of meat and cereals—and fast. On the same day, she alerted John Landquist at home in Sweden, who in turn contacted the National Food Supply Committee to issue the licenses required for the export of food. The wait for their decision turned into a race against the clock. Every minute lost could cost lives.

"Swift help needed. Children dying from starvation. Clear message when?"

The telegram sent to Elin the next day, March 9, was desperate. In a report to the national archivist, Ester Blenda wrote that "the famine is critical." She was not aware that the National Food Supply Committee had already rejected several license applications from the Famine Relief Committee for bread and cereals.

In the evening, she penned an article that she sent to the editor of her old newspaper, *Svenska Dagbladet*. It was an appeal to the public and a situation report in equal measure.

> If there ever was a time to speak of famine, this is it.
>
> Alas, it is all so hopeless! Small children who have died of starvation—whole families about to perish. Cattle that dropped dead from the lack of fodder, and every-where, seed grain is taken for bread [. . .] It affects per-haps a thousand lives. It involves a small sacrifice of our own abundance, which, at the very least, is better than the bare essentials, when you see how these poor people starve. Couldn't we possibly help? Is there none among us who would voluntarily part with some of what they have, perhaps with some sacrifice, perhaps with some difficulty? Give of your own volition; give as little as you like; give *soon*; give everything you can—coupons, money, food, anything at all that can be sold and exchanged for food. It is urgent—think of all the children dying from starvation, who may not live until the summer when fish and game could be procured from lakes and forests. Wouldn't you help them, please? Oh, hurry!

> From an article in *Svenska Dagbladet*, March 15, 1918.

The day after the article was published, *Svenska Dagbladet* received 7,679 kronor from Swedes who wanted to help. Just less than a week later, the total reached 14,000 kronor, equivalent to almost 266,000 Swedish kronor today.

The evenings in the cold room at the inn in Pajala were heavy and lonely. To pass the time while waiting for information about export licenses and food, Ester Blenda wrote a letter home to Frithiof.

> I am as one cast away on a desert island. The priest is gone, and there is not a single mouth that can speak a word of Swedish. It's absolutely awful.

The head of the National Food Supply Committee, Henning Elmquist, also rejected the submitted application for meat exports to Kolari. Instead, he sent cargo loads of dried vegetables that the Swedes had rejected. After a week, John Landquist had an infuriated Ester Blenda on a crackling phone line from Finland: "Tell the committee that the Finns would rather die than eat your grass!"

> I went to Clason at the National Archives and presented Ester Blenda's message. He smiled, furrowed his forehead, and said, "There may be a way around Elmquist. We will address the government directly. Call Edén!"

> From John Landquist's memoirs, *I ungdomen. Scener ur den förlorade tiden* [*In Youth. Scenes from the Lost Time*].

Nils Edén was the sitting prime minister. John Landquist did as he was told. He called the country's prime minister directly and was asked to submit an application for two thousand pounds of meat, which he was promised would be swiftly approved by the council. Just a few days later, Ester Blenda received word that the food could be picked up in Övertorneå village, ninety-three miles away.

> I had driven my reindeer to the point of him gasping from exhaustion. He could hardly walk the last bit, and the sledge had swerved so much that I thought the trees in the woods would fall on me from all the shoving. But we were in a hurry, and it was worth the effort. Bitter, blunt faces lit up—slow, dull movements filled with life—eyes brightened and loud voices spoke, people came from all over [. . .] My sluggish, labored Finnish emerged too slowly to keep up—they spoke so fast, I could barely understand them.

From an article in *Svenska Dagbladet*, March 25, 1918.

Just over one ton of fresh, fatty beef. It was rationed out by the food committee under the supervision of Ester Blenda and the parish pastor who considered each family's number of children and general physical health.

At a grand ceremony, the municipal chairman later gave a speech thanking Ester Blenda. He was so moved that his voice broke when he asked her to humbly thank all the Swedes who helped save their lives. Around them, the war raged on; shots from firing squads rang out in the forests. In the southern parts of the country, the White faction took Tammerfors city in a series of bloody street battles. Red prisoners were sentenced and executed in the county courts established among the ruins.

Pajala, March 28, 1918

Beloved brother—thank you for your very welcome letter. You know how happy one gets on hearing from home, and you in particular know this to be the case when in Pajala. Can you believe I have been here for three weeks today. Well, I'll be damned! I cannot believe that I am alive and have my health—can you?

From a letter from Ester Blenda Nordström to Frithiof
Nordström, March 28, 1918.

A few days after sending the letter, she turned twenty-seven. There was no mention of any celebrations of the occasion in any of her remaining letters.

Money continued to flow into *Svenska Dagbladet*'s fundraiser. During the first week of April, the second major relief shipment came with almost seven tons of cereals, vegetables, and tubers. The food was divided equally between Kolari and the neighboring parish, where the need was just as great. Around the same time, German war machinery rolled into Helsinki, and the German battleship SMS *Westfalen* entered the port. The German troops had come to assist the White side.

When other northern Finnish parishes heard about the Swedish journalist's heroic efforts, she was contacted with cries for help. Ester Blenda tried to get into the villages with food, but the mud made the roads impossible to travel on. Shortly afterward, terrible news came from home: the National Food Supply Committee refused to issue further export licenses. Deeply disappointed, the Swedish famine commissioner began to plan the trip back to Stockholm, conscious of the fact that she would be leaving several people behind to die. On May 4, in a report to her client, Sam Clason, she wrote that she "must consider [her] work completed." Barely two weeks later, on May 15, 1918, the civil war was over. White Finland, comprising the upper classes, had won. Finland would become an independent republic—at the cost of a traumatized population, divided families, and dark, shameful secrets that would be passed down through generations.

On the way home, Ester Blenda made a stop in the Swedish part of Lapland. Carin came to meet her. They planned to hike the mountains with Frithiof and a friend of his, the prominent insect researcher and explorer René Malaise. Frithiof and René Malaise both collected large Nordic butterflies and had plans for an entomological collaboration.

From Altevand, she set her sail
With Carin fairest at her tail
They'll meet the brother and Malaise
At the maison, oh yes.

But reckonst thou it was to be?
Alas, upon the marshy sea;
A message back: No, meet us not
At home, forget the lot[.]

From a poem by Frithiof Nordström to Ester Blenda Nordström in connection with a mountain hike in 1918.

Beloved, quiet, solitary Lapland. For ten days, Ester Blenda and Carin walked across golden-yellow bogs, swamps, and clusters of willow, hour after hour. Ice-cold baths on the shores of Lenavand. Brewing coffee and cooking over an open fire.

As the time to meet Frithiof and his friend approached, they realized that they regretted having arranged this; they wanted to keep being just the two of them. Hence the miffed lines in Frithiof's poem. Instead, Ester Blenda and Carin were thinking of taking the Hurtigruten cruise to Norway. The boats went almost every day, and you could have supper on board.

In the evenings, they camped wherever they thought it was beautiful. Made a fire under the covering of a birch grove, let the heat dry wet socks, and fought off a million mosquitoes. Ester Blenda tended to Carin's feet, which were covered in fluid-filled blisters. Then they fell silent, side by side. Carin with a book, Ester with her pipe. Sometimes they had crispbread crumbs and chocolate for dinner: that was what happened when you skipped past stops for refilling provisions. When you decided you wanted to blaze your own paths, paths that no one else had chosen to walk.

They stayed in a hotel; eight kronor for one night in a real bed before they went on to Ester Blenda's friends Johan and Fine, who owned a farm nearby. The smell of grass was intense; Ester Blenda drew it in through her nostrils along with the clear, high air. Felt the calm fill her lungs, after her months spent in Kolari with the constant presence of death.

The notebook in her hand was small. So were the letters that filled it, arranged in densely written pencil strokes.

> Aug. 9
> Sitting on a lawn outside the farm in Hanglid, writing.
> Carin sleeps next to me. The sun is shining. Johan U. is
> driving in hay. Fine cooks for us and life is quite lovely.

That same summer and fall, Ester Blenda started writing an autobiographical manuscript. It resulted in only eight handwritten pages before she suddenly stopped. They are all about the same thing: her rebellious temperament as a little girl, her recurrent antics, and the family's increasingly exhausted attempts to nurture and shape her according to the strict ideals of the time and their social class.

The memories that seemed to have made the most profound impression, and which took up the most space in her writing, were those from her time with Uncle Håkan, the vicar, when Lotten and

Daniel gave up and sent her away from home. The more careful and detailed the descriptions of her memories, the darker her tone. The little teen girl's pain was plain for all to see. The wounds felt fresh and raw.

At the beginning of September, she sent the pages to a former colleague at *Svenska Dagbladet*. On the back of a small business card, she wrote:

> Here's more drivel once again. I haven't the energy to change anything in it. I'll leave it as it is. Feel free to sign it "Bansai" if you prefer—makes no difference to me whatsoever. Bye!

What exactly was the purpose of the text? It was never published, and none of Ester Blenda's papers included a reply from Märta Lindquist, the colleague she sent it to. But the text clearly sowed the seed for something else. Ester Blenda started talking about a girls' book with her sister-in-law, Gerda. She had an idea for a different kind of heroine, one who *must* not be anything like the other typical girls' book characters. But before she had time to start, some longed-for news finally reached her: she was to be the only woman ever to have been admitted to the country's biggest agricultural school, the Hagaberg Nordic Agricultural School.

Once again, Ester threw herself between diametrically opposing worlds: from the witnessing of starvation and desperation in the middle of a civil war, to a life of quiet study on a large farm located in a birch grove outside Jönköping.

> I am alone with 112 men—all churlish, more or less, but somewhat decent. The rather severe rules of conduct state: "the consumption of alcoholic beverages, card games, immorality with women, and any other indecent behavior is forbidden for students both within and without the

student accommodation." So there you have it: It says nothing about immorality with men in any case. So you cannot rest assured of anything with me.

From a letter from Ester Blenda Nordström to Frithiof
and Gerda Nordström, November 21, 1918.

She specialized in small-scale farming, a passion that Ester Blenda shared with the charismatic founder, Per Jönson Rösiö. There was something of the iconic Swedish author and playwright August Strindberg about him, with his thick hair that often shot straight up and bushy eyebrows that pointed upward too. He also had Strindberg's notorious temperament.

Rösiö was a well-known figure in the country, both as a writer and speaker. Before he started this program, he was one of Sweden's most successful agricultural columnists; he was given regular column spots in over two hundred newspapers, and at his peak, he delivered up to 353 annual lectures on farming and cultural issues. Among small-scale farmers, he was the closest thing they had to a revival leader.

Under the clear influence of August Strindberg, among others, Per Jönson Rösiö pursued an agrarian ideology that aimed to counteract the harmful effects of industrialism on the culture of the people. He was also a forward-thinking man with a great interest in all the new science; Hagaberg, for example, was the first in the country to work with experimental fields and testing of legume grafting.

Per Rösiö taught, and Ester Blenda loved his lectures; you could never predict how they would end. He ran, marched, jumped, and stirred up chaos, bellowed and whispered about anything and everything in front of the students. But you had to watch out not to laugh out loud. The principal was also cross-eyed, so there was no way of telling whom his watchful eyes had settled on.

There was only one other woman at Hagaberg: Natàlia, the dorm mother. She kept an extra-close eye on the only female agricultural student; she would not have been pleased to know that Frithiof and Gerda had stuffed Ester's recent parcel with cigarettes, on the occasion of her name day (a remnant from Catholic saint veneration that continues in a number of European countries). In her thank-you note, Ester remarked that the dorm mother forbade her to smoke, but that she found a way to continue without being discovered. She "sticks her head in the tiled stove and puffs her heart out" when the urge grew irresistible.

In November 1918, the First World War was finally over. It would take a few more months before the first peace documents were signed in Versailles, but the difference was already felt at Hagaberg. For dinner, two different soups were served, one of which always contained meat.

Coffee was still being rationed, but Agda and Carin's acorn coffee had not been successful. Carin lost all her invested money. Ester Blenda had no time to comfort her. Agricultural studies were demanding. She locked herself in her room and was determined to fight. She did so with good results. For the big fall exam in physics, she got an A plus. She expressed her pre-exam anxiety and post-exam glee through small stick-figure drawings placed in letters sent home to family.

Gerda in particular loved the tiny illustrations and encouraged her to draw more. She sent small gifts to Hagaberg. Candy. Chocolate. More cigarettes. Homemade cookies. On such occasions, Ester Blenda ran to Natàlia, the dorm mother, and asked to use the gas stove to brew coffee in her copper pot. As a thank-you, Natàlia was then invited to have some coffee in Ester Blenda's room. It was small and simple, but there was room for the typewriter. Alongside her studies, she started working on the manuscript for her girls' book—the first fictional work she had ever written. But Ester Blenda didn't completely depart from reality, either. The main character was named after Frithiof and Gerda's eldest daughter, Anne-Marie, who was now six—though with a slightly modified spelling. She wrote home to Gerda:

With regard to an illustrated girls' book, I have just started work on one. Not illustrated, of course—now, *there's* an idea—but a girls' book. You're probably right that I should do the drawings too. They are truly original and fresh; no one can claim otherwise.

From a letter from Ester Blenda Nordström to Gerda
Nordström, November 30, 1918.

And thus, Ann-Mari Lindelöf emerged. An impulsive wild child who usually acted before she thought, who always seemed to get into trouble because she refused to live and behave as society both expected and demanded. The adventurous girl with grass stains on her knees, dirty hands, and tiny nails in her pockets, who longed for the freedoms that boys and men enjoyed as a matter of course—just as Ester Blenda herself always had.

She was standing up straight in a white dress with a blue ribbon around her waist. Light blue socks and a blue bow in the hair. She was so pretty-looking that she thought herself disgusting, but that could not be helped—she had to suffer through it. After dinner, when she felt a little less watched, she disappeared. Straight down to the river. Just to see what it looked like! It was more tempting than usual—a huge piece of timber had got stuck in the middle of the tiny stream, and a bunch of log drivers were using axes and pike poles to try to loosen it. New logs came swirling every minute, and it seemed so completely impossible to get it all under control that Ann-Mari stood and jumped with zeal and delight. Rudel was out there too, and he waved and screamed at her. The pike pole lay tempting her on the beach. If she could just take off her dress and run out and help for a bit! Then she could not soil it, and no one would consider that she was gone until it was time for coffee [. . .]

Ann-Mari never considered anything for long. Within a minute, her dress was off, and she was out on the logjam in a petticoat and bodice. No one had time to think about how she was dressed or to even look at her. They had all put the pike poles in a barricading log and pushed with all their might. "Hi, ho, hey let's go!"

Ann-Mari wedged her pike pole in next to the others and sang along. Slowly, slowly, the log began to move, then slid forward for a bit, and the pike poles sank into the next [. . .]

"This is the life," thought Ann-Mari. If she were a man, she would be a log driver all her life.

From *En rackarunge* [*A Little Rascal*].

Surely that's little Ester herself coming through between the lines. Later in life, she would go on to confirm—in both private letters and public interviews—that the character was based on her. Ann-Mari was never still, did not care about her appearance, and was bold enough to laugh and to cry until the snot got smudged all over her face. She felt incredibly warmly toward friends from all walks of life, even a convicted murderer. And marriage was not the "obvious" end goal; her dream was to live as she pleased and to one day become a self-sufficient farmer with her own farm.

Ann-Mari was forced to live with a strict and cold pastor so that she could grow up to be an obedient and kind girl. She constantly challenged his authority by coming up with new tricks and ended up in all sorts of trouble.

And there it was: Ester Blenda's revenge on Uncle Håkan who'd once placed her on his lap, pulled up her skirt, and hit too hard, for too long. Fourteen years had passed, but there was no question who the evil pastor was. Ester Blenda described him as "strict, cold, and slow to forgive."

We will never know how Uncle Håkan reacted to Ester Blenda's book. But relatives, friends, and everyone in Villstad—anyone who knew that the famous journalist lived with him for a period of time— could see that the character of the evil priest was based on him.

When Frithiof and Gerda had their fourth child at around the same time, they made Ester Blenda the godmother and named the girl Ester Blenda Gunilla. The new aunt was with Agda and Lotten when she heard about their name choice. She excused herself for a moment. Once alone, she gave in to her emotions.

But Agda followed her and watched. What she secretly witnessed was such a rare sight that she wrote about it in a letter to Frithiof. From her apartment on Kungsholm Square, Ester Blenda also wrote to the extended family that she meant to dedicate her soon-to-be-finished book to the baby. Her wish for the newborn was that she "live and delight in the book, and that she may cook up better and far worse schemes than her aunt did in her modest youth." She also promised that if the book was a success and reached more than five print runs, revenue from the sixth would go to her namesake as a baptism gift. However, the letter ended on a somewhat gloomier note, as she announced that this gift was unlikely to come to anything, as she could not envision more than one print run of the upcoming book. "Unfortunately for me and for you and for her." Her confidence in herself and her ability to write fiction was obviously weak.

The agricultural program ran two years. But the joy of being accepted didn't last long. It never did. In the spring term of 1919, Ester Blenda traveled back to Stockholm more and more over the weekends. She took care of her mother, who was seriously ill. There were many night vigils in the big house by the Åland Sea. Lotten, almost seventy years old, survived; once Ester got back to school in Jönköping, the calm and the routines felt increasingly suffocating. The restlessness distressed her, seemed to torment her worse than it had done in a long time. Ester Blenda wrote to Gerda, telling her that she felt down.

No wonder that her bored and frustrated gaze got stuck on the *Svenska Dagbladet* article. She reacted immediately because she knew the man being described: René Malaise. He was going on a long scientific expedition to Kamchatka, a secluded peninsula in a volcanic region in northeastern Siberia. A two-year adventure among roaring bears, barking sled dogs, and rumbling volcanoes.

She could almost hear her heartbeat racing. The very next day, a letter was sent to Frithiof:

> Lind on February 24, 1919
> Frithiof—do not laugh at me now. I am serious. I absolutely must accompany Malaise to Kamchatk [*sic*]. I have read quite a bit about it in the newspaper today and went completely wild. It is just the thing for me! [. . .] Tell him that I am a good friend who is as strong as he is at the very least, and who is far more used to hardships than he is. I could probably also get them some money through my rich acquaintances—ten thousand or thereabouts—and I would, of course, pay for my own travel and subsistence myself. Will take all responsibility myself, of course, and sort myself out, but will also help them a little with odds and ends. Mend clothes and such. Having a woman along can be a good thing—tell him that. I can shoot too.
>
> *SvD* could send me. Goodness, imagine the kind of book you could write after! He must not refuse me. Ask whether he will take me with him if I promise them ten thousand to help? This is serious. Have a serious

conversation with him about this, and tell him to keep from laughing for once. Reply soon.

Letter from Ester Blenda Nordström to Frithiof
Nordström, February 24, 1919.

But René Malaise's expedition lacked neither resources nor the presence of women who could assist with practical tasks. The adventurers and explorers of the time were hailed as heroes, and the financiers had to get in line to support the work. Various sponsors had showered the team with clothes, preserved food, skis, cameras, gunpowder, chocolate, toothpaste, and everything else that might be required in the wilderness.

At the time, Swedes rationed alcohol purchases per person on a monthly basis, and the purchases were tracked meticulously in something called a *motbok*. Malaise's venture was so well supported that the crew members had even received a full motbok ration for a three-year supply of 96 percent alcohol—with the promise of not opening any of the boxes until the boat had passed Nyckelbojen in Gothenburg's seaport.

The artist Anders Zorn, who was also Ester Blenda's friend, contributed SEK 10,000. René Malaise was said to have succeeded in personally persuading him to assist them with the very generous sum one particularly wet evening at Den Gyldene Freden (which translates as "the Golden Peace") restaurant in Stockholm.

The other two participants, birdwatcher Sten Bergman and plant geographer Eric Hultén, would be bringing their wives with them to work as field assistants and housekeepers. But Ester Blenda was determined. René Malaise was unmarried, and she proposed a sham marriage to him in order to get a valid place in the expedition. He declined on the advice of Sten Bergman. She cured the feeling of defeat and her worsened mood the way she always did. Her nights spent partying while in Stockholm grew in number, length, and intensity.

Ester Blenda and the renowned seafaring troubadour Evert Taube met and became friends around that time, somewhere among Stockholm's tavern crowds in 1919. He had recently had a national breakthrough following a few high-profile performances. Since then, Evert Taube assumed an obvious place in the spotlight.

Two attractive, young, incredibly charismatic celebrities, they were almost the same age and shared a love of music, Swedish tunes, and wine. There were many striking similarities between them. Both grew up in musical families; despite uncertain schooling careers with mediocre grades, both went on to realize that they were linguistically gifted and had passed through the newspaper district in Klara to develop their talent. Ester Blenda was already a bestselling author, and Evert Taube was well on his way to becoming one.

They were both drawn to the new and unexplored and were unafraid to part with convenience and money in order to experience adventure. At eighteen, Taube went to sea and managed to make stops in Australia, South Africa, the Red Sea, and South Asia during his first voyage. Admittedly, this was done under duress from his father, who would rather see his son work as a fireman at sea than live the bohemian life in the capital, but the latter turned out to suit Evert well.

Having secured a place on the English wheeled steamer *Princess of Wales*, his next aim had been South America, where he supported himself as foreman at the canal construction in Córdoba and on the Pampas, and as a bottle washer, tram conductor, illustrator, and journalist in Buenos Aires. Had it not been for the First World War, and for conscription back in Sweden, Evert Taube would probably have been traveling instead of drinking wine in Stockholm taverns with Ester Blenda.

The newly minted friends often sat together, playing their guitars, singing, and telling stories. Ester Blenda started inviting Evert Taube to dinners with her closest friends and to her mother's home. Lotten was thrilled; in a letter to her daughter, she asked for more of his company. Ester Blenda listened raptly as he told stories of his escapades on faraway continents. She was particularly fascinated by the poetic descriptions of the emerald-green plains of the Pampas, and of the absolute freedom to be had as a gaucho on the plains that stretched up toward the Andes. Her sense of curiosity and longing was aroused. She wanted to go there too.

All her old friends took note of the new, intense friendship. John Landquist was starting to get annoyed. Maybe even slightly jealous.

> One evening at our place, she sang a song by him, of which
> I remember the refrain (turalleri turá). The tune was good,
> as was her singing. It should only have been a joy to hear.
> But I felt that she was about to transition into a world
> unknown to me. During a visit to her home—should be
> at the end of 1919—she announced that she was planning
> to travel to South America in order to write travelogues. A
> sense of anxiety rose within me. She could have sat quietly
> in Stockholm or Kiruna as the wife of a prominent man,
> and now she was going to embark on a journalistic prole-
> tarian trip to South America while completely defenseless.
> She was not as strong as she was cocky, and she was softer
> than she was aggressive. I presented my case to her, that she
> had nothing to gain from writing any articles about South
> America. She probably did not know much about that part
> of the world. She would simply overexert herself, and she
> would expose herself to danger. She did not listen to this.
>
> From John Landquist's memoirs, *I ungdomen. Scener ur
> den förlorade tiden* [*In Youth. Scenes from the Lost Time*].

No, Ester Blenda didn't wish to "sit quietly as the wife of a prominent man." She wanted to go out into the world, to experience and

discover. You needed to have enough freedom and courage, or possibly foolhardiness, to be "defenseless." And no man, no matter how prominent he might have been, seemed to be able to give Ester Blenda the life that she wanted.

During a holiday with Ester Blenda's motorcycle and newly purchased sidecar that same summer, her constant passenger Carin wrote a love poem in their shared travel diary:

> Her gaze is the most beautiful gaze there is, and her beach
> the most beautiful beach one can set anchor on—and her
> goodness is immeasurable.

It appeared between the notes in the diary and was written in Carin's unmistakable handwriting, elegantly ornate and childishly rounded at the same time. Those tender lines were the only documentation of their love that was not hidden away or erased from posterity. But the little notebook remained, possibly forgotten, and it was heavy with emotion. During the week, Carin and Ester Blenda quarreled and fought on the Swedish country roads, made up, separated, and felt incomplete without each other.

They were headed south toward Nyköping city. Carin was sitting in the new sidecar. She had bought herself her own helmet and goggles and was starting to get so used to the motorcycle that she wanted to try riding it herself.

> Carin got her second driving lesson and did excellently on
> difficult, tricky roads for distances of up to eighteen miles.
> Very proud and smug! In Nyköping, we had dinner, and
> then the headlights came on while traveling to Norrköping
> where we arrived at twelve midnight. The bike runs like
> a god.

Later in the diary, Carin admitted to running the bike into a ditch. Ester Blenda took over again. On the way to Vadstena, which they both wanted to see, they drove out on rural roads and ran about until they got lost. As the sun set, the headlight broke. The road ahead was only traceable as a faint, gray ribbon. After twelve uninterrupted hours at the handlebars, Ester Blenda suddenly stopped in the middle of nowhere. She was so hungry that she refused to drive another yard.

Break for coffee and a pipe during a motorbike trip with Carin.

Carin swore and cursed, but I still sat down in a rain puddle on the road and fried ham and potatoes. Had a bit and was happy. As was Carin, eventually. But it was pitch black all around.

It was impossible to see all the deep potholes in the roads at three o'clock in the morning. After pushing the bike up a steep hill, they broke the rear wheel and had to get off it again. They groped around for their tools in the dark; Ester Blenda got down on her knees, trying to see. In the end, she managed to patch it back up to driving standard. It was still pitch black as they rolled into a very quiet Motala. There, they assigned each other tasks. Carin was to find a room; Ester Blenda would locate a garage and workshop.

Once she'd left the motorbike behind, she walked around and around for hours, carrying the heavy bag and looking for Carin. Her arms ached. The feeling of exhaustion was intense. As was the feeling of being alone and abandoned. She fought the desperation that only seemed to arise when Carin wasn't by her side.

> It was awful. I sat on a staircase and cried for a bit. In the end, I walked toward a brightly lit lamp with an assured joyous hope that I had finally found a hotel. Like hell it was! It was an old dump of a grocery store. My language was supernaturally coarse. I was so tired I could die. Then I suddenly saw a sofa under a tree and lay on it for a blissful moment. Then a policeman walked by and said that it was "forbidden to lie on that sofa."

They first reunited at dawn, slumbering anxiously for three hours in a hotel bed before another traveler was due to take over the room. The repair bill stung. They were rewarded with a couple of beautiful days of rural idyll with a fully restored motorcycle before driving back to Stockholm.

This was how Carin constantly appeared in the documentation of Ester Blenda's life, often between business trips and other more long-term commitments. Suddenly Carin reappeared, in photographs and travel notes. The best friend to the outside world, but the love poem and photographs revealed something deeper. In the small fragments that remained, the contours of a romantic relationship started to grow increasingly discernible.

The book publisher Wahlström & Widstrand acquired the girls' book manuscript that had started taking form at Hagaberg. The contract was written on July 4, 1919, just a few weeks after the decision on universal suffrage in Sweden had been voted through in the Parliament House. The contract stated that the first print run would produce five thousand copies. While the new children's author completed her agricultural training in Jönköping and planned for her own personal conquest of Evert Taube's beloved South America, the book titled *En rackarunge* [*A Little Rascal*] was published.

The country's young girls immediately embraced Ann-Mari, who was the exact opposite of how they were usually represented in fiction, both as children and adults. They were typically presented as weak, inferior, docile, controlled, almost without exception.

In the wake of women's emancipation with the newly won right to higher education and professional careers, there had been calls for more independent female characters. Ester Blenda was hailed as an innovative girls' book author—although it should be pointed out that a couple of the reviewers were also found in her personal circle of friends, once again. Elin Wägner, for instance, wrote in the magazine *Idun* that "Ann-Mari restores the honor of her gender." However, despite the possibly biased favor among Swedish critics, there was no doubt that Ester Blenda had produced groundbreaking work. She was even praised by male, conservative reviewers. Eventually, a whole series of books about Ester Blenda's fictional counterpart would come to be.

This was even followed by radio and film productions.

The first print run wasn't enough. The next one sold out. And the next. The money started rolling in. Ester Blenda could start paying off her debts. She should have been all relief, happiness, and excitement as she stepped aboard the MS *Balboa* a few months later, heading toward

South America with several newly purchased sailor suits in her suitcase. But there was also a sadness over an unresolved, painful matter. Things had gone wrong with Evert Taube before her departure. He had suddenly stopped answering letters and phone calls.

At my house on January 5, 1920

I will be leaving in a couple of days. Would you do me a big favor? Write down *"Farväl, Farväl"* right away and send it to me. If you would be so kind! Just the words, I know the music.

I guess I won't be seeing you anymore. I suppose you are upset with me for something I cannot help, so you would rather not see me anymore. All right! When I come to Buenos Aires, I certainly will be thinking of you.

Goodbye, goodbye for the last time.

I do bid thee farewell—

Thank you, dear boy, for all the songs, for all the strings you plucked on my lute, and for all the strings within me that you—without knowing it—have caused to reverberate once again. Be well!

EsBl

Letter from Ester Blenda Nordström to Evert Taube,
January 5, 1920.

Had Evert Taube, like several of the men who had gotten close to Ester Blenda over the years, developed feelings that were more than friendly? Was he yet another of the many rejected and hurt men around her?

It was minus four degrees Fahrenheit, and there was a snowstorm as MS *Balboa* departed from the Norwegian capital Kristiania (current day Oslo). She wrote to him again at the first stop in Hamburg. A few

tentative lines on two postcards with motifs of the large harbor said that
he could still reach her if he wrote to the Swedish consulate in Buenos
Aires. But no reply ever seemed to have come through. The two cards,
postmarked on January 28, 1920, appeared to have been Ester Blenda's
last correspondence with Evert Taube, ever. He went to Paris the same
spring and met Astri Bergman there, the woman who would become
his wife and the mother of his four children.

Just a few days before leaving, Ester Blenda received a letter from
another man who never seemed to lose hope of winning her heart.
Hjalmar Lundbohm had started writing this letter several months prior.
Formulating line after line about the sorrow and joy that Ester Blenda
filled him with during their time together, about the harsh words she
had once written to him, and about how there was actually a grain of
truth in them. About the joy of her welcoming him back into her life,
and the crushing fact that he would never be able to stop loving her for
as long as he lived. About how her beautiful depictions of Värmland in
the letters from her time in Bön had made him cry. But when he had
finished writing it, he destroyed the sheets, having surmised that they
were pointless, that this was in the past. He revealed this in the new
letter, the one he chose to send, and the one she received and saved for
the rest of her life.

Hjalmar seemed to know her so well that he could tell that she was
carrying something that she didn't have the strength or desire to share,
even with him.

> You are traveling now as you did when you went to
> Lapland, to escape something that torments you. I do not
> know what, for I have never wanted to pry. But I hope that
> you succeed. I hope that you find the calm path that you

seek to walk, although I hope that you will come back, so that I may see you again.

From a letter from Hjalmar Lundbohm to Ester Blenda Nordström, January 4, 1920.

Was Ester Blenda plagued by her secret and illegal love affair with Carin? Or was it the pain of not being able to live openly, in public? There is no way to find out. We can only guess and interpret the air of sorrow that her nearest and dearest could see so clearly around her but did not understand. Ester Blenda was tormented by something and was constantly trying to run away from an inner sense of anguish. She ran fast. For an outsider, the speed at which her life moved forward, and the number of accomplishments she achieved along the way, was almost inconceivable. She was twenty-nine years old and had already managed to revolutionize Swedish journalism, live with the traveling Sami population for six months, write two acclaimed reportage books and the first part of a girls' book series. She had thrown herself into a civil war and saved thousands of people from starving to death and trained as a farmer at the country's biggest agricultural school as the only female student among 112 men. Still, it was just the beginning. Now she intended to become an adventurer as well.

CHAPTER 11

On Muleback across the Andes

She instantly captured the captain's attention, and he clearly liked what he saw. Soon, Ester Blenda was often seen accompanying the captain, a short, stout man with a thick, dark mustache. His name was Frans Grundberg, but she gave him the nickname "Papa."

They were photographed together several times while on deck: as they leaned side by side over the railing looking at the white foam around the ship's hull, he with a loving look in his eyes at a happy Ester Blenda who was playing his accordion, and then outside the captain's cabin where he placed his arm around her and pulled her close to him, with a satisfied expression on his face. His grip around her had something desperate about it. It was so firm that his hands seemed to cling on more than they sought to hold. Her smile was slightly strained; her head was tilted toward him as she pinched the burning cigarette between her middle and ring fingers.

In the same photograph, Captain Grundberg had his other arm around a tall, dark woman in a light, beautifully embroidered dress. Her name was Alice Thorne; she was an illustrator and part of a group of Norwegians on board. Alice and Ester Blenda had a mutual friend, Hjalmar Lundbohm, the "King of Kiruna." The two women quickly found each other. Alice became a person who occupied a lot of space in all the letters Ester sent back home both during the rest of the trip and over her coming six-month stay on the new continent.

Ester Blenda in work overalls on the deck of MS Balboa headed to South America.

Ester Blenda had, of course, not left Sweden unnoticed. *Svenska Dagbladet*'s readers had been gifted a major farewell interview and the promise of several upcoming exciting freelance reports from the destination. From the text below, it was clear that her leaving the country was major news:

Ester Blenda Nordström is not just one of our most read authors, she also has the rare gift of attracting a level of interest around her personality that is far warmer and more heartfelt than fame alone could account for. Along with the great rumors, she has the dubious pleasure that everything she has done, intends to do, currently does, and does not do is discussed and explained ad infinitum; as these things are extensive in number and variations, one has an explanation as to why people are so preoccupied with her.

From the article "See South America and write about Sweden. A farewell interview of Ester Blenda Nordström, by Bris," *Svenska Dagbladet*, January 18, 1920.

The start of the seven-week journey turned more dramatic than they would have liked. The night after MS *Balboa* passed the Kattegat, at maximum speed and in pitch-black darkness, three ships traveling the same route were blown up by mines. Shaken, they arrived in Hamburg, Germany, where they stayed longer than planned due to a winter storm. Ester Blenda went ashore and blew a substantial amount of her travel fund on gifts for her family and herself.

For once, I've felt what it's like to be a millionaire. My God in heaven! I had seven hundred kronor. These have won me six beautiful dresses, a coat, a guitar, a lot of silk socks, a lovely leather briefcase with a lock, six pairs of shoes, three pairs of dreamy trousers with thick crepe-de-chine undershirts, undergarments (hand-embroidered), sewing accessories, many miles of silk ribbons for the aforementioned, cigarettes, an electric lantern that remains burning for 120 hours, suede photograph frames, fifty gramophone records (there is a lovely gramophone here), films, binoculars, stationery, meals that you couldn't even imagine, wine, liqueur, cognac, and a lovely sapphire ring. *Mein Liebchen, was willst du noch mehr!* It is beyond wonderful—in any case, all my money's gone. So I ask that you immediately send a check by rapid post to the Swedish consulate in Buenos Aires worth what you owe me.

From a letter from Ester Blenda Nordström to Gerda
Nordström, February 1, 1920.

After a few days of spring at sea, MS *Balboa* steered straight into the heat. Once at the equator, Ester Blenda and Alice got to experience the fluttering, exotic 104-degree heat from the shade. They lay completely still in deck chairs or hammocks. Thoughts gently floating, eyes fixed on the blue sea.

It was never boring. The sailors often threw spontaneous dance parties on deck: cranked a gramophone, threw on fancy dresses, and got their heels clattering so wildly against the wooden deck that the gramophone needle jumped and scratched the discs. And although the ship was one of the newest productions of the shipping company Nordstjernan, still dazzlingly white, there was always work to do on board for those who wanted to. Ester Blenda wanted to. She put on work overalls over her sailor suits and helped chip rust, wash, scrape, and paint.

She had this idea on one of these days: The ship had two cylindrical pole masts that towered about thirty feet above deck. You could only reach the top of the masts by climbing straight up a narrow steel ladder attached to the outside of the pipes. There was no protection once up there, nothing to hold on to.

People rolled up their sleeves and pant legs. She kept her white sun hat on as she started the climb. When Ester Blenda reached the windy top, she sat on the pole mast, let her legs dangle freely and the strong wind tear at her hair. There was barely anything to sit on; the tube's diameter was just about enough to span the width of her hips. Alice did the same. They were photographed, each sitting on a mast top. There was nothing but sky and sea around them.

In the distance, they saw the low white houses with flat roofs in Pernambuco, Brazil, starting to take shape. At the harbor, wagons with millstone-sized wheels rolled forward, attached to long-eared mules. Clusters of small fishing boats bobbed in the water. Ester Blenda and Alice joined them out on several trips, paddling the canoe and then stepping out to stroll around shops. They photographed narrow cobblestone alleys that streams of people floated past on streets lined with simple food stalls. Along the curbs lay heaps of garbage and food scraps.

They couldn't resist the exotic shop spreads, or even the silk monkeys no bigger than a hand with long, dancing tails. They bought three monkeys, named them Noak, Efraim, and Tjingtjing (pronounced "Ching Ching"), and took them on board when it was time to travel onward a few days later. The monkeys were as tame as dogs by the time they reached the next port. Ester Blenda let them climb around on her head and shoulders, held them in her hand, and confided in her new friends.

They instantly fell in love with Rio de Janeiro. "Like a fairy tale, a dream, where it lies sandwiched between the gray rocks of the most astonishing formations," she wrote in one of her reports. Bansai offered new scintillating reading material from places on earth that most of her readers would never ever experience, other than through her text and photographs.

In Brazil, the visit by the famous Swedish journalist and successful author made headlines. Several newspapers wrote about her presence in the country, and Arne Holmberg, the Swedish consul, rolled up in his car and took Ester Blenda and Alice on a trip up the mountains. He seemed to want to impress and drove at a dizzying speed on unprotected roads lined with bananas, bamboo, and acacia trees. No one in the car raised any objections.

Pole mast ascent on MS Balboa.

The ship took them onward, through the coffee town of Santos, Sao Paulo, the seaside resort of Guornja [*sic*], Rio Grande do Sul, Montevideo . . . then Evert Taube's Buenos Aires. Alice's cousin, who lived just outside the city, invited Ester Blenda and Alice to a few days of unbridled luxury and partying with some upper-class Norwegian friends.

Each room in the large brick villa by Laguna Yamahuida had its own bath with both hot and cold water, toilet, bidet with running water, and a marble sink. Sumptuous dinners were served in the evenings. After-dinner bridge games turned into decadent parties with wild dancing. A few hours of sleep and early-morning horseback rides, each on their own beautiful thoroughbred that remained at their disposal throughout their stay. Everyone in their crew went hunting, played golf, and competed against each other in pistol shooting.

Five-course luncheons were served with wine, beer, and spirits. Everyone let go, let life be a game. Ester Blenda's camera was always with her. Someone snapped a photo; it didn't matter who. Young and beautiful people dressed in summer-white party clothes lay in a large pile, having fallen straight onto the grass. A woman with her head on Ester Blenda's belly could not keep from laughing; she giggled uncontrollably as she looked straight into the camera. Ester Blenda herself had pulled down a white sun hat over half her face. A man with his face turned away from the camera rested his head against her chest.

All this extravagance and revelry were merely temporary. Only the most essential items could be brought along on their next escapade. They packed the warm ponchos received as gifts from Alice's cousin. The plan was to ride on muleback over the annular Cordilleras mountains, from Argentina all the way to Chile through the winding paths of the ancient Inca Empire. They were going to really explore the mountains. Not escorted in a car driven by a well-dressed consul; and not by rail, like the other well-to-do tourists wanting to take in the Andes.

Travel permits were issued by the governor of Mendoza, and visas from the Chilean legation were ready. Had it not been for the Swedish envoy Carl Hultgren's terrified look when they told him about their plans, they wouldn't even have considered securing protection. Ester Blenda had procured a short-barreled revolver, knives, and a small-bore Winchester rifle that were among her packed items. That clearly didn't do much by way of easing Hultgren's mind. He knew all too well how ruthless the *bandoleros*, mountain robbers, were toward their victims. When they struck, there were no survivors. And assuming you managed to avoid robbers, there was still the looming risk of freezing to death in a snowstorm, being crushed in a landslide, falling off a steep edge, or losing your life due to an overestimation of access to food and water. Just to name a few.

The Swedish envoy immediately contacted Argentina's president, vice president, and secretary of state. This was shortly followed by an invitation to Vice President Villanueva's huge estancia at Uspallata. Ester Blenda and Alice traveled there and were given two documents to carry with them for the rest of the trip. One of them ordered all officials throughout the Argentine Republic to make themselves available to assist or protect the visiting women if needed. The second one was an order issued to Chilean authorities by the Chilean minister in Argentina: they must immediately offer all imaginable forms of assistance that the women deemed necessary.

The Argentine government also sent a staff of four people to ride with them across the mountains: a police commissioner, a gaucho, and two uniformed gendarmes with rifles, revolvers, and sabers.

> I wonder if any other country's government would go through so much effort for two stubborn girls! But I also don't think that any country's representative would have received and assisted a female compatriot the way Carl Hultgren did in Buenos Aires [. . .] If even the Queen of Sheba herself, in all her splendor and glory, had come up with the wild idea of sojourning over the Cordilleras on horseback, I hardly think she could have been afforded more terrific arrangements.
>
> From "Over Cordilleras on donkey back," *Svenska Dagbladet*, July 11, 1920.

The travel party left on a roasting hot Saturday morning. From a distance, no one could tell that the two of them were Scandinavian women. They were dressed just like the civilian men in heavy boots with spurs, cotton shirts, kerchiefs around their necks, and bombachas. Underneath, they wore knitted men's undergarments. Wide-brimmed hats protected them from the scorching sun.

The first gallop lasted until lunch. Narrow, winding paths between rolling mountain ridges were lined with dusty cairns. They passed by vestiges of the army commander José de San Martín, who, with his troops, eliminated Spanish rule in Argentina in 1812, in Chile in 1818, and in Peru in 1821.

There were animal carcasses everywhere, sometimes so fresh that the vultures still circled them. Small crooked wooden crosses lined the roads, quickly thrown together to preserve some scrap of dignity for all the human lives that met their ends in the barren, stony landscape. Neither Ester Blenda nor the others had saddles. Some sheepskins and a beautiful ornate leather blanket covered the mules' backs. The stirrup leathers creaked. The hooves clattered. Silver spurs jingled.

At the bank of the Mendoza River beach, Ester Blenda and Alice lay on their backs and listened to the sounds of the water. They were offered chicken skewers covered in red Spanish pepper, buns, butter, and sardines. A bottle was passed round, and red wine flowed from it generously. Their throats were dry, and water was not an option. It was deemed hazardous to the health; even having a sip was too dangerous.

There were another four hours before they reached where they would stay for the night: a farmhouse located a good way up the mountains. The mules walked across rivers, fields of pebbles, and canyons. Sometimes they lost their footing and slipped uncontrollably. Ester Blenda thought to herself how Scandinavian mountains were truly no bigger than dung heaps and that a single tiny step in the wrong direction would send her down the path of earning herself one of the many crucifixes they passed along the way.

Hordes of wild horses rushed over the fertile plains of the Pampas. The camera came out; she took several pictures. A few cactus shoots were placed in her bag as a memento. They still stand more than a

hundred years later, now as huge ornamental plants at the homes of two
of her siblings' grandchildren.

> A lone condor sails above us—like a black dot against the
> eternal blue of the sky; a faint little wind blows with the
> scent of cactus flower; there is life in every breath we take.

> From "Over Cordilleras on donkey back," *Svenska
> Dagbladet*, July 11, 1920.

*In 1920, Ester Blenda rode with her friend Alice Thorne on muleback between Argentina and Chile,
along the paths of the ancient Inca Empire.*

There were days when the sun never rose behind the black mountain walls. When the sky was black and gray, and the wind blew so strong that they had to crouch over the mules, noses buried deep in their manes. They continued onward and upward anyway.

They stopped at Hotel Las Cuevas to thaw their frozen bodies on a day like this. The gendarmes and their gaucho named Ramon sorted out their animals and baggage while Ester Blenda and Alice entered through the low door; the room had sloping ceilings and crumpled iron-plate walls filled with dents and holes from revolver bullets. Rotten nailed boards took the place of windowpanes—these were also riddled with small round holes from quarrels gone wrong.

The bartender was wearing a dirty white coat and a mottled apron that also used to be white. He was small and pale and languidly served a couple of men cloudy liquid in two glasses. The only two women in the room asked for coffee and bread. They had to wait a long time before it was served. The earthen floor was damp and cold. Their feet never had the chance to warm up before it was time to get back on the mules.

Ester Blenda occasionally wrote home to Frithiof and Gerda using stationery that had been slipped into the suitcase back at the Savoy Hotel in Buenos Aires. Talked about Ramon, how they had eaten unfamiliar foods and bought red country wine from peasant families along the road, families that had also provided places to sleep for the night in stone houses that were as low set as they were crooked. She sent simple pencil drawings with speech bubbles along.

The photos shared with the family back home were hardly comforting. Ester in a full cowboy uniform with a hefty knife *and* a pistol tucked into her belt. The men keeping her company, while wearing hats and ponchos and seated leaning against rocks, were thirstily emptying bottles. And then the robbery situation that was recounted in one of her letters: two men with raised weapons aimed at Ester Blenda and Alice. They were both on their knees with big eyes and gaping mouths. Turned out that the heavily intoxicated gendarmes hadn't realized that

they were trying to hustle their own charges out of their warming ponchos, under gun threat.

But we are doing well. Aside from the fact that the money
has run out. We don't even have enough to get to B. Aires.
But the Lord is with his people—and we are hoping for a
miracle. It is incredibly beautiful here. One day, we rode
uninterrupted for ten and a half hours. This was when
we embarked on crossing the highest peak on the road—
fourteen thousand feet. This is where the border between
Chile & Argentina runs, and a bronze Jesus statue has been

placed there for the sake of peace, so insanely awful that I unwittingly remembered the famous expression of Daniel, of blessed memory: "Damn what an ugly Jesus!"

[. . .] Mules are amusing creatures, believe me. They have minds of their own. Right in the middle of a hearty gallop, they stop, causing you to fly headfirst onto the ground.

From a letter from Ester Blenda Nordström to Frithiof
and Gerda Nordström, April 21, 1920.

The scars from riding hurt. When they stopped for a break, Ester Blenda and Alice took turns lying on their fronts with their buttocks in the air while the other dabbed her friend's backside with cotton balls and put on bandages. One evening, when it was Ester Blenda's turn to be a nurse, the bandages had dried up and she lit a match, hoping that the heat would soften the glue. The match got a bit too close to the cotton on the friend's sore bottom.

Burned like gunpowder under [Alice's] hoarse scream. She later said it was as if she had a volcano in her rear. And we will not even speak of the riding wound! But if you can imagine what it must feel like to have burning cotton on your behind, I am sure you can also guess how wonderful the spectacle was. Nowadays, [Alice] views me with a deep-rooted suspicion and claims that I definitely did it on purpose. But you who know me so well know that such a thing could never be the case. Toodles! Essan.

From a letter from Ester Blenda Nordström to Frithiof
and Gerda Nordström, April 21, 1920.

The fever and diarrhea came suddenly. Ester Blenda got so ill that they were forced to take a break. They were escorted back to Alice's cousin, where she received medical treatment and was closely cared for by her new Norwegian friends. They were all male. They took turns keeping her company. When they were not dabbing her forehead or feeding her rice and water, they lay down on the chaise longue in her room, chain-smoked, and got so lost in their own philosophical ramblings that they didn't take notice of how the swaying columns of ash fell straight to the floor. But Ester Blenda saw. She took a mental photo, the way she always did when she wanted to hold on to a particular moment.

One of the men came by more often. It was soon clear why. She recognized the gentle look, the undivided attention, and thought of his wife who was out there somewhere. It was a very difficult balancing act, that of rejecting someone you cared for, while wanting to remain friends. Ester Blenda was starting to turn it into an art form, weighing her words, touches, and smiles with great care. Frithiof and Gerda were let in on this secret, but Ester made sure that they didn't go hoping for marriage. She was starting to get good at that too.

Among her packed items lay a small black leather photo album with space for four photos. Her mother was in one and her brother's children in two. The fourth photograph was a beautiful profile picture of Carin with a longing gaze, taken in Italy in 1919. The travel album followed Ester Blenda everywhere.

The big house in Yamahuida served as their base over the coming few weeks. More golf, horseback riding, and hunting. Ester Blenda loved to shoot with shotguns and rifles. One day, she returned to the house with fourteen wild pigeons that were then cooked in cream with their heads still on. She became the hero of the evening when they were served for dinner.

The photograph of Carin that Ester Blenda carried with her in the travel album during all her trips around the world.

It was nice not to have to find new ways to dodge hotel bills. But despite a desperate shortage of funds, Ester Blenda and Alice couldn't resist the invitation to a ball in Buenos Aires. They booked a train ticket and got going. On the way, they passed the wine district of Mendoza, a lush paradise at the foot of the Andes, twenty-six hundred feet above sea level, with endless plantations of fruits and vegetables such as tomatoes, olives, apples, apricots, and peaches. In the French-inspired city center, cafés and restaurants were densely packed in rows among squares framed by lush chestnut trees.

I will not speak of how we stopped at Mendoza while the train held, and ate supper for the last of our earthly money, and then the train left us. [Alice] latched on and screamed, but I stood and stared next to our baggage and uttered a number of words in pure Swedish that would cause a Stadsgården dockworker to place me, and the rich possibilities of the Swedish language, in the highest esteem. [Alice] jumped off in time and uttered some things to my hearing that I will be burying in the black night of oblivion. But Norwegian also has a great deal of rich items—I know that now.

When I get home at some point, I will tell you about this evening, and that night, and the money we raised. I haven't the energy just now. But there are Swedes in Mendoza, Argentina, too, and we did damn well.

We did not get to the ball, but it's all the same to me. In any case, we came to Yamahuida after a great number of telegrams about money and such little things. And so here we are now [. . .] I have received a letter from "Papa" today. He also loves me. I owe him 466 kronor. Please pay it and set up a bill on my account. I miss you all.

Your poor, lonely, and destitute, but not pregnant
Ester Blenda

From a letter from Ester Blenda Nordström to Frithiof
and Gerda Nordström, May 7, 1920.

Soon, the publisher would pressure her to write a sequel to the girls' book success, *A Little Rascal*. In the summer of 1920, Ester Blenda traveled back to Sweden. She was joined by a parrot and the silk monkeys Noak, Efraim, and Tjingtjing. She barely made it ashore before the letters from all her new acquaintances in South America, both women and men, began to arrive, filled with admiration and longing. Some were simply nothing more than love letters filled with yearning.

Captain "Papa" was on his way home from Buenos Aires and wanted to meet up in Stockholm. A Norwegian passenger from MS *Balboa* described his frustration over how he never got to say goodbye to his "Kjere EB" (Norwegian for "Dear EB") after the trip. Another called her "My dearest songbird." The Norwegian adventurer A. R. Hvoslef mentioned his friend, the great explorer Roald Amundsen, and encouraged Ester Blenda to go on similar expeditions, so that "we common, blind people can see with your eyes for a bit." He sent this with words urging her not to "get lost or lose your healthy moral compass."

She saved all the letters. Put them in her big green suitcase where she had started to gather pieces of her life. Alice, however, only seemed to have made an intense, but brief, guest appearance in Ester Blenda's life. There were no further traces of her beyond the time spent in Chile and Argentina.

The weekly *Vecko-Journalen* got in touch; they'd heard that she had brought exotic animals home from her adventures in South America, and they wanted to do a report on her. Ester Blenda wore a nice black dress with wide sleeves. They took a photo of her holding one of her unusual pets. She looked down at the little black monkey, with love in her eyes.

On August 22, 1920, the artist Anders Zorn died. Barely six months had passed since the acclaimed artist turned sixty. After the birthday party, he wrote to sisters Hildur and Ester Blenda Nordström:

> For kind remembrance of my sixtieth birthday, I hereby wish to express my warm, deeply felt gratitude. Thank you so much for your kind remembrance yesterday—the flowers will wither in due time, but my gratitude and affection will not.
>
> Yours, Zorn

Now a new bouquet was sent, this time with black ribbons. After the funeral, the new widow, Emma Zorn, wrote from their farm in Mora:

> Miss Hildur and Ester Blenda:
> Thank you, dearest, and God's blessings.
>> Best wishes to you,
>> Your devoted

Christmas passed. It was always celebrated at Frithiof's home, with Gerda and their children. The family gathered around the huge Christmas table. Everything was as usual. The two-foot-long ornamental pig with real pig bristles stood in the middle of the set dining table. The kids loved to lift the tail and activate the built-in music box. Frithiof did too, just as much as he loved his other strange table ornament: the wooden crow that always had a cigarette placed in the corner of its mouth. Ester Blenda gave another one of her celebrated speeches.

Stockholm was both familiar and foreign. Immediately after the Christmas celebrations, she packed her sturdiest clothes, typewriter, and instruments before taking the train north, toward Kiruna and her beloved Lapland. On Boxing Day, December 26, she opened the door to the small log cabin in the middle of the forest in Soitola by the Torne River. The nearest train station was forty miles away. The cottage had a room that was shared with the hired maid, Mina. It was very simple but hot and dry; the moss that lay between the rough beams formed a tight seal against the cold. The thick sheepskin fleeces that were scattered everywhere were a gift from Hjalmar Lundbohm. Outdoors, it was minus four degrees Fahrenheit.

Ester Blenda looked out of one of the small windows framed by red curtains and thought about how it looked just like a Christmas card. In a letter to Gerda and Frithiof, she described the interior and surroundings in detail. She concluded with the words, "Now brewing some coffee. See you in a while." Then she sat at her typewriter and started working on the next book about Ann-Mari.

Winter turned into spring. When she wasn't writing, Ester Blenda went skiing out in the woods and up on the fells. At times, she stayed in Hjalmar's large villa called "Lundbohm Palace." And then Carin, of course, came to visit. She stayed for a long time, sharing in the isolation and the simple, almost ascetic life in the Lapland forest.

Left to right—Ester Blenda, Carin, the maid Mina, and an unknown Sami woman in the log cabin in Soitola.

During a joint visit to Hjalmar, Carin had an accident. She slipped and fell down an icy staircase after a dinner party at a friend's place. A doctor stated that she'd broken a vertebral process in her lower back. Ester Blenda did not leave her side. She gave her morphine powder, changed covers and beddings when needed. She only voiced her concerns in a letter to Gerda and Frithiof in which she wrote that "the first night was awful with fainting spells and terrible pain" and that Carin was in so much pain that "she could neither sleep nor eat." A week went by before she started feeling better and was able to go home. Ester Blenda was left alone again, with only the maid and her beloved instruments for company.

Her thirty-second birthday passed in March. The family sent gifts, and Frithiof's children each wrote a letter to their favorite aunt. She flipped between laughing, giggling, longing to see them, and crying as she read the letters in her voluntary state of isolation.

It is so lovely, when one is far away, to feel a warm breeze from those who are close to you [. . .] Annami's love letter made me long for the child ever so fervently, and Kjell's comradely, cheerful creation was all my heart could wish for [. . .] On my way home. Or traveling south. Maybe I should say that instead, because I will not stay in Stockholm for long. My book has progressed so much that I cannot write much more of it up here—I may still have a week's work left, but then I'll probably have to leave for some little fish camp on the east coast. The environment has given what it can, and I am left rather helpless as I write about fishing and sailing and the archipelago, all of which I really know very little about. So I will go somewhere to get all that, along with some language and characters. Writing is going terribly slowly this time—it will not be an eleven-day book, but it is also much more difficult and takes a lot more sensitivity. A girl of fifteen and one of thirteen, that's a damn sight different! Whether it will be any good, I cannot say [. . .] In the evenings, the new moon is in a pale sky, and it is not really dark at any point—the white nights have returned little by little.

I should think it's probably already summer down where you are, but I'll be there soon to have a look.

From a letter from Ester Blenda Nordström to Frithiof
and Gerda Nordström, April 17, 1921.

The book started taking shape. Ann-Mari had turned fifteen. She was still just as temperamental and constantly aware that she could never fit into the template of how a teenage girl should behave, aside from having a crush on a teacher, a girls' book trope. Ann-Mari carried within her a constant desire to escape, didn't hesitate to use her fists if necessary, and, of course, wound up in fights.

Its title was *15 år. Några blad ur en rackarunges liv* (*15 Years—A Few Pages from the Life of a Little Rascal*) and it was published in the fall of that year. More praise. More public affirmation. Renewed restlessness. Renewed wanderlust. She withdrew from her friends, not least Elin and John. She never really resumed contact with John again. Her friendship with Elin temporarily cooled. The couple was going through severe marital problems. Elin longed to have children and a place to find peace that was outside Stockholm. John was not interested in traditional family life, and the discussion about a summerhouse somewhere in the country usually fizzled into nothing.

My divorce from Elin Wägner began in February 1922. I did not encounter Ester Blenda ever again after this time. For three years, she was like one engulfed by the earth.

From John Landquist's memoirs, *I ungdomen. Scener ur den förlorade tiden* [*In Youth. Scenes from the Lost Time*].

CHAPTER 12

Train Hopping in America

But no, Ester Blenda had not been swallowed by the earth—just by America.

This massive country, rapidly filling up with aspiring settlers, was her next destination. She wanted to continue to bring her own curiosity and her readers out into the world. In 1922, her plan was to follow in the footsteps of Swedish emigrants and trace some of all the hopes and dreams of a better life on the other side of the Atlantic.

She had lived as a maid among maids. Then as a nomadic teacher with the Sami people, where she adopted their way of life for six months. Now Ester Blenda was to take on another role: that of an emigrant living their everyday life in the new country.

The ticket for the SS *Hellig Olav* was stamped "third class." And although the book and magazine publisher Åhlén & Åkerlund had paid the very generous sum of five thousand kronor (roughly USD$15,000 in today's currency) for fifteen American articles in their popular magazine *Vecko-Journalen*, her wallet had no more than the fifty dollars required on disembarking the ship. The other men and women packed around her at the Scandinavian-American Line office in the port of

Copenhagen on May 18, 1922, had little more to start their new lives with, and Ester Blenda wanted to travel on those same terms.

In the Småland of her childhood, several families dreamed of America; even members of her own family had settled in Minnesota. Ester Blenda had grown up seeing the loss and sadness in the eyes of aging parents in small cottages suddenly turned infinitely large after their children emigrated. The mass exodus from Sweden had always fascinated her. Now she was going to experience some aspect of it for herself.

The day before departure, third-class passengers were ordered to attend a medical examination and vaccination clinic. A young doctor waited at the bottom of the paved hall, behind a screen. He started with their hair and scalp. It took time. He lifted, turned, and parted endlessly. The rest of the body was examined with the same degree of scrutiny. No part was left unseen or untouched.

Ester Blenda left the room with a stamp of approval in her inspection card, and her chest seething with humiliation. But it wasn't over yet—another inspection awaited before she was allowed on board. Meanwhile, passengers in first and second class could step straight onto the black giant as it rested at the quay. The last time she traveled on a ship of this size, she herself had been one of them.

Minutes before departure. Heavy rain. Ester Blenda stood pressed against the railing on the emigrants' deck, looking down over the crowds, noises, and chaos. Wobbly arms carried suitcases from the baggage store to the ship's hold. Several different national anthems boomed throughout the boat. Babies screamed in strollers surrounded by fitful farewells. Tears, laughter and crying, admonitions. Arms full of flowers. Then a bell rang. The moorings were thrown off. The steam whistle released three deafening signals.

> Slowly, slowly we left the quay. The music played, and
> some tried to cheer. But it didn't really work; it only

amounted to a bit of hoarse screaming. We jostled and
shoved on the middle deck—everyone wanted to get to
the railing and look for as long as a beloved face remained
even somewhat visible. And everyone waved. Some wiped
their tears with their hands and used their handkerchiefs
to wave with; others blew their noses in their fingers for
the same reason, and some just stood still without even so
much as moving a single muscle in their face, just looked
straight ahead with pensive and sad eyes; they did not even
bother to push their way through to the railing. They must
have gone through all of that which now was taking place
in front of them at some small railway station in the home
parish—they had the worst of it behind them, although
they probably ached from the memory of it. In their but-
tonholes and coats remained half-withered flowers, and
the hands, which held tightly on to sacks and duffel bags,
trembled somewhat.

From *Amerikanskt* [*American*].

There were between two hundred and three hundred emigrants on
board. But only about twenty of them were Swedes, most of whom were
from southern Sweden. About one million compatriots, both men and
women, had already emigrated to the huge country in the west where
the arable land was abundant and cheap following the Homestead Act
of 1862—and where there was freedom of religion and military service
wasn't compulsory. A democratic political system and the chance to
get a well-paid job in one of the fast-growing industrial cities also drew
people to the place. The expansion of Swedish railways and regular
transatlantic passenger traffic made the relocation wave possible.

The emerging emigration industry was huge. America was in great
need of a bigger population. State authorities had employed Swedish

emigrants as migration agents whose job was to attract more compatriots. There were plenty of handbooks and guidebooks to choose from for those who'd made the decision. A few of the books were aimed at women who had chosen to take the critical step on their own. These women were relatively few in number.

In the wake of the mass exodus, Chicago became the second-largest "Swedish city" after Stockholm. But dreams of a better life were not limited to Sweden. Soon, about thirty-five million Europeans would have emigrated to North America.

Not unexpectedly, single women were in the minority on SS *Hellig Olav*. Ester Blenda was alone in her cramped two-bed cabin in the sheets she had brought with her, just like all the other third-class passengers. The door could not be locked. Every morning at 4:30 she was brutally awakened by a cleaner who came in to scrub the wooden floor. It made no difference; the stench from all the seasickness on board couldn't be washed away. To escape all the wailing, she was mostly out on deck. Smoked cigarette after cigarette. Looked at the other passengers from under her men's felt hat. The trench coat flapped in the strong wind. Beneath, she was wearing a shirt and tie.

A large travel party of Russian Jews sat bunched together on a tarp on the hatch, wrapped in shawls and blankets. Day after day, night after night, in the exact same spot. No one talked to them. Ester Blenda approached them, showing them her camera. The children smiled, and the women looked curiously as she took a picture. Her heart twinged as the bitter cold, storm, and rain forced her back inside while they remained out there on the tarp, tightly packed.

Meals, sleep, more walks around the deck—the days soon blended into each other. There was no idle moment. A poker team formed on board. It consisted of men only, with the exception of Ester Blenda who'd been invited. The maximum bet was ten öre. In the evenings, spectators stood closely around the table and watched the game as it was played in complete silence.

The dance on the middle deck was lively; brandy bottles were passed around to the sound of the accordion. Waltz, tap, jazz. Everyone tripped and fell about in the dark on the wet deck. There were lanterns and lights not too far below them. Above them, first- and second-class passengers danced to a live orchestra.

Most third-class passengers got to know each other within a couple of days. Origins, travel itineraries, goals, and marital status had been clarified through at-times-comical language miscommunications, especially between Swedes and Danes. Ester Blenda got to know Elof, the farm boy with two shiny gold teeth who'd never been outside Småland County, and who believed that the port wine served for Sunday dinner was sauce. She listened at length to the old man who stated that he was going to look for his daughter, Hulda Nelsen; he hadn't seen her for twenty years, but she had written that she lived "close to Nuyork." She supposedly had her own car as well. And then Sonja with the balalaika, who never stopped singing.

The closer they got to the new country, the more a sense of fear spread among the passengers. They'd heard and shared many stories about the huge station on Ellis Island, the island at the mouth of the Hudson River that was known for its harsh treatment of lower-class newly arrived passengers. About how you could get locked up without reasonable cause and detained for months.

Some were said to have fallen ill in this miserable state and died at the threshold to their new lives.

The stories didn't seem exaggerated or fictional once the SS *Hellig Olav* reached New York and they crossed the gangway to solid ground, on shaky legs. The nightmare began right from the harbor. Here, customs officers turned carefully packed suitcases upside down. Threw embroidered pillows, seashells, home-woven linen tablecloths, and framed photographs onto the floor in the arrival hall.

Emigrants on the deck of the SS Hellig Olav. Possibly Ester Blenda at the far right in the second row up.

Tears welled up in her throat when Ester Blenda saw the mess they'd made. Kalle, a young boy who was on the boat, sat on his empty suitcase with his head in his hands and cried. In one hand, he held a painting with the well-known illustration "The Life and Age of Man. Stages of Man's Life from the Cradle to the Grave." She helped him gather his belongings, noted the carefully folded shirts made of unbleached fabric, and the heavy boots that some local village shoemaker must have spent several hours making.

So much of everything a mother could think to equip her boy with, when he is going out into the world on his own for the first time, far from home, and from being taken care of. I packed and packed, and a tear would fall into it all every now and again, but this made no difference as it did not take up any space. And when I finally got everything back in, and Kalle and I joined in using all our weight to push the lid down, they began to scream and shout that we should line up in marching order. And so we were herded onward—I could not possibly use another word, because it was certainly as if we were a herd of cattle. If anyone stopped for a moment to get a better grip of their duffel bag or to adjust their hats, they got barked at or squeezed by the arm, and so it continued. Out onto the ferry that would take us over to Ellis Island.

And we felt even more like a herd of cattle there. No benches apart from a few narrow ones next to the chimney, no windows apart from a few windows on each side, and so dirty everywhere that one would prefer to be suspended in the air if one could.

From *Amerikanskt* [*American*].

They stepped onto the dreaded island in long silent rows. Sweaty, dirty, hungry, through passages that looked like chicken coops. Kalle with his freshly packed suitcase. Sonja with her balalaika pressed hard against her stomach. The old man looking for his daughter, Hulda, was so exhausted by the journey that he needed help to stay upright. Orders on where men and women were to go for enrollment were screamed overhead. Nobody understood the language. Ester Blenda translated for those near her.

Once in a crowded locker room, they were forced to take off all their clothes. There were no hooks, and vermin crawled all over the walls. The stench made several people vomit. Another inspection awaited them. A small lectern served as a checkpoint; here, the passengers were to present their papers and funds. A Swedish-speaking man stood next to the guard, demanding to see documents. Hundreds of small blue passport books were held forward and examined. Inspections proceeded quickly until Ester Blenda showed her cabinet passport. She was interrogated about her name, place of residence, intended destinations in America, names of the relatives and the friends she planned to visit. The guard grew increasingly scornful and unpleasant. He insinuated that the relationship with the male acquaintance in New York whose name she gave was inappropriate in nature and a means for a common maid desperate to get out into the world. When he asked how she got ahold of fifty-odd dollars, her patience ran out.

The horror didn't dawn on her until a guard locked the door behind her. Adults and children from different parts of the world were crammed into the cell among heaps of empty bottles, chewing gum paper, and old fruit peels. A woman sat crying in one corner, practically unreachable by the outside world. Ester Blenda was led to her by a Norwegian acquaintance from the boat who'd also rubbed the passport inspector the wrong way. The woman turned out to be from Skåne County. Her name was Johanna, and she didn't know a word of English. Seeing that things were bad, Ester Blenda tried to console and comfort her, but her words didn't reach her at all. The only time Johanna reacted was when the door opened and a towering Black man stepped in with a piece of paper in hand. Then she made the same desperate dash toward him as all the other prisoners did.

Once a person's name was called, they were free.

The new arrivals mostly sat quietly, side by side as the hours crawled by. Then the big man with the paper suddenly returned. Johanna Johansson's name was called. Life returned to the weeping face. Ester Blenda looked at her for a long time as she left. When even her Norwegian acquaintance from the SS *Hellig Olav* disappeared out the door shortly after, she was close to tears herself.

Her idea of passing the time by writing letters only made things worse. Homesickness hit her, hard. She begged the guard to let her write a telegram and ask for help. He finally said yes but gave her no reassurance that it was being arranged outside the cell.

Then suddenly Johanna returned. A female friend had pretended to be her relative, and since Johanna didn't know any English, she wound up back in captivity.

> Both accused of lying and fraud and awaiting our judgment. It certainly was not pleasant, but I was not as sad as poor Johanna in any case, because I had merely gone out to see and experience something new, and I have certainly succeeded to that end. And *I* would certainly be able to get out with the help of Swedish authorities [. . .] We sat and stared down at the dirty stone floor and philosophized about the evils of the world.
>
> "If this is supposed to be America, and they treat you like this everywhere you go, then I can do without!" Johanna said at last.
>
> From *Amerikanskt* [*American*].

They could hardly believe their eyes or ears when a white-haired older man stuck his head in through the door and asked if there were any Swedes in need of advice and help.

The Swedish pastor Axel Helander listened intently to Ester Blenda's presentation of her ongoing mission to travel like an emigrant to America and portray the lives of Swedish settlers. He laughed at the mess she'd wound up in and promised to sort things out. After just a few minutes, he was back with permits for both her and Johanna.

While Johanna was being pushed back through the chicken-coop-like hallway, Ester Blenda was escorted to a uniformed man, seemingly high-ranking. The pastor informed him that she was a Swedish journalist who had traveled to Ellis Island to investigate how newly arrived immigrants were treated. The rest of her path into American freedom was lined with friendly smiles, curtsies, bows, and welcoming words. Afterward, she was told that a female American journalist went through Ellis Island with a false passport only a few years earlier, in order to write about the reception process. The articles led to Senate hearings on how immigrants were treated, along with decisions on improvement measures.

Johanna and Ester Blenda found their way back to each other and were escorted to the Swedish Lutheran Immigrant Home of New York City, run by the pastor. Seventy-five people were housed in twenty-seven rooms. One bed remained. When Ester Blenda explained that she was happy to head into town to find a room with a bed for herself, she was told that no woman whom the pastor had received into the immigrant home was "released" until he had seen papers proving her employment as a maid. They weren't even allowed to go and look around without an escort, the porter from Skåne authoritatively explained. Johanna started crying again. The feeling of being a prisoner for a second time was too much. When no one was looking, Ester Blenda took her by the arm and slipped into the noise of the city, heading toward Broadway.

The bustle of the street overwhelmed them both, Johanna in particular. With her mouth open, she looked at well-stocked shop windows, various eateries, and dizzying skyscrapers. She tried to digest the fact that Black people were a natural part of the cityscape. Tram brakes screeched, car drivers honked for all they were worth, and coachmen were forced to violently pull their reins as Johanna walked straight out into street after street. Her gaze became increasingly wild and terrified—the Immigrant Home might not be such a bad idea after all.

They were both stunned by the young women who passed by along the sidewalk: their makeup nothing like modest; nor was the length of their skirts. Their socks were rolled down over bare knees. In shock, Johanna remarked on the length of the skirt and, remarking on the thick layer of white powder on their foreheads, noses, and chins, said, "They look like they dipped their faces in a bread trough right across the cheekbones."

As it was five o'clock in the afternoon and they were filing out of offices, banks, and shops, Ester Blenda realized that they were self-sufficient and leaving their jobs for the day. They were witnessing the liberated, modern, twentieth-century American woman, the flapper. They both looked at her with clear fascination and amazement—even though Ester Blenda was seen by herself and others as a similar type of pioneer back in Sweden. But they were in the US now, where the world's first women's association, the NWSA, had been formed in 1869. That same year, the territory of Wyoming granted all adult women the right to vote, regardless of socioeconomic status and ethnicity. Since then, the territories and states had followed suit, one by one.

Admittedly, it wasn't until 1920, when the Nineteenth Amendment to the Constitution was passed, that women in all states were given the right to vote in presidential elections. But many of the women Ester Blenda and Johanna encountered on Broadway were living proof that American women had taken their liberation further than Swedish women. After fighting for voting rights, careers, and contraception, a new generation had taken over.

Flappers were taking the Roaring Twenties experience to the fullest. They cut their locks into wavy page hairdos, discarded long dresses in favor of loose, comfortable fits. Their arms and legs were exposed. They danced to jazz music in provocatively high heels, and they went on dates (preferably nonexclusively). With the improved economy, finding a job and earning your own livelihood wasn't hard to do, especially not in the big cities.

Their lighthearted approach to life permeated their every action; they challenged societal norms and stirred things up. Johanna and Ester Blenda couldn't take their eyes off them.

> The whole business of painting is just for sport, I suppose—
> this is now a "flapper's" prerogative, as is flirting and jazz-
> ing about, and dressing with a certain eccentric elegance,

without losing a single ounce of one's dignity [. . .] I should think our grandmothers would cross themselves and be gripped with horror were they to set their eyes on them, but nowadays no one crosses themselves over anything, and no one is struck by a bit of paint, or a couple of generously exposed legs, or jazz, or such small trivialities. Still, it is incredible how expansive the opportunities for human development are [. . .]

People swept back and forth around us, laughing, talking, screaming. Suddenly, I felt Johanna's grip tighten around my arm, and when I looked at her, I saw glistening tears slowly run down her cheeks.

"It's a long way back to Sweden now!" she simply said.

"Very far!" I replied, swallowing past a tightening of my throat.

"If I didn't have you just now, I would have started crying already."

"We're tired," I said. "Let's go back home to Luther."

From *Amerikanskt* [*American*].

After a long persuasive speech, Ester Blenda convinced Pastor Helander to give her permission to move to her own room at a nearby hotel. Before he let her go—with the porter from Skåne as an escort—he made inquiries about vacant rooms. Johanna didn't let go of her until she solemnly swore to return the next day.

A new walk through bustling neighborhoods. It was easier to enjoy without having to practically save the life of a peasant girl from back home every fifteen minutes. "Positively no bedbugs!" read a sign that immediately caught her eye in the cramped reception area. The room that Ester Blenda was shown to was deplorable. Greasy, stained wallpaper; a torn-up carpet; windows without curtains. At night, she had nightmares about the cell on Ellis Island.

Three days later, Johanna got a job as a cook in a millionaire's home on Long Island. They said goodbye to each other, aware that they would probably never see each other again. Ester Blenda traveled to Chicago to carry out an assignment given to her in Sweden. Before the trip, she was contacted by Alma Hedin, city council representative and sister of the famous explorer Sven Hedin who pulled strings behind the scenes of the 1914 peasants' march. When Alma Hedin heard that the famous journalist was going on a trip to America, she asked that Ester Blenda deliver a gift to a friend in the city. The friend wasn't just anyone. Few in Sweden had not heard the name Othelia Myhrman, despite the fact that she had emigrated from the tiny industrial town Finspång at the tender age of sixteen. Now, she was sixty-five and had become the very poster child of making it as an emigrant. She was often referred to as "the most famous Swedish woman in America."

Othelia Myhrman ran the very successful Free Swedish Employment Bureau in Chicago alongside her husband. The agency, which provided Swedish immigrants with jobs, was one of the city's largest and was known for being the first choice of the most distinguished and wealthy families looking to hire help. The couple's home had become a meeting place for Swedes in the city, and Othelia also worked hard to preserve Swedish cultural heritage, serving as chairman of the Swedish Ladies of Chicago, organizer of large midsummer parties, and driving force for a Swedish theater house. Swedish artists and actors who were trying to make a name for themselves in America could breathe a sigh of relief under Othelia Myhrman's patronage. If, for instance, the ticket sales of a play were sluggish, she would take over and make sure that every single seat was sold.

The Swedish government acknowledged her efforts with several awards. But even among Americans, she was seen as a prominent citizen whose name was sought after in election campaigns and by companies that worked on various kinds of propaganda.

White haired and standing tall, she welcomed Ester Blenda into her office. Afterward, Ester Blenda wrote to Alma Hedin that Othelia initially looked so grim and stern that she almost scared her. But Othelia Myhrman seemed to thaw fast. It was a meeting between two strong women. Their sense of mutual respect laid the foundation for an immediate friendship that would last even beyond Ester Blenda's time in America. Othelia Myhrman was planning a return trip to Sweden the following summer and would go on to have an unexpected role in a dramatic event that shook the entire Nordström family.

The next stop on her trip was Minneapolis. Ester Blenda bought a ticket for a night train and was rocked into heavy, dreamless sleep by the train's movements on the way to the city where she would visit her emigrated relatives. The individual who entered the sleeping coach and expertly rifled through her baggage was able to do so without interruption.

Writer Robbed in July

Miss Ester Blenda Nordström truly has quite the luck with experiencing convenient adventures, a talent that has remained with her ever since she made her debut as a maid among maids in Taninge.

A few months ago, Miss Nordström traveled to the USA to write a book for Åkerlundska Publishing, and also in part as correspondent for *Dagens Nyheter*, and already it has come to our knowledge that Miss Nordström, in pursuit of her journalistic curiosity in an American first-class home distillery, has been skillfully robbed in Minneapolis, forcing her to become not only a window cleaner, but also an assistant on a German farm in the region.

Her only loss is that she was not also chloroformed in the course of the robbery; for Miss Nordström is hitherto non-chloroformed. But her time will come. One thing at a time.

From an article in *Dagens Nyheter*, July 10, 1922.

She did not discover the theft until she took out her wallet to find a note for a store that she had been told sold cheap socks. The address label was where it should have been, but the rest of the wallet was completely empty.

The rocking chair in which Ester Blenda sat and contemplated her fate was of the most exclusive kind. The hotel room walls were silken; the carpet was thick and soft; the bathroom was covered in marble. Her commitment to the emigrant experience had clearly lapsed; on arrival in Minneapolis, she opted for a night in a luxury hotel.

She had four dollars and twenty-five cents at the bottom of her bag. That wasn't even enough for a telegram home to ask for more money. The only thing of value that Ester Blenda had brought with her to America was the 18-karat gold wristwatch, but the pawnbroker she showed it to seemed to prefer to call the police to find out if she'd stolen it.

"Waitress Wanted" was written on a sign in front of a little joint that she walked by after fleeing the pawnshop. She stayed there for one day, was unable to stand it any longer, and made just enough for an emergency telegram home. Hungry, poor, and lonely—desperation was near. In a newspaper, she saw an ad for cherry pickers on Müller's farm on the outskirts of Saint Paul. It took an astonishing number of cherries to fill a completely empty stomach. Ester Blenda left the farm in the evenings with two freshly earned dollars in her pocket, and her hunger was replaced by a stinging ache from all the fruit acid. But she at least had something to write home about for *Vecko-Journalen* magazine readers.

Minnesota was reminiscent of Småland. Dark forests, rolling cornfields, red cottages with white trim framed by birches and aspens with rustling foliage. The first Swedish farm Ester Blenda visited was a mile from the train station. A farmhand picked her up with a horse and buggy. His name was Gustav, and he'd arrived by boat from Sweden only a month prior but had already started to season his Swedish with American expressions. Gustav had never been outside his home parish before gaining employment from emigrated Smålanders Erik and Karolina in northern Minnesota.

The smell of coffee was heavy throughout the gray log cabin with a turf roof. A red wax tablecloth lay on the table in the small kitchen. The cups were already out, and Ester Blenda noted that the butter for the rye buns was so fresh that it still gleamed with small white beads of buttermilk. Memories from Jogersta came flooding back. Even though her hands no longer looked like those of a maid, she knew exactly how long you had to churn to see the color of the cream change from white to a buttery yellow.

Bible passages and photographs from Sweden hung on the walls. Out in the yard, some hens pecked around a magnificent, brightly colored Swedish rooster, a foal played by a water trough behind a well, and a couple of cows lowed on the hill at the farm.

> I dipped, ate and drank, and talked and talked, while I took in every detail of the kitchen, the furniture, the two old people who never tired of listening. I looked at their faces—friendly, calm, with that very trait of assured dignity that is so particular to our Swedish farmers—at their hands that rested on the table, gnarled and broken by labor; at their eyes, which seemed to look so far, far away, with the

resigned fatigue of old age. Maybe they were seeing their childhood district in old Sweden, which they had both left so long ago and never seen again, would never get to see again. As they left, God knows why, to start anew in a foreign land, to begin the same work and toil over again, to clear land and break ground for a new home for themselves and their children.

From *Amerikanskt* [*American*].

The five children had flown the coop; their last daughter had done so very recently. Ester Blenda asked how they'd come to make the decision to leave their Lövhultet cottage back in Sweden, a house that had a prominent place of honor in one of the frames on the wall. It was very similar to the one they were sitting in now; in fact, it was almost identical. Erik looked embarrassed as he answered that they barely knew, themselves. Maybe it was all the testimonies about how beautiful America was. How much money one could make. How there was enough firewood for a fire to burn and keep them warm for the rest of their lives. Or how there was no stone in the fields. "Yes, I think that's what it was about, about how there was no stone, because my God, there were so many stones in my fields. Yes, I broke stones until I nearly broke my back," said Erik.

The boat tickets were paid for by the sale of the farm, the chattels that were sold off at auction, and relatives who sacrificed some of their own savings. The Swedish consulate arranged for the land in northern Minnesota where Erik and his eldest son, Adolf, built the cottage and barn with trees that they felled by hand. It took almost a year to prepare the house and its interior. During that time, Karolina and the other children lived at the home of a relative in Minnesota.

Since then, they had lived in the tiny house and farmed the surrounding land, just like they had done back home in Sweden. And almost exactly just like Erik's father, grandfather, and great-grandfather had done before him in their own tiny homes in Småland. Well, except for the hard work with all the stones then, which they'd since escaped in their new homeland.

As the children grew up, they made attempts to modernize the farm to make life easier for their parents, but the only thing they had managed to introduce in all those years were a couple of time-saving agricultural machines that had really only freed up more time for other work. And then the washing machine, of course, which Karolina had reluctantly accepted; she had also reluctantly acknowledged that it had helped with the constant back pain from all the years spent on her knees over the washbasin.

Ester Blenda had proven her expertise in farmwork by lending a hand with various tasks on the farm since she arrived. The blue work overalls were left to hang in the attic late at night and were put back on in the early hours of the morning. She mentioned alkaline fertilization of the soil as an idea for speeding up crop growth. She got to learn all about it in her agricultural training. Erik sniffed at her new ideas. Not contemptuously, he was too kind for that, but impactfully. He had also sniffed at his sons who had taken matters into their own hands and built a new, nice house for their parents a short distance from the cottage, on the land owned by the family.

Ester Blenda was impressed when she was shown around the house. It was spacious, bright with high ceilings, spanned two floors, and was built in modern fashion with floorboards, planed pine panels, and a cement basement.

> But does anyone perchance think that Erik and Karolina moved? Absolutely not—ten years later, when I came, the house was left standing as it stood. Large and airy and cool in the summer heat, with planing benches and separators and all sorts of rubbish that had gathered over the years

[. . .] Oh, Smålanders—oh, Swedes! There is nothing quite like you! Stubborn and single minded and unshakable once you have got something stuck in your mind! Still, I understood Erik and Karolina so well—maybe I would have done the same myself.

It was with a heavy heart that I left Erik and Karolina a few weeks later [. . .] I had seen Sweden live, eternally and stubbornly, right in the middle of America; I had learned that a faithful heart never fails.

From *Amerikanskt* [*American*].

In the three months she'd so far spent in the huge country on the other side of the Atlantic, not one drop of rain had fallen. The sun blazed relentlessly, incessantly; there were cracks everywhere in the ground; dust flew everywhere, getting into eyes, ears, hair, and skinfolds.

Back in Sweden, the summer of 1922 was unusually cold and rainy. There was a record low of meteorological high summer days in Stockholm, an unwanted record that would remain for the next forty years. Film director Fredrik Andersson was one of the many people having to wrap their coats more tightly around them while walking to and from work. He ran the production company Filmfred Produktion and was waiting for Ester Blenda to come back from America. He planned to convince her to have her first girls' book about Ann-Mari, *En rackarunge* (*A Little Rascal*), turned into a movie. He was certain that it would be a huge success.

At around the same time, a few hundred miles from Minneapolis, the author got off a train in the middle of nowhere. She had chosen the station completely at random, knew nothing about the place, and had no intention of staying. The map she carried with her was of no use; she put it aside and decided to improvise and ask for directions along the way. The plan was to go on a long hike and to eventually get to the widely known and widely publicized Mormons in Salt Lake City.

Male drivers slowed down as they cruised by, stuck their heads out of the windows, called her things like "sweetheart," and offered rides. Sometimes, she rode along—if she wanted to get out of her chafing shoes for a bit or wanted a break from the huge dirt clouds and exhaust fumes from all the cars on the road that settled like a thick carpet in her throat, or wanted to simply get a bit closer to her goal. It took longer to get to Salt Lake City than Ester Blenda had imagined.

One of the men she chose for a momentary travel companion turned out to know a lot about life as a tramp, not unlike the existence Ester Blenda was living during her ongoing wander. His name was Sid, and he tipped her off on how to travel for free on freight trains. He suggested that the roof or unlocked coaches could work. But it was easy to get caught, and the consequences weren't fun.

According to Sid, the very best way to ride for free and without risk of detection was to lie across the brake rods under the train and to hold tight. He suggested bringing a plank with you to avoid lying directly against the rounded and rather uncomfortable poles. To successfully sneak under the train unseen, it was important to hide really far out on the railway line, at a water stop, behind a bush, or in a deep ditch and wait for a train to stop. Ester Blenda listened with fascination. Curiosity quickly trumped reason. Such an experience would really be something for the readers.

How conscious was Ester Blenda of the fact that she was constantly raising the bar on the element of surprise in her articles? For over ten years, she had spoiled her readers with increasingly sensational articles. Was she starting to feel compelled to constantly cross new boundaries and break norms? Had she created a persona that she was constantly pushing herself to embody in the real world? Later that year, when Ester Blenda came to summarize her articles from America in book form, she herself wrote that she wondered why she embarked on a laborious hike

in the desert heat when she could have ridden trains with electric fans
and been served ice water. She even admitted that she felt compelled to
do things that an "ordinary" person wouldn't dream of doing.

The shrub she selected was a rather feeble specimen that had survived in the dry sand along the track. But it was close to a water stop that
the trains along this track always stopped at, and it was bushy enough
to hide someone within its branches. She screamed and stomped before
crawling in; rattlesnakes were common in the area. The early-morning
air was soon replaced by the familiar heat as she lay in wait and listened
intently for the sound of the rails singing from an oncoming train. She
was unbelievably lucky. The last carriage on the next train that passed
by stopped right in front of the bush she was hiding in.

> I had not brought a plank with me—I thought it would
> look so strange to people I could run into on the way
> here, and what's more, you can never find a plank when
> you really need one [. . .] There were four or five—I have
> forgotten how many—narrow bars, which ran along
> the carriage, and I was now to place myself across them.
> Lying on my back, of course. There was not much space
> between the bars and the floor of the carriage—I could
> easily reach the bottom of the carriage, to a point where I
> could stretch half my arm upward, and there was a scent
> in the air around me that vividly reminded me of a barn.
> It wasn't just a scent, by the way. I heard the mooing and
> the trampling of anxious hooves and knew then that I had
> ended up on a cattle train, or under it, to be precise.

> From *Amerikanskt* [*American*].

The idea of using her backpack as a pillow probably saved her life.
Later, Ester Blenda recounted that the jerking of the train leaving was

so powerful that she was thrown along the poles under the carriage. She didn't stop until the backpack strap hooked onto a joint, with a second forceful jerk. She discovered that she had ended up exactly where Sid had told her to avoid ending up—where the rods slid through iron brackets and where the risk of getting catastrophically trapped was the greatest.

With great effort, Ester Blenda managed to somewhat squeeze herself away from the danger zone. The speed of the train increased. The cars tossed and swayed round the bends. With every shard of stone encountered, she felt like she was being run over a mountain; the pain of the increasingly hot rods cutting into her back overwhelmed her. In the chaos, she managed to think that she would give everything she owned to have that plank to lie on. And the noise, the cacophony of screeches, thundering, and a loud rhythmic thump—it was so deafening that she was convinced that her eardrums would burst.

The freight train, on its way to Colorado, flew along the track. No one would think to imagine that a young Swedish woman from a prominent family, with fame and a successful career to boot, was lying under one of its carriages. She clung on for dear life and closed her eyes to protect them from all the debris that fell on her face.

> In the end, I tried to turn around to lie on my stomach, but once I finally got on that side after a thousand movements and efforts and opened my eyes to see what it looked like, I had such a feeling of dizziness and nausea at the sight of all the rail beams being passed over at an insane speed, that I was forced to undergo the same torture to turn to lie on my back [. . .] The only thing that made me somewhat happy was that the speed caused such a wonderful breeze that I at least felt cool. But that was all. I was so overwhelmed with torment and dust and thirst that I could not think a single thought, and could merely moan

and groan and hold on to the brake rods for dear life and
with both hands.

From Amerikanskt [American].

When the train finally stopped, Ester Blenda fell onto the embankment, exhausted. She couldn't stand upright and simply lay there,
stretched out in the sand with a throbbing head and body until she
heard a voice from somewhere above her. The man wore a hat with the
railway company's initials and emblem. He swore angrily and asked
why she couldn't simply have hitched a ride inside a carriage instead.

It turned out that the man was a brakeman. He told her to sneak
into his carriage a bit farther toward the front of the train and wanted
a dollar for his secrecy. A moment later, Ester Blenda stared into a pair
of cow eyes, moved through a herd of animals, and sank into a high
dirty bundle of straw in one of the carriage's corners. The braker sat at
the other end of the same carriage and sang quietly to himself. She fell
asleep immediately, with one hand on her short-barreled revolver.

And before the train stopped, I took the long backward
jump that Sid had so highly recommended and landed
calmly and quietly on the embankment. This is how I got
to Colorado.

From Amerikanskt [American].

Train hopping turned out to be an effective way to reach her new
goal. But Ester Blenda was careful not to end up in the wrong cars.
She had the most fun with a family with three children and a Danish
wife who was overjoyed that Ester Blenda knew her favorite song, "The
Princess." The woman listened to it with her eyes closed and her head
longingly tilted to one side, almost without interruption, for two days.

Then the temporary songstress grew tired of it, thanked them for the ride, and walked on along the road.

It soon became clear that the Swedes were everywhere in America. Coincidence and fortune led her to them. She ticked off emigrant farm after emigrant farm on the road to Salt Lake City. A few days of work and lodging, then on she went. Everyone seemed to agree that the new country was certainly not that much better than Sweden, but it was bigger, and they stayed put for a chance to make money and give their children a better future.

In the evenings, all the conversations that she had between stretches of hard labor, and all the impressions she had formed, were turned into long articles. She got help photographing herself in work clothes on several of the farms where she stopped. Barefoot in a sturdy shirt with rolled-up sleeves and carpenter's pants, at a pump, in the process of filling a bucket with water. Cigarette break in the shade of a large tree. Always with a sun hat on. She sent some of these pictures along with her letters to the *Vecko-Journalen* editorial office.

In the articles, she made sure that the Swedish settlers were heard and included long quotes written in the subjects' distinctive rural Swedish dialects. Their stories were told almost like fairy tales built on courage, curiosity, joy, faith in the future, melancholy, and homesickness.

However, despite the fact that the writer had chosen to stand on the side of the marginalized people throughout her career, she was obviously influenced by the ignorant and racist view about people of color at the time. Before Ester Blenda herself understood the extent of Black people's unfair living conditions, with racism, violence, and restrictions, she repeatedly described them in condescending ways and voiced her suspicions about them. A sense of compassion, and a questioning of the country's unexamined and inherently white supremacist culture came to her in time, but not for a good while during the first part of her trip to America. A racial reevaluation would come only after she'd been repeatedly questioned and personally judged based on her gender and the roles she'd chosen to take on.

August 26, 1922, was a big day, both for Fredrik Andersson, director of Filmfred Produktion, and Ester Blenda. For her, funds increased by fifty-five hundred kronor, which was significant; for him, it was because everything was in place for the movie production of the successful book *A Little Rascal*. The contract seemed to have been finalized despite the geographic distance between them. The ninety-two-minute-long feature film had secured Elsa Wallin, a most of-the-moment Swedish actress, in the lead role.

The streets of Salt Lake City were dirt-free; the facades were beautifully white; and the parks were both lush and well kept. The unexpected beauty and cleanliness of the Mormon capital made Ester Blenda momentarily forget her dusty clothes, her heavy backpack, and that she herself smelled of sweat.

The houses were single story, but everywhere, spires from Mormon churches loomed above the greenery. Her time in Salt Lake City would be both more fun and more interesting than she'd expected. Ester Blenda stayed for several weeks, much longer than she'd thought she would, lived with Mormons that she turned out to get along with wonderfully, and in her articles poked holes in myths about polygamy and meals made from living children. Mormons lived by their own rules—just as she herself had always done.

When it was time to travel on, she was handed an unexpected gift by one of her new friends: a romance novel that was bold, to say the least, by the infamously scandalous writer Elinor Glyn.

In Las Vegas, she saw a huge nugget of gold displayed in a shop window. But that was the only fun thing about the city, which had only one street with a few small low-rise houses, a tiny café, and a few shops with dusty wares in their windows. Just a few hundred yards away, the desert took over, expansive and still. She went on a new train journey, with a new desert landscape outside the train window. Native

Americans stood along the Santa Fe rail line, selling handmade items as souvenirs. Ester Blenda grew bored by the Southwest after a stop in El Paso. She headed back to Chicago and arrived alongside the fall season.

The house was by Lake Michigan on Astor Street, the city's most splendid street, and was reminiscent of the Nordström family's large villa, Ekefors. Ester Blenda's baggage was heavy and wet; she, too, was soaked through from the pouring rain. She walked past the beautiful entrance and onward to a narrow, dark passage in the basement—the servants' entrance.

In Chicago, Ester Blenda once again took a job as a domestic servant under a false identity, eight years after the month in Sörmland that changed her life forever. Back then, she had been a twenty-three-year-old maid; she was now a thirty-one-year-old sous-chef. She'd gotten this job through Othelia Myhrman's employment service. The cook, Emma Karlsson, who'd emigrated from Sweden thirty years ago, critically examined her substitute helper, eyeing her from top to toe. Repeatedly looked at the card with name, salary, and length of service listed. Made sure she could really peel potatoes and wasn't afraid to sleep alone. Then she showed Ester Blenda to the room in the attic where she would be staying. It was pure paradise in comparison with the narrow and hard sofa she'd shared with Sigrid and the lice at Jogersta North Farm.

As 1922 drew to a close, Ester Blenda worked in the large house on Astor Street. No one knew that the new maid was journaling at the time, describing her daily toil and life in recurring articles in one of Sweden's biggest newspapers. She kept a deliberately low profile, pretending to understand only a few words of English when she was around other staff members. And the hard work kept the demons at bay:

> Nothing on earth gives such joy as physical labor; nothing has such an ability to calm, still, and, as it were, cleanse everything within. One has no room left for thoughts that would worry and torment—one white-knuckles it until

the day ends, then sinks down into a chair like a train stopping; the only thought one is able to muster is "now I am truly exhausted, thank God that it's evening."

From *En piga bland pigor* [*A Maid among Maids*].

In November, a strong feeling of homesickness struck once again. She had been gone for six months this time. The oil-fueled turbine engine of the SS *Drottningholm*, Swedish American Line's ocean steamer, took her back across the Atlantic to Gothenburg. It was the same ship that star actress Greta Garbo would soon buy a ticket for, going to New York with her director, Mauritz Stiller.

While the boat slowly left the harbor and headed east, Ester Blenda went up on deck. She raised her hand, then waved goodbye to the Statue of Liberty and contorted her face into an ugly grimace at Ellis Island. Then America disappeared into a compact, gray mist of rain.

Back home, she immediately reunited with Carin. They went on a skiing holiday together, to Storlien in Jämtland County, right next to the northernmost part of Norway. Ester Blenda had her camera with her, and they photographed each other up on the mountain. Ester Blenda squinted at the camera lens in the bright sunlight. She had her hat and gloves in one hand, and turned her body up from the skis her booted feet were strapped in. Legs wide apart, her other hand casually tucked into her jacket pocket. Her head was slightly tilted to one side when Carin clicked the shutter. Then they traded places.

Carin also had her skis on, with a pole in each hand. She wore a hat with ribbon and a bow at the front. Elegant sports trousers with fabric buttons that ran down from her knees right to her ankles, rag socks folded down over her boots. She posed with her gaze dreamily fixed in the distance. Around them were nothing but mountain peaks and empty expanses that would have been dazzlingly white were it not for the black tree branches standing dormant for the winter, spruces in small clusters, and protruding rocks that the snow had been unable to cover. It was so quiet. So undisturbed. Maybe that was why they were brave enough.

Carin began to unbutton her knee-length coat, belted at the waist. Took off her light blouse with its wide collar. Twisted herself out of her sports pants. She smiled gently at the camera as she began to pull down the black stockings fastened with suspenders in the white pantalettes. A petticoat strap had slipped down one of her shoulders. She didn't pull it up. She kept sunglasses and a hat on. One hand on her hip. Click.

Ester Blenda took everything off; only the watch remained around her right wrist. The cold from the snow was staved off using a pair of sheepskin slippers that she pulled out of her packed baggage. She sat straight down in the snow, naked, pulled her knees up to her chest, and clasped her hands around her shins. Peeked up from under her short-cut, unruly curls. Smiled happily at the camera, at her Carin. Click.

She stood up, still naked, raised both hands to the bright sky as if taking off to fly, lifted her right leg, and burst out laughing. Click.

For the last photo, they used the self-timer. Both were completely naked. Carin leaned against Ester Blenda. One of the poles cast a dark shadow over one of Carin's breasts. She still had the hat with the bow on. Ester Blenda had a bruise on one shin. They sat close together in the snow and smiled shyly at the camera. Click.

When they got back to Stockholm, Ester Blenda had the photos developed in a shop on Drottninggatan. She wrote the place and date on the brown envelope and hid it away from view.

Writing the last American article continued in tandem with Ester Blenda's work putting together the texts from her trip for a reportage book. As usual, this couldn't be done in Stockholm, where other temptations held far too much sway. Sitting at the typewriter and working suddenly became so boring compared to everything else. Especially when there was money in the account. From a farm in Dalarna, Ester Blenda wrote an unusually merry letter to her brother:

Bäcka, Orsa, Feb. 10, '23

Dear brother—received the issue you raised on the ninth of this month, and am immediately hurrying to respond to it. Well, damn it, of course you can borrow from me, God knows you can—what else is money for if not to be spread among us, increasing the general level of prosperity in the country. I have written a check for the desired thousand—you may think it awkward, to have a checkbook and the money at the bank! And I don't believe I shall need to bother you for a return until sometime this summer. As far as I know at this point. I have had a new print run of *A Little Rascal* out as well—the next will be Gunilla's, for this was the fifth one—so I am pretty well-to-do. Moreover, I have paid off debts totaling four thousand, so I feel sort of relieved. I am just thrilled to be able to help you for once—for all the times you lent to me in the halcyon days of my penniless youth. I can still see your old fluffy, black-checkered cursed book coming out of your back pocket to show me how thoroughly trapped I was in a web of fifty-öre coins and kronor. I dreaded it [. . .] Oh yes. Otherwise, I feel quite well; if only I did not have to write articles. It lowers my mood.

From a letter from Ester Blenda Nordström to Frithiof Nordström, February 10, 1923.

May 7, 1923. Slow movements. Her head felt tight. Mouth dry. A dull, throbbing pain over the front and back of her head. How much could she remember from the previous night? From all the glasses that were emptied. The bottles that filled the table. The note next to her gave her some answers. She'd apparently wanted to keep track. Maybe because

Albert Engström was paying for the whole do. The note was small, handwritten in pencil; the handwriting was her own:

> 2 bottles Eng. Porter
> 2 bottles II
> 2 5: cl purified spirits
> 2 glasses of port wine
> 1 bottle soft drink
> Given by Albert Engström
> Certified:
> Correctly written, as solemnly declared by
> Albert Engström (signature)
> May 6, 1923
> Bye!

This night of partying together was probably not their first by any means. They had known each other for a long time and had several mutual friends, including Evert Taube, René Malaise, and Hjalmar Lundbohm.

Albert Engström was one of the great cultural personalities of the time. Illustrator, author, artist. Member of both the Swedish Academy (chair no. 18), and the Royal Swedish Academy of Fine Arts. He started out as a student of Carl Larsson at the Valand painting school in Gothenburg at the end of the nineteenth century, with a great talent for creating illustrations. During the early twentieth century, his drawings, which were cutting caricatures of authorities and figures such as Kolingen and Bobban in the self-edited satirical magazine *Strix*, had become both famous and popular. He also had an impressive list of books to his name.

They shared a love of drinking. Albert Engström even weighed in on a Swedish referendum to ban drinking to the point of intoxication, a ban that divided the country in 1922. Election day was in the middle of the national crayfish party season that year, and Engström did not waste time seizing the opportune moment: by drawing a poster in which he portrayed himself pointing at a schnapps glass next to the text "Crayfish require these drinks! If you do not vote no on August 27, you will have to abstain from crayfish." It had a decisive impact. After the election day count, the no-votes had it by an extremely small margin: 50.8 percent.

In the Nordström family, concerns about Ester Blenda's drinking habits grew. Anxious gazes darted around her at dinners and events during which her glass was never empty, when her eyes went from clear to glazed over. At the many dinner parties at Frithiof and Gerda's home in the spacious apartment at Kungsholm Square, the guests were often prominent and famous to varying degrees. The three oldest children, Kjell, Anne-Marie, and Birgitta, had gotten so big that they had to help serve drinks. They'd been taught to walk with straight backs, and to serve the wine from their right. The dinners were merry; they often ended with everyone spontaneously doing the Charleston on the hall floor. But once the others got to a point of feeling they'd had enough to drink, Ester Blenda carried on. She was always in the center, radiating and shining dazzlingly bright—just like the "goddamn sunshine" she'd always been called.

If she didn't receive the attention she wanted, she made sure to get it. On one such evening, Ester Blenda went out into the kitchen and refilled everyone's champagne glasses. On the way back into the hall, she stood in the doorway with the heavy tray in her hands, waiting for the guests to react. No one came her way; everyone was busy talking and dancing. Suddenly, the party was interrupted by the deafening sound of a silver tray hitting a hard floor and several glasses breaking all at once. Instant silence. Everyone looked up toward the doorway. Hundreds of shards in wet puddles lay around Ester Blenda's feet. A big smile spread across her face.

Her niece Birgitta was in the room and would carry the mental images from that night for the rest of her life. She recounted the moment to the author Otto von Friesen when he interviewed her in the early 1980s about her once-famous aunt whom no one seemed to remember anymore. His goal was to write about Ester Blenda Nordström in his forthcoming book *Tio reportage som förändrade världen* (*Ten Reports That Changed the World*), where he highlighted names such as Ernest Hemingway and August Strindberg.

But back to 1923, a time when Ester Blenda Nordström was still one of the country's most famous people and the family grew increasingly distressed about her alcoholism. Because by now, many years of partying had turned into a full-blown addiction. This was also the first time that Othelia Myhrman from Chicago reappeared in her life. Ester Blenda seemed to have taken refuge with her friend after some sort of scandal that she was central to at an event while Othelia was on her long-awaited visit to Sweden. Everyone agreed that something had to be done, otherwise it was "all going straight to hell," as Agda put it in a letter to sister-in-law Gerda:

> Little Gerda—how grateful I am for your nice, kind, good letter. So grateful that I kissed the dry sheet of paper. It feels so good to know that someone can appreciate and understand our hell here, and say a few words of comfort in this misery. I am currently just like an animal being hunted. I do not cry and do not rock back and forth as Mother does; I don't even feel like normal. I'm just tense night and day, constantly suspicious, constantly ready to take action, constantly looking to avoid further scandals, and concerns, and accidents. Ester Blenda will soon grow to hate me for all the wondrousness I deprive her of, but I must bear it, for her own sake, and for the sake of us all.
>
> Maja calls almost constantly and desires to take care however she can in her own way. She is said to have had a few choice, sharp words for E.Bl., particularly with

reference to the scandal of Wednesday night. Ester was with Maja, sober and lucid, and is said to have taken it all without any reply, as usual.

Today she is in with XX [illegible crossed-out content] and Othelia—Othelia at Alma Hedin's home, where Ester was to fetch her at half past four. I am now tense about the state in which she will return. However, as Othelia has not called, I hope all is well. Fr-f is here now, waiting to talk to the girl, especially about the book, which he is very worried about. This, too, requires resolution in some way, otherwise it's all going straight to hell.

Dr. Söderström, whom I was with yesterday, will be visiting tomorrow. He did not sound hopeful but has promised to do what he can. I just wish Fr-f would stay here and lead it all tomorrow, but I do not want to ask him; he needs to be away from all that is tiresome, poor boy. But I don't know how it will go, whether she will put up a fight or run away, or stay put and defy the doctor.

[. . .] In any case, the guests from this past Wednesday, they will certainly remember that party.

From a letter from Agda Nordström to Gerda
Nordström, summer of 1923.

Did this attempt at an intervention lead anywhere? Did the immediate family, Ester Blenda's lifeline for so many years as she balanced on an increasingly thin tightrope, manage to have the difficult conversations about her alcohol abuse in full? In the end, did she listen to them—Dr. Söderström who was summoned, or the woman referred to in the letter as Maja (probably a friend of the Nordström family)? Or did Ester Blenda choose to "defy and run away," one possible outcome presented by big sister Agda in the letter?

It would have been so easy. To just close her eyes and let herself rest on the great professional successes that dominated the fall of 1923. November 22 saw the premiere of *En rackarunge* (*A Little Rascal*) at the major cinemas in Stockholm. The movie took up a lot of ad space in the papers. Almost simultaneously, the book *Amerikanskt* (*American*) was published and was called the biggest book success of the year, the printing of the ten-thousandth copy making for major headlines.

The newspapers wrote stories. Ester Blenda's name and face were everywhere. She handily posed in front of the photographers' cameras. Wide smiles, squinting eyes—just the way readers recognized and liked her. In one of the pictures, she was lying on a cement floor under a car, wearing overalls and sticking her head out. Her hair flew around her face; she smiled wide. The caption read, "'Everything suits a beauty,' says Ester Blenda Nordström, clearly showing how it was pure slander to say that women daren't do the dirty work on cars."

At the same time, her family members were riddled with constant anxiety. And they would soon be given more to worry about. Frithiof's friend, entomologist and explorer René Malaise, had just returned from the Kamchatka trip, which Ester Blenda had been refused access to. He had been celebrated as a hero and already planned a return journey.

During the short time spent back in Sweden, he and Ester Blenda met on several occasions. She didn't have much opportunity to pull off what was, by all accounts, a carefully thought-out plan to make René Malaise fall in love with her. It would take marriage to get a spot on the expedition, and her suggestion of a sham marriage failed once before.

When René Malaise's book *Jakter och jordbävningar: öden och äventyr i fjärran östern* (*Hunting and Earthquakes: Fates and Adventures in the Far East*) was published in 1924, it was dedicated to Ester Blenda. Around the same time, she announced to the family that she would spend the next two years in the volcanic region of northeastern Siberia— and the journey would begin with her and René getting married.

This was no excursion for the faint of heart. Of the approximately 150 volcanoes in the area, thirtysome were active. And you needed to be a skilled shooter with a steady hand when it counted. Wild animals such as wolves, lynx, wolverines, and brown bears roamed freely between the villages in the raw mountain landscape with deserted plateaus, forested valleys, and rivers with crystal clear water. The brown bears measured over nine feet in length and weighed up to fifteen hundred pounds. There were plenty of them, about thirty thousand on the peninsula spanning nearly two hundred thousand square miles.

Ekefors, July 10, 1924

My precious little darling!

I must write to you today, my little friend, whom I have been thinking about for so long! Baffled, surprised, by your last two letters. Dearest one, the fact that you intend to marry without love as you say. How is that going to turn out. Sure, the boy is lovely, but when I think of your changeable nature, how would things turn out for the poor boy who loves with all his soul [. . .] Of course I am saddened that you are traveling away from me, so far away to this horrible Russia, but then I think to myself that it might also be beneficial, in many respects, for you. It is my highest and sincere wish that you will always be well; I have grieved so much over you—you know this.

Now, you may well escape from it all and return healthy of mind and body. May God make it so! My dear, beloved child! But it gets so empty and dark and cold when you are away. It will be so long before I get to see

your happy face again. Whether we meet again is in God's
hand, as they say [. . .]

    Your very own Lotten

From a letter from Lotten Nordström to Ester Blenda
Nordström, July 10, 1924.

Was Ester Blenda purely driven to leave by her appetite for adventure, or was she once again experiencing an acute need to escape the
pedestal on which she'd been placed in her glittering Stockholm life,
so as not to go under? To her friends, she appeared to be someone who
gladly refused fancy parties and glamor in favor of a more authentic life
in unassuming settings. John Landquist described this in his memoir:

> Her participation in social life, where she shone like a star,
> and her own love of isolation in nature and her propen-
> sity to thrive among simple, even primitive people [. . .]
> constitutes a complication of her nature that is unusual
> among human beings. As far as I can tell, she did not
> long to return to the hectic social life once she would
> leave it. She had a fundamental desire for coziness within
> that was warmer and stronger than the joy and triumphs
> among artists and socialites. I have witnessed how easily
> she abandoned social life in Stockholm, without any sense
> of missing it.

From John Landquist's memoirs, *I ungdomen. Scener ur
den förlorade tiden* [*In Youth. Scenes from the Lost Time*].

CHAPTER 13

In the Shadow of a Volcano

It is by no means an overstatement to say that *Vecko-Journalen* has never before in its long history been so richly equipped to face a new year, or had such valuable and attractive news to offer its readers as it does at the transition into 1925.

We can already reveal some of the valuable news we are offering in the coming years [. . .] Ester Blenda Nordström will embark on a trip to Kamchatka during the year, and we hope that *Vecko-Journalen* will not be accused of indiscretion for noting that the trip will also serve as the highly esteemed author's honeymoon. Tales from this journey will color *Vecko-Journalen* throughout the year of 1925.

From a self-advertisement in *Vecko-Journalen*, no. 51
(Sunday, December 21, 1924).

Åhlén & Åkerlund, the publisher behind *Vecko-Journalen*, had signed a new contract with their star reporter. They'd doubled the fee this time: 10,000 kronor, equivalent to about 260,000 kronor or USD$29,000 today, for travel items and rights to a book about Siberia.

René Malaise and his new assistant Carl Sjöblom were already in place. Almost a year had passed without Ester Blenda joining them. She didn't seem to be in a rush to enter her pending marriage. After securing her spot on the expedition, she spent the entire spring behind the steering wheel of a car in Spain. She was not alone. Carin sat next to her.

After Spain, they landed in Sweden for a while before traveling on to Asia via New York, San Francisco, and Hawaii.

Contract signing with Åhlén & Åkerlund before the trip to Siberia.

Then on to China and Korea. They stayed in Japan for five months. Ester Blenda collected material for a journalism book she planned to write. Together, they experienced unique environments and their cultural heritages. They also witnessed and were shaken by human tragedy.

Like the girl in the small village of Kinosaki. She was no more than four or five years old when they found her alone, sitting on a pile of boards, the remains of her home and family that had just been destroyed by a powerful earthquake.

The whole village was more or less wiped out. There were smoldering piles of ash everywhere, and an unbearable stench from half-charred bodies. Ester Blenda lifted the camera, captured the girl's scared, lost gaze. There was a dizzying contrast between this and the luxurious hotels, views from mountain peaks, religious celebrations, and Buddha statues in every conceivable size that their eyes had passed over as they'd been carried around in rickshaws.

They would have preferred to avoid all the typical tourist excursions, but there would be no Japan book without them. And few people around Ester Blenda seemed to believe that she would really be able to put one together—not even Åkerlund at the publishing office. But Carin regularly forced her to sit at the typewriter, just as firmly as Elin Wägner had when *Tent Folk of the Far North* had to be written. In a letter home to the family, Ester Blenda lovingly called Carin a slave driver.

Tokyo was boiling hot. Kyoto was no milder. It was rarely below eighty-two degrees in their room. The fans were constantly on; the window was always wide open. The sweating verged on the unbearable.

They could bathe every day at the hotel, but the water in the low wooden baths was almost 120 degrees hot and wasn't followed by a cooling ice bath. If they were lucky, they could wash their salty bodies in peace, but they were often accompanied by male hotel guests.

In a letter to Gerda, every little detail was described. The letter was long; there was so much she wanted to share. Like how they'd both learned to master the art of using Japanese train toilets—a balancing act where you had to step up on a porcelain podium, stand wide-legged over a small crack with your feet on each special footplate, and stare at the wall ahead to maintain your aim while the train twisted and turned.

Or the trip to the monastery with the paradise garden up in the mountains where they bathed in a private bathtub and met a gorgeous priest who said that he drank five bottles of sake a day while joined by different geisha girls.

> After the bath, we went to bed on a pile of lovely silk mat-tresses, dressed in clean cotton kimonos that are always made available to a guest in a Japanese house, and slept like the dead until five in the morning, when we had to shuffle out in slippers [. . .] The priests who were standing in long lines sang a strange, rhythmic, babbling, monotonous mel-ody, accompanied by a drum and cymbal; we had to shuf-fle to the altar, where our shiny tablets were placed upright in front of the Buddha's fat and content face, kneel and bow to the floor, and light up some sweet-smelling incense, lie for a while in silent meditation, break our spines to get our foreheads down to the floor again, and squeeze back into our spots.

> From a letter from Ester Blenda Nordström to Gerda Nordström, July 19, 1925.

The tone was lighthearted and humorous, but both Ester Blenda and Carin felt weighed down. Their farewell was approaching. Japan was their last stop before they separated and traveled in different direc-tions, Carin back to Sweden and Ester Blenda to an isolated peninsula, nine time zones and six thousand miles east of Moscow.

Carin and Ester Blenda in Japan.

They knew that they wouldn't see each other for two years and that Carin would have to address her letters to Mrs. Malaise from now on. Ester Blenda told her that it was only for the sake of the expedition and the Japan book, referring to her husband-to-be as a little boy. He seemed to have already run out of the money she'd sent him—which was her entire travel fund, more or less—and hadn't even responded to her latest telegram. That was the advance for the book, and there wouldn't be more money until she submitted a manuscript to Åkerlund.

> Thanks to René's most peculiar behavior, to say the least, the money I set aside for Kamchatka has had to be spent in Japan and China, and only God in heaven knows what it will be like when I finally get there, because I don't. He apparently has no money at all (René I mean, not God) [. . .] I don't know, but it looks a little strange. I will send you one of his letters, and have you see for yourselves. It is written in such a nonchalant tone that I became truly furious on receiving it [. . .] I shall have to give the boy a talking to once I get there, so he can hear what I have to say.

> From a letter from Ester Blenda Nordström to Gerda
> Nordström, July 19, 1925.

Carin was anxious, not just about the financial situation, but about the whole idea of the expedition and the marriage that made it all possible. She, if anyone, knew how deeply a setback would affect Ester Blenda, who was already in a fragile state.

As usual, the prospective expedition participant herself tried to laugh it all off, saying, "I've made my bed and now I have to lie in it." But even she began to worry. The idea of calling it all off had crossed her mind, but it had since left again. She wanted to spare her family the scandal. Her past scandals had been more than enough. She had yet to receive any letters from them.

> I feel so strange and abandoned, when I see how many letters Carin receives from her mother. At first, I cried and was so sad that I was inconsolable, but now Carin has

told me that you probably sent a letter to Petropavlovsk addressed to Mrs. Malaise, and I'm starting to believe this, too, because you cannot possibly have completely forgotten me in the time that has passed, and you certainly do not care so little about me that you should punish me so severely.

I do not think I would be able to cope with that, although I certainly do not deserve better treatment than such. This I know.

From a letter from Ester Blenda Nordström to Gerda Nordström, July 19, 1925.

Ester Blenda and Carin traveled around Asia for six months. This picture was taken in Korea.

By this point, the Nordström family had begun to understand that the relationship between the two women was more than friendly. Maybe this had already been explicitly confirmed to some of them. There were signs of this being the case, including an undated letter to Gerda from one of all the many trips that Ester Blenda and Carin took. Only parts of the letter remain, but one can see that Gerda was asked to hide something she knew. Carin was also said to have read something that was not intended for her eyes and was upset. The remaining lines were almost desperate and suggested conflict within the Nordström family over the forbidden relationship.

> She read the card and became so sad. And she has been so infinitely sweet to me this trip that I want you to just love her and thank her and like her. Not a word about this, because then she will never be good to me ever again.

> From a letter from Ester Blenda Nordström to Gerda Nordström, undated.

Carin and Ester Blenda went to the famous springs in Miyanoshita in their last few weeks spent together. After their walk around Fuji, René was meant to come and meet up with his future wife. But he never showed up at the agreed time and place.

The bag that René Malaise packed with his finest clothes remained untouched in a harbor warehouse in the town of Petropavlovsk where the boat that was supposed to take him to Japan arrived. He sent it there in advance to have everything prepared. But as the boat then left the harbor, René was fighting for his life up in the mountains.

The journey home from his and Carl Sjöblom's monthlong stay with the Siberian nomadic people known as the Lamuts (currently known as Evens) began with a bit of bad luck and ended in disaster.

All the broken skis, unexpectedly dramatic thawing of snow that destroyed roads, and many snowstorms would have been bad enough. Once all of this passed, the region's largest volcano began to spew hot ash that settled in a half-inch-thick layer over the landscape and burned the soles of their shoes off. A cool west wind then caused the snow surface to have a rock-hard crust that they froze to with their heavy equipment. After leaving behind everything that wasn't vital for their immediate survival, they managed to get over the last peak with the help of their dogs that were also starving to death.

Sick from scurvy and starvation, they wandered around in the snow for days. With only a can of grease and some tea for provisions, they started the final climb back down toward civilization.

The journey back from the nomadic people was only supposed to have taken a few days. Fifteen days after the journey began, René Malaise and Carl Sjöblom stumbled into the base town of Klyuchi with a single surviving dog. René rallied quickly; he was an experienced adventurer who had survived both earthquakes and real volcanic eruptions during his years in Kamchatka. But the boat to Japan and to his fiancée had left; there was nothing he could do about this.

Ester Blenda was completely unaware of what had happened—and of the fact that similar challenges awaited her once she traveled the last bit toward Kamchatka on a thousand-ton barge.

It was dirty, full of cockroaches, and tilted so severely that she suffered from severe seasickness despite being accustomed to boating. She lay in a cabin under a dirty blanket that smelled of mold and vomited until her throat stung, with tears running down her cheeks. Or that was, at least, the nightmarish scene she painted of the trip in one of her travel reports.

Her legs trembled as she stepped ashore, pale, thin, and furious. Two days later, on August 31, 1925, Ester Blenda, thirty-four years old, married René, who was younger than her by a year. The Soviet marriage bureau was in an old shed, and all it took was them signing a piece of paper. Outside, a bright red flag flew.

They had drawn up a prenuptial agreement confirming that they would maintain separate property. In the evening, Ester Blenda wrote in her Kamchatka diary:

> Monday, August 31
> Got married. Dinner at Vetkovski's. Played bridge. Rain and dull.

The marriage—albeit loveless on one side—could have had a better start. But René still seemed exuberantly happy as he wrote to his new brother-in-law, Frithiof:

> Ust-Kamchatka, on Sept. 8, 1925
> Dear Brother and In-law,
> After a whole summer of impatient waiting, Ester-Blenda has finally come here to Kamchatka [. . .] While we waited, we exchanged "love letters" that grew more and more per-fumed as the waiting period lengthened [. . .] I have clearly gotten myself a very good wife. She finds the new condi-tions perfectly agreeable and is very domestic. The expe-dition will benefit greatly from her, particularly through her natural ability to steal firewood. First on the order of the day is the expected arrival of her clothing and travel provisions; though somewhat late, it is, however, much awaited. She now walks about in a narrow skirt, which will soon become as stained as my clothes [. . .] Over the past few days, we have also made decent purchases for the winter. It looks like I have gotten myself a rather dear wife. We have lived on fish offal from the cannery all summer, but as she thought this too fatty, she has tricked me into

buying several pounds of rancid pork, so now we live in the lap of luxury, as if every day were our last.

Ha, ha, oh well. Being married certainly has its difficulties, all right. My wife admonishes my speech and way of expressing myself and claims that my Swedish language is not sufficiently cultivated. She herself gives examples of how it should sound when we, and I in particular, beat her in our evening card games. The Swedish Academy's dictionary clearly needs to be extended [. . .]

Bye for now and greet everyone warmly from me.

Your friend René

From a letter from René Malaise to Frithiof Nordström,
September 8, 1925.

He didn't write about how they were still living on the beach in a temporary tent camp consisting of heavy cloths strung up between a few wooden boats. Nor about how they had to boil water in a saucepan over an open fire so that they could wash themselves and change into their wedding clothes.

The family wouldn't see Ester Blenda's own pictures from their first "home" until afterward. Carl and René standing topless and shaving themselves with a Mora knife. Ester Blenda stooping over plain wooden buckets by the shore and cooking over the open fire with laundry hanging off a thick-cut wooden stand in the background. The sheepskin slippers—the same ones she wore when she and Carin dropped their clothes in front of the camera in Storlien a few years prior—kept her feet warm in the cold, damp sand.

They were members of "the new Kamchatka expedition," a wilderness adventure that was followed with great interest back in Sweden. Malaise and Sjöblom were going to carry out ethnographic studies and had brought along equipment to capture both moving and still images of nature and people.

Calle, as he was called, was a trained engineer from Falun and had actually planned to spend the coming years in the desert, not Siberia. He had longed for one of the coveted spots in Sven Hedin's Swedish-Chinese expedition to central Asia. But Calle was rejected, then recruited by Malaise instead.

René Malaise was nowhere near as famous as Sven Hedin but was nevertheless a big Swedish name among explorers. The firstborn son of Augusta Söderkvist and the Frenchman Edmond Malaise, head chef at a renowned Stockholm restaurant, René became obsessed with botany at an early age. His grandfather had been a gardener; René was said to have developed a love of insects during a summer stay with relatives in France, where much of his time was spent running around with a net and fortifying a cousin's collection of butterflies.

The butterflies were soon replaced by a burning interest in the unusual sawflies. Like his new bride, René Malaise had spent a lot of time in Lapland, where he made his first three expeditions.

His interest in hunting and weaponry also came early. Malaise himself was said to have told the story of how, as a child, he often took up a position as a sniper by a window in his family's apartment at the exclusive Östermalm Square in Stockholm. From there, he would use a blowpipe he made himself to blow sharp darts that settled in the hat plumes of passing ladies, with continuously increasing precision.

Ester Blenda was to complement the group as a still life photographer. But before the expedition could begin its research work, they needed to arrange a sensible home for themselves in the small community.

Just under five hundred inhabitants were scattered across the houses that stood lined up between the foot of the volcano Klyuchevskaya and the wide Kamchatka River. The place was seventy-five miles from the nearest sign of civilization and was completely free of cars, trains, and proper roads. It was really only a collection of simple, gray houses, one more dilapidated than the next. A school, a church with an accompanying priest, and a barn that had been converted into a people's house where Lenin, Trotsky, and other revolutionary heroes were plastered up on the walls.

The newlywed Malaise couple in their house in Klyuchi, Siberia.

The Klyuchi settlement was living on borrowed time, constantly threatened by the roaring volcano and the river that dug deeper and deeper into the shoreline every time the ice thawed, carrying one or more buildings with it into its black, frothy spring-flood whirls. Life was governed by nature's terms. The average temperature dropped with ease to minus forty degrees during the long tundra winters.

Wild animals roamed freely between the houses, even out on the main street. The horses in the region were ragged and unkempt and fed themselves until they were captured by the men to be used in mountain hunts. The barking sled dogs that filled every yard still had wolf blood in their veins.

Fall flew by for the "new Kamchatka expedition" with hard work on the house that would serve as their base for the next two years. It was shabby, drafty, and run-down. Two bedrooms and a reception area.

The newlyweds didn't share a bedroom. René and Calle slept in the living room. Ester Blenda moved into the smallest room in the house. She could fit a bed and a small desk in it. On the desk stood a portrait of Carin.

They built furniture and set up the interior, working intensively to be done by Christmas. A packing case became a bookshelf; a sturdy tree stump became a smoking table next to the mantelpiece. Ester Blenda did her best with patterned pillows, tablecloths, and rugs. She hung up curtains in all the windows. She photographed the result and sent pictures to Frithiof with short, descriptive captions.

From the kitchen window, she could look straight out at the huge volcano.

> Klyuchevskaya, it storms up at the sky. It is as if it knew itself to be the largest volcano in the whole world and therefore wanted to reach even higher; as if it raged over being bound to the earth and broke up through space to reach all the way to the heavens in its wild, immeasurable vanity [. . .] One forgets that one stands there, far below, and that one is just a small human insect in a black and dilapidated village. One forgets everything, except that life is wonderful to live and that the air is easy to breathe; one forgets that one can be reached by something that is earthly and pathetic and ugly. But one is reminded when

the gleaming white summit up there wraps hazy veils around itself and hides from one's eyes behind a mantle of mists. Then everything becomes as usual again. So earthly and monotonous.

From *Byn i vulkanens skugga* [*The Village in the Shadow of the Volcano*].

The villagers gave Ester Blenda a new name: Elizaveta Danilovna. One of her new Russian friends made a candlestick from old rifle parts and presented it to her as a gift. It was given a place of honor on a kitchen shelf.

Ester Blenda in front of the Swedish expedition's house on the village's main street.

On the outside, it looked much like any other residential building in the area. Unpainted horizontal logs, small mullioned windows, corrugated roof, and a simple wooden fence. But there was something unavoidably different about their particular house. The expedition members hung a Swedish flag from a long stick attached to one of the attic windows. It proudly swayed back and forth along the main street.

Soon, their yard was also filled with sled dogs, a must for getting around the barren terrain. To begin with, they had twenty-four Siberian huskies. They purchased number twenty-five with high expectations. Kraska, a bitch that was said to be of the finest sled dog breed, cost them two Mora knives, several yards of steel wire, and two spools of white sewing thread.

Ester Blenda had primary responsibility for the pack and grew to have her own favorite, Loften. She called her "my sweet" and "my finest," buried her nose in the soft fur, and played with her in the yard. The villagers laughed at her. The sled dogs in Kamchatka were there only to carry out their assignment—to pull heavily loaded sleds across the snow six months a year. They got just enough food to be able to run without tiring. Shards of ice made deep cuts in their paws. If they fell, they were made to get back up with blows, strikes, and kicks.

At night, the village's roughly one thousand dogs joined in lamentation. Their howling made for a marvelous, sorrowful, hopeless concert. Animal lover Ester Blenda was awake and listened. Her heart ached when she thought about their hard life.

The men in Klyuchi were gone for long periods of time, busy with the work of filling food stores with salmon and meat from wild reindeer, bears, and mountain sheep for the winter. Ester Blenda, René, and Calle packed weapons, ammunition, bearskin sleeping bags, tents, and provisions in the form of rice, potatoes, and bread; they also set off several times between the renovation projects.

You didn't always have to go too far up the mountains to hunt wild game. Sometimes, you could hunt bears right down in the village, among the townspeople walking about. But this was still so unusual that such an event was big news even in Klyuchi. In the fall of 1925, the man who was on his way up a salmon-drying scaffold in a courtyard when he killed a huge, black bear became a hero. Not least because the hunt was preceded by the murder of twelve cows, all of which had fallen victim to the fearless beast that autumn. The last one had been found half-eaten on the church embankment in broad daylight.

Everyone wanted to see the dreaded beast. A neighbor knocked as Ester Blenda had her hands deep in a washbasin. She wiped the soapy foam off on her apron while they half jogged out together.

> I left the washing and everything without a moment's hes-
> itation. He was already cut up into pieces by the time we
> arrived—an imposing big bastard with a carbon-black coat
> and feet that were a foot and a half each.
>
> We ate some of him in the form of steak and cabbage
> dolmas. He was very fatty and very, very hard to chew.
> Peace be upon his tenacious memory!
>
> From *Byn i vulkanens skugga* [*The Village in the Shadow of
> the Volcano*].

A bear cub that strayed down into the village was tamed and became everyone's special pet. Ester Blenda was photographed playing with it outside the house.

As winter set in, the expedition ran its dogsled team everywhere. Ester Blenda had her own. She learned how to prepare the various lines before attaching all the dogs in pairs on either side of the gangline. The lead dog was the last one to be put in place.

Driving a sled required speed and raw strength in both arms and legs, and there was no room for hesitation. The first part, right after she shouted the dogs' starting command, was the hardest. The sled driver always ran next to the pack for the first hundred yards as the dogs set off at a maddening speed. After that, it was important for the driver to first spring into the sled exactly at the right second, then quickly start zigzagging between the houses on the village street. Any delay introduced a high risk of tipping right over into a gatepost or a house wall. It was the work of a moment and was often associated with physical pain; Ester Blenda learned that the hard way. She had to lie in bed for several days with a compress around an intensely aching knee and, on another occasion, for a sore stomach and chest after a wild journey where she fell out of the sled and was dragged by the reins across rocks and bushes, refusing to let go.

During the sled rides, she sat wrapped in a thick layer of fur and reindeer hide, with the brake lever in a firm grip in her right hand and her gaze darting between the road and the team. The three-person expedition embarked on many excursions. The sled carriage wound its way up between the mountaintops like a long black snake. If feed was in good supply, they could run seventy-five to ninety miles in one day without any problems. The night runs were challenging; it got so cold that the expedition members lost all sensation in their feet and sometimes had to run next to the sleds in the moonlight just to stay warm. They stopped only to sort out tangles or mediate if fights broke out between the dogs.

They stopped for the day only once the lactic acid buildup in their arms drowned out the desire to push on a bit farther. Then they made a fire and roasted meat or fish before falling asleep in their sleeping bags in the open air.

Everyday life in Siberia. Ester Blenda is cutting Calle's hair with the household's only pair of scissors.

They were offered semi-raw meat in wooden trays out among the nomadic people who lived in the most remote and inaccessible mountains. No salt, no bread. The blood was still running from the steaming hot pieces, down their chins and between their fingers as Ester Blenda, René, and Calle ate.

After dinner, Ester Blenda picked up the camera. The pictures she took of the blazing fire and the mountain people who gathered around it had a suggestive air, reflecting her own mood in that moment.

> One felt like one were in the Stone Age in some strange way. And pagan. As if there were nothing on earth but this wilderness [. . .] Far, far away were people from the twentieth century, thousands of years away. Were they missed? No, hardly. At first it was perhaps strange to live in a country where a train had never rolled through; where car wheels had never made their mark; where paths trampled by forest animals were the only possible access ways. But one easily got used to it. One soon found that one could live just as well without all that was previously thought necessary [. . .] It was so simple, so real.
>
> From *Byn i vulkanens skugga* [*The Village in the Shadow of the Volcano*].

Soon, they developed a sort of everyday life in Siberia as well. Cooking, washing dishes, reading books in front of the fireplace, playing cards, writing letters, making grocery trips to the small shops . . . Much of the housework fell on Ester Blenda. She cut hair, sewed, did the laundry, and cooked but was not very entertained by it. She trial-ran a rotating schedule for doing dishes and laundry. In her magazine articles, she mocked Calle and René for their lack of housekeeping skills.

Life in Kamchatka and the daily routine back in Sweden were still miles apart. The problems that arose were completely different in nature. Would the lead dog's foot heal in time for the next field study? Would showers of ash ruin the laundry currently hanging out to dry? Would the next batch of yeast be good to bake bread with?

Letters from home served as reminders of that other world; they were typically painful reminders, causing Ester to feel homesick. In her diary, Ester Blenda wrote that the first letter to arrive at her new address was from Carin. Another early letter was from Elin Wägner, with whom Ester Blenda didn't seem to have had any contact in a long time.

> My beloved friend!
> I wonder if you will ever receive this. In any case, I will make an attempt to reach you. Yesterday we heard from Agda that you were getting married the same day, so at dinner at Andrén's we offered a toast in your honor [. . .] So you've simply gone and made a lightning tour through China, you strange girl. I read an article; it is fantastic that you have reached the most interesting point on earth, then left after just one tiny article in *Vecko-Journalen*! But Malaise was waiting, we understand.
> [. . .] In any case, life is empty without you, but this has been the case for many years now. When will you come home?
> Yours, Elin
>
> Letter from Elin Wägner to Ester Blenda Nordström,
> September 2, 1925.

Her time in Kamchatka would come to breathe new life into their friendship. In the letters that followed, they didn't appear to keep any secrets from each other. Emotional lives, exhaustion, and moments of humiliation and of everyday joy were transmitted in densely written lines between Siberia and Sweden.

Elin told her about her new house, Lilla Björka, which she'd bought in the Småland County neighborhood where she'd grown up, and where she now stayed for long periods of time with her housekeeper, Linnea; about her work on the last two chapters of her next book; about her longing for Ester Blenda to come and join her, "happy and full of stories." She wrote that her ex-husband, John, sounded so tender, funny, and kind when they talked to each other on the phone, to the point that she became tearful every time, while she had also given love a new chance with Swedish author Sigfrid Siwertz. She preferred to keep him out of the public eye because her divorce hadn't yet been finalized, but "still all of Sthlm knows that we have joined together." The relationship was not without its complications. Fatigue had taken over her life: "I feel then that I haven't the energy to have a lover, yet it is probably what one most wishes to have energy for . . ."

It is clear from reading the replies that Ester Blenda was as open as Elin was, but the exact content of Ester Blenda's letters is unknown. They are nowhere to be found in any collection left behind by Elin Wägner, despite the fact that her life was otherwise unusually well documented. Were the letters from Ester Blenda deliberately erased? If so, was this because they contained sensitive information about Carin? Obviously, Elin knew that the two had a love affair. An upcoming letter will soon show this.

The three Swedes had entered a village community and a local culture where the consumption of large amounts of alcohol was customary. You took every chance you got to break up the monotony of everyday life with something strong to drink. There were plenty of holidays, or *prazdnik*, and if there wasn't an official holiday, people took to celebrating a name day or commemorating a deceased father or mother. Even a funeral presented an excuse to get drunk.

It didn't take long before the locals discovered that the female expedition participant was very similar to them on that point. She liked to entertain at her house with guitar and vocals. Guests joined in and played balalaikas. A new friend, Tamara, danced Russian folk dances to a huge round of applause. The floor tiles shook. Someone took pictures. Misty gazes, gathered in a steamy, warm room in Siberia at the transition into 1926, were immortalized.

René, Ester Blenda, and Calle made home brew using their own recipe and generously invited their new friends to partake. People from China, Korea, Russia, Japan, Latvia, Estonia, Lithuania, and Czechoslovakia sat tightly packed in the dim light around the Swedes' kitchen table.

Everyone carried their story of how they wound up in the remote Siberian village. As for the Russians, some had fled the revolution, but everyone knew that most of them were wanted criminals who had searched for the most inaccessible place they could find and taken new names and gained new lives once there.

Some had ugly eyes—eyes that hid thoughts that could not withstand the light of day; others had gentle, sad eyes that looked inward as if they were constantly searching for a constantly elusive memory, without ever finding it; and still others had cheerful, bold eyes, and at first one would think they were beholding life as if it were before them always—until one would suddenly catch them with a look so heavy and dark and hateful that one could not help but watch them to see whether one might have been mistaken after all. But one was not mistaken—right then, the cheerfulness and joy in their eyes would break, and they would darken into a bottomless woe, an indescribable torment, and a hatred, hatred, hatred . . . [. . .] It is true that the Russians happily speak about themselves with a great and childish delight, but one did not learn much even so, certainly nothing that their eyes could not remain silent about. They also talked about each other, in silent, mysterious whispers in nooks and crannies [. . .] They dished up horrible stories of murder and robbery and theft and bestiality, allusions to deeds so disgusting that one refused to believe them for the sake of one's own peace, if nothing else.

From *Byn i vulkanens skugga* [*The Village in the Shadow of the Volcano*].

They were all survivors, just like Ester Blenda. Did she recognize her own gaze in theirs, her own mood that swiveled so violently from cheerfulness to darkness?

She lived, as many of them did, with a dark secret gnawing at her chest: the fact that the woman in the photograph on the desk in her bedroom was not just her best friend. Carin was her life partner, the one she depended on and always returned to. Carin was the person she couldn't live without but wasn't allowed to live with. The consequences of the discovery of such love weren't just stigma and shame—they risked imprisonment, penal servitude, or detainment in a mental hospital.

The Russian vodka settled like a layer of cotton around her brain, numbing the longing inside. Sometimes, she let go and let the tears flow. In Kamchatka, no one cared.

Sergei Konstantinovich Müller, one of their neighbors, had his eye on Elizaveta Danilovna. He was a short, chubby former steamboat machinist who still always wore his sailor clothes. At the parties, he pressed himself against her, whispering incoherent secrets in terrible German in her ears. No one else in the village spoke German and understood what he was saying to Elizaveta Danilovna. She closed her eyes, let the words go in one ear and out the other without listening.

René Malaise and Ester Blenda on a horseback ride in Kamchatka.

It did not matter at all that I would intermittently be completely absent and the only replies he would get were long sniffs. Sergei also smiled. He would hit his small round knees, and one huge burst of laughter after another would pour forth from his tiny rosebud of a mouth. And the people would stand around, looking puzzled and curious, and would simply listen [. . .]

"Do not tell anyone about this, Elizaveta Danilovna! Promise me!"

From *Byn i vulkanens skugga* [*The Village in the Shadow of the Volcano*].

Working with a headache was nothing out of the ordinary. Hangovers were a normal condition in this part of the world. Without them, life would be too "sad and dry" as Ester Blenda wrote in her reportage book from Kamchatka, based on the long travel reports in *Vecko-Journalen*. They didn't start publishing her pieces until almost a year after Ester Blenda's arrival. Her texts, which had been sent to Sweden, had been stopped by Soviet censorship.

The diary was also proof that there would be many wet evenings. It consisted mostly of snapshots from everyday life, just a few words, and short straightforward notes about weather conditions and excursions. Things like doing a big load of laundry with Calle, or a dinner with friends where she was "eating herself to death." Or a note about how they arrived in Klyuchi after eleven hours of driving a dogsled. She pasted small photographs next to the inked sentences.

The parties stacked up like pearls on a string: An undated event where "vodka flows in streams." "Wednesday, January 21. Russian Prassnik [*sic*]—Anniversary of Lenin's Death." "Sunday/Monday, January 25. Big celebration at the doctor's place. Tach name day." "Wednesday/Thursday, January 28. Yurro's birthday. NB. Party in the evening—Yurro and Chihopp." "Saturday, February 21. Spectacle and *vechorka* at the People's House. Played violin in the orchestra. Boring event." "Saturday/Sunday, March 7. At Militia's for wedding. Spectacular party . . ."

And the diary went on and on. Page after page, day after day, month after month. At the same time, the money started to run out. Apparently, the "new Kamchatka expedition" had not received the same degree of financial support as the one in 1920, when money was more or less showered on René Malaise. Diary entries showed that they started to sell their personal belongings in order to be able to buy meat, bear traps, and other necessities. Calle and René were forced to give up their much-needed Mora knives; Ester Blenda had to sell her jewelry. She telegraphed home asking for money.

The camera became an accidental savior. It had attracted both attention and curiosity ever since they arrived, and the villagers now offered to pay to be photographed. Those who couldn't pay in cash gave them milk and potatoes. The orders came hard and fast. Weddings, funerals, child portraits. The priest in the village, Bátuchka, also wanted to be immortalized by Ester Blenda. He stood completely still inside the church; the darkness called for an exposure time of twenty seconds. He didn't even blink.

Suddenly, the villagers also got the notion that people who had just died should be photographed. Ester Blenda thought the idea was repulsive and refused—until an acquaintance, Imilia Tíschanovna, came to beg for a picture of her dead mother.

> When a neighbor, from whom I am perpetually borrow-
> ing a sewing machine, comes and asks—with tears in her
> eyes—for this one little favor of photographing her dead
> mother, you cannot refuse for long. Not in Kamchatka.
> Not I. So Imilia Tíschanovna got the macabre photograph
> that she wanted, and I found it less difficult than I thought
> I would to point the camera at the tired, gentle, old face,
> which was beautiful where it lay with the icon on her
> forehead.

It was not as easy every time. And not as beautiful. But if I had photographed one, I could not deny the other without arousing much bad blood. That is not the done thing in Siberia. In a small village, where you only have each other, where all is shared equally. So I went with death in my heart and photographed death in all ages and forms. In the end, I got so used to it that a corpse hardly meant any more to me than it does to a funeral home.

From *Byn i vulkanens skugga* [*The Village in the Shadow of the Volcano*].

On April 2, 1926, Hjalmar Lundbohm had a stroke and collapsed at his brother's home in Fritsla, about forty miles east of Gothenburg. Two days later, on Easter Sunday, he died peacefully, at the age of seventy-one. The funeral service was held in Hedvig Eleonora Church in Stockholm—without the presence of one of the most important people in his life. No one knew how Ester Blenda mourned the "King of Kiruna," whose coffin was transported in a specially built railway carriage to his hometown and life's work. There were no notes in her diary, no remarks in any remaining letter. But René Malaise could see as clear as day that her heart was heavy with the news of this death. He interpreted it as heartache. Many years after his time as a married man in Siberia, he told Yvonne Malaise, his niece, that Hjalmar Lundbohm had been Ester Blenda's great love.

Hence, it appears that René didn't have a clue that her heart belonged to Carin. Barely six months after Hjalmar's death, she received more terrible news from home; this time, Ester Blenda did not recover. The heaviness settled like a lead weight in her body. On the worst days, she barely left her bed at all. She wrote, in a few words in her diary, that she just lay there.

Can a human implode? Break from within? Is this what happened to Ester Blenda in the late fall of 1926 in Kamchatka, when she found out that Carin had remarried? Her diary showed a sudden incidence of physical ailments. Fever. Stomach problems. Aches and pains here and there, completely without logical explanation.

Carin's new husband was Gustaf Hellström, the accomplished *Dagens Nyheter* correspondent and author who had been one of their common acquaintances since the beginning of the 1910s. Ester Blenda had gotten to know him during her time at *DN*, and Carin and Gustaf had had mutual friends in Stockholm's most affluent circles since youth, including the banker Ernest Thiel and his family.

How exactly did Ester Blenda get the message—and from whom? Was she completely unaware that this was going to happen? Did Carin choose to wait until Ester Blenda was far enough away from her every-day life, and for long enough? The questions pile up, but there are no answers. The sources stop here. None of the remaining material gives us any clues about the dramatic entanglement. Gustaf Hellström was never mentioned in letters or other documents that were saved from Ester Blenda's life up to the time in Siberia. He did not seem to have been a part of their shared life at all. But beyond this point, what was clear about Gustaf Hellström, aside from his prolific output, was that he seemed to have been known as a womanizer with a messy private life and a taste for booze.

During her most desperate moments, Ester Blenda looked up departure times of boats to Vladivostok where you could take the train to Moscow, then on to Helsinki and Sweden. She knew the exact moment when yet another boat would leave the harbor, when another chance to leave Siberia was lost.

In Kamchatka, there was no consolation to be had. You cannot be comforted for that which was not allowed to exist.

The letter she sent to Elin Wägner shortly afterward was desperate. No words could heal a broken heart, but there was some relief in sharing the pain with someone who knew how it felt. Elin's new love had just abandoned her with the clichéd words "I'm not the person you thought I was." Elin's answer also showed that she had been made aware of the secret relationship.

> My beloved friend,
> [. . .] That which has hurt you so much from the outside, I understand. This matter has only interested me from your perspective, and you can be sure that I agonized about you at the time when you were to have been informed. It's simply tragic, to the extent that she invests anything in this, and I suppose she does, poor devil [. . .] Yes, poor us who cannot help but hope that gambling for happiness will render us profitable in the end. Strange how we remain little toddlers [. . .] In your letter, I felt the solidarity and, as you put it, that we are in "the same boat." I am not comforted by the fact that you feel terrible, but it is partly a faithfulness and tenderness in your letter that makes me feel infinitely good, and partly a willingness to cope with the damn thing and to not give up.

She made something of an attempt to elevate the misery they shared to something higher and greater:

> It is often in grief that one perceives the most powerfully. So-called happiness makes one so self-absorbed. Sorrow makes one kind, once you have made it through the initial awful period, and it also makes one clairvoyant [. . .] I am in part writing to convince myself of this as well, that being beheaded has its benefits.
> You can come to me and stay with me next year, even though we are not really old women yet [. . .] What if you

and I could sit at our own machines once again with our backs to each other and plod on [. . .] Come home and let us be together.

Yours always.

From a letter from Elin Wägner to Ester Blenda
Nordström, December 11, 1926.

The cold pierced her face like a thousand needles. The rest of her body simmered under layers of reindeer hide as she shouted out her commands to the dogs pulling the sled over the trackless snow. She drove them on until they ran like crazy, as if they were afraid of their own shadows. The speed was dangerous, but physical pain no longer scared Ester Blenda. It was almost as if she wanted it, as if she were trying to evoke it.

Kamchatka's tundra bathed in the moonlight. Both the dogs and their driver were completely exhausted, down to every last muscle, by the time they finally returned to their yard. Ester Blenda stumbled out of the sled. A lone lamp shone over the kitchen table inside the house. She had no choice. She had to go in, pretend like nothing happened, and continue her life with René and Calle for one more year.

The ultimate adventure had proved incredibly costly. Ester Blenda married a man she didn't love to gain a spot in the historic expedition—and had to pay with the loss of her love. Now she was stuck in a shabby log house in a gray village in Siberia, alone with pitch-black thoughts and homebrew in her glass, having to photograph corpses to raise money for food.

CHAPTER 14

A Farm of One's Own

Days went by; weeks turned into months; winter turned into spring and summer. Ester Blenda resisted all her impulses to go back home. It was too late anyway. She'd lost Carin. There wasn't much else to come home to, either. Her friends in the League were busy with careers and marriages with varying degrees of happiness. Agda had been married for a few years now and had given birth to her first child, her daughter Cajsa, at the age of forty-four. Hildur had also found love late in life, gotten married, and moved to Borås, a village in the western part of Sweden, far away from Stockholm. Her nieces and nephew, Kjell, Anne-Marie, Birgitta, and Gunilla, were busy with studies, travel, girlfriends, and boyfriends. They no longer had time for their favorite aunt, Essan.

Ester Blenda and René's empty marriage was filled with frustration and opposing views. Both wrote long letters home to Frithiof, without telling the other what they had to say about their shared lives. Some letters were even written on the same day. The tone was intermittently harsh from both sides. René gossiped about how little his wife was working on her commissioned Kamchatka book and questioned whether it would ever come to anything. He was clearly no longer so in love that he was blind to the palpably loveless relationship. In one of the letters to Frithiof, René remarked that he probably received very different reports from each of them. And he was absolutely right. This was clear in several letters that remain and were preserved by one of Frithiof's grandsons after they lay unpacked and forgotten in a moving box up in an attic for several decades—the same box that held the answer to what happened to all of Carin's letters to Ester Blenda.

> Klyuchi, October 22, '26
> Dear, beloved little Fretsöpp—Many thanks to you for your annotated photo album. I can't think of a more suitable gift to send to your poor sister in exile.
> [. . .] I have captured some butterflies for you this summer, but René says he will send them, upon which he probably "forgets" to inform you that I had some part in capturing these. He usually prefers to take the credit himself, whenever the opportunity arises. "We have done all this ourselves," he says proudly when someone loudly admires our little dollhouse. But when "we" toiled until we nearly dropped last fall to get what we wanted—Mr. Malaise didn't do a thing other than go and get furious that the work was never completed. All he has done, as far as I can ascertain, was put hinges on two doors and burn a couple of cabinets with the blowtorch. But now, it turns out that he has done everything. His "we" can truly irritate. Often, as we are en route, he will lose something important—a whetstone, or some tongs, or something else that we cannot be without. Then when he is asked for the item, as he had it last, he calmly says, "*We* have lost it." Yes, goodness! He is so unbearable that it is almost dangerous to constantly have to carry such rage within.
> [. . .] He can never decide—it ultimately falls on Calle and me to tell him the best course of action. He is so

completely without any will himself that he prefers to obey someone else, someone stronger. I am happy to admit that I am in large part to blame for his remaining here, but I cannot help but realize that it is the most sensible thing for him. He is unable to do anything, would be no good in the labor market competition at home—he could possibly earn one hundred kronor a month to sit in a museum and tinker with butterflies, but he cannot subsist on such work [. . .] And I do not wish to take it upon myself to support him, either—I do not like him enough to do this. And that is exactly how it would go: he would go about being unhappy and useless, a horror to himself and others.

> From a letter from Ester Blenda Nordström to Frithiof Nordström, October 22, 1926.

Her last winter in Klyuchi turned out to be as unbearably long as Ester Blenda had feared it would. She had lived in Siberia for a year and a half—longer than she had stayed anywhere in her entire adult life—all while grief had eaten at her. It was as if it fed on her life force; there seemed to be a bit less left of Ester Blenda with each passing day.

In the spring, they started planning the trip back to Sweden; "the new Kamchatka expedition" would be disbanded. It was decided that Ester Blenda and Calle would leave Siberia together. René stayed put, with vague plans.

> Tuesday/Wednesday, June 9
> C. and I left Klyuchi forever, followed by friends and acquaintances who filled the beach, crying. The farewell was preceded by magnificent giftings of old clothes, etc.

Thursday/Friday, July 2
The train left Vladivostok.

From Ester Blenda Nordström's journal from her time in
Kamchatka, 1925–1927.

They traveled third class, all across Siberia to Moscow. From there, they went on to Finland. The journey back home took a month. Two and a half years had passed since she boarded the night train going south on an April evening and rolled out of Stockholm Central Station. On the way to the great adventure. The one that would become her last big journey.

The journalists were waiting, cameras ready, as the small pontoon plane from Helsinki landed in Stockholm. There was widespread clicking as she took her first gingerly steps down the steel stairs. Suit, hat, heels. Holding on tight to her welcome bouquet.

The star was back. But she no longer smiled as she usually did at the cameras. Her facial expression was pinched, almost irritated. There was something shy about the woman with everyone's eyes on her. Ester Blenda returned to Sweden a changed woman, with two heavy losses in her heart: Hjalmar, her best friend, and Carin, the love of her life. Soon, she would be forced to endure a third.

The picture adorned the cover of the forthcoming issue of *Vecko-Journalen*. Ester Blenda Nordström's return was major news. She was showered with questions. What had she missed the most? Where was her husband, René? The old Ester Blenda first came through when her travel suit, described as "ultrachic" in the article, was mentioned:

> Only four or five dresses were brought along to Kamchatka, and can you imagine I have not worn a single one. I have not worn a skirt in two years—always, always pants, wonderful! When I left, I gave the dresses to my neighbors' wives!

A journalist asked what she would do now. She responded: go home to some peace and quiet out in the countryside back with her mother, and write her Kamchatka book.

Back to Lotten, the constant anchor in her life. Back to the unconditional motherly love that stood as unshakably as ever. Mother Lotten, who, ever since the birth of her youngest daughter, had her as a favorite child and repeatedly told her as much in secret. In a letter, Lotten had written about their special relationship, saying things she urged Ester Blenda to keep quiet about when around the others.

Ester found the peace to work at the Ekefors mansion, where she discovered the words to describe her transformative time in Siberia. It was in many ways a poetic travelogue, filled with strong feelings about the beauty of nature and life outside of Western civilization with its imposed norms and conventions. But there was also a noticeable melancholy, heavily colored by the lonely village life where she was stuck with an aching heart.

> Nothing will ever be beautiful after this! Had this thought on the final night, when I stood on our porch step and watched Klyuchevskaya glisten in the moonlight, the white mountain slopes on the other side of the dark river. Nothing will ever be so dizzyingly, unbearably beautiful! Nothing as glorious as this desolate, wild, hospitable land, which receives with generous and open arms and gives with generous and open hands.
>
> When I think about it now, I see a lone trail over a snow-heavy tundra, a lone dog team pulling ahead on it, like a shadow passing under the stars. And in the silence, I hear a thousand sled dogs joining up to cry, causing a wailing and a wildness to fill the white expanses. The ground trembles—it is the volcano that erupts: it thunders in the air—it is the purge, which comes roaring.

A small village lies there, poor and miserable, slumbering in undisturbed peace. One narrow track leads there;
one leads out.

There was no more than this.

The epilogue in *Byn i vulkanens skugga* [*The Village in the
Shadow of the Volcano*].

René Malaise became the director of a Soviet sable farm in the
village of Yelizovo near Petropavlovsk. Strangely, he seemed to hope
that his wife would come back. In December 1927, he wrote in a letter
to one of his aunts: "Do not think that Ester Blenda and I separated as
enemies; on the contrary, and I am very certain she will return here."

But Mrs. Malaise had no plans to reunite with her husband. She'd
gotten what she went for.

Ester Blenda and Carin seemed to have completely ended all contact. She was not mentioned in any letters and was not found in any
photographs from this time. Gustaf Hellström had moved with his
second wife into the huge house with a view of Humlegården park. The
couple spent part of the year in the Stockholm archipelago, in Carin's
summerhouse on Utö. Gustaf thrived on the island; he had spent a lot
of time there in his bachelor years.

Was their marriage ever a happy one? Gustaf Hellström had his
own writing cabin on their plot of land where he shut himself in, often
all day, to work on his novels. Carin devoted herself to gardening. They
never had any children, but her nieces and nephews often visited them
on the island. They have since stated that Gustaf "despised them."

He still spent long periods in England as a correspondent for *DN*,
where he stayed with Carin's brother, Sven. Sometimes Carin joined
him, but she seemed equally happy to stay put in Sweden.

Ester Blenda's comfort from being reunited with her mother was
short lived. She was to be her third major loss. Lotten was seventy-eight

ESTER-BLENDA NORDSTRÖM
kommer hem från Kamtschatka,
se vidare artikeln inuti numret
Foto: Holmén

when she passed away in 1927. The child who had returned was sud-denly left alone in the big house—without money or any company.

The bitterness in her heart grew, and she did nothing to hide it; many family members have since testified to this. Family relations hardly improved when a majority decision was made to sell Ekefors. The siblings wrote to each other about how they needed to resolve Ester Blenda's housing situation before they sold it. It looked like they continued to take responsibility for their little sister, even though she was now thirty-six.

Once again, much of her everyday life was all about raising money, of which Ester Blenda was perpetually short. While writing her book, she "sliced off" new articles for several newspapers and magazines about her various travels. She also received shorter writing assignments: in her characteristic style loved by readers, she described what it was like to go see a real boxing match or to subject oneself to the hysteria of Christmas gift shopping.

The payments received for her articles kept her afloat—no more, no less. And she didn't write with any desire or joy. She hadn't done so in several years.

> Truth be told, I know nothing worse than writing. But once you get on that path and once people are kind enough to buy and read what you write, then [. . .] *Tent Folk of the Far North*. That was really fun to write. Actually, I think it is the only real book I have written—the only one that had a real point.
>
> From an interview with Ester Blenda Nordström in *Aftonbladet*, February 16, 1925.

In 1929, René also left Kamchatka and traveled back to Sweden. Their divorce was finalized that same year. Shortly afterward, the book *Byn i vulkanens skugga* (*The Village in the Shadow of the Volcano*) was published. Ester Blenda chose to write a dedication in the book about her time in Kamchatka:

> To My Big Sister
> With Love and Gratitude

This was her way of thanking her big sister Agda, one of the people who had most consistently been there for her through the many crises of recent years. René Malaise was not mentioned anywhere in the entire book.

> Ester Blenda Nordström: *The Village in the Shadow of the Volcano*. Bonniers. 6.50. It's been a long time since Ester Blenda Nordström came up with a book—a remarkably long time, one must think on reading her now-published Kamchatka tale, because she retains all her old storytelling joy and all her radiant quickness. But she has simultaneously matured. Granted, she never fell for the temptation succumbed to by her less intelligent successors in the girls' adventure industry: that of bragging about her own skill and initiative-taking. But there was previously something of an undeniably small conscious, though hardly distasteful, glimmer of self-satisfaction in her ability to brilliantly handle the most stressful situations. There is no trace of this in the book from the small gray village on the Siberian tundra. The author's own life and how it's lived have completely faded into the background—she is pure eyes and ears.

> From a review of *Byn i vulkanens skugga* [*The Village in the Shadow of the Volcano*] in *Dagens Nyheter*, December 15, 1930, signed E. B.

The health problems that had begun to emerge while in Siberia were getting worse. Throbbing headaches. Sudden fever spells. Toothaches. Hour-long, cramping stomach pains that came and went.

In the medical records, "poor diet" was noted as a possible reason. The cough and chest pain turned out to be tuberculosis. She spent eight months at the sanatorium (an early form of the present-day hospital) for nitrogen treatment.

In the Nordström family, the anxiety about Ester Blenda and her alcoholism was part of everyday life again. The day before New Year's Eve 1929, Hildur and her husband, Hjalmar, invited her to their home in Borås, along with Aunt Sofi from Varberg. It started off so well. Ester Blenda was in a good mood, singing and playing and telling everyone about her adventures. Everyone was happy, secretly relieved that it seemed that it would be a quiet New Year celebration. But once again, it ended in chaos and woes. This shows in a letter written by Hildur to her sister-in-law, Gerda, shortly after the visit:

> Yes, the little child [. . .] it was fun to have her here, and it went well, but I remained in an all-consuming state of anguish that something would happen, and I did not depart from her side for the entire day.

The next day, they accompanied Ester Blenda to her train and waved goodbye. Four hours later, she called and explained that she missed the train in Falköping. Her condition caused Hildur and Hjalmar to abruptly end a dinner party and throw themselves on a train headed in the same direction.

> And this was just as we were about to sit at the table and eat our little New Year's meal in peace and quiet. But this would turn into a different New Year's Eve than the one we had looked forward to. As luck would have it, the afternoon train up to Herrljunga hadn't yet departed, so we caught up with it at a brisk pace. Admittedly, she had threatened us over the telephone that if we intended to go up to Falköping, she would probably disappear from there

before we got to her, but we took this lightly, as she had no money—we advised her to go to bed instead.

They eventually found her in a hotel room, and she let herself be cared for.

No major disaster appeared to have occurred. However, I believe we are less clear on what could have happened if she had been allowed to stay there alone. Yes, poor little dear child—I do not believe that she will ever recover from this disease.

> From a letter from Hildur Nordström to Gerda Nordström, dated Day of Epiphany, 1929.

A maid among maids found

Where is Ester Blenda Nordström? Has she gone to a convent? She is not in any of the nation's telephone directories? Does she not intend to do something else? What is she occupied with? What are her whereabouts? What are her plans for the future?

It is Ester Blenda Nordström's audience asking. As you know, the audience has never been satisfied. It has long since consumed the book about Kamchatka, and now it wants a new one.

In a way, it is true that Ester Blenda Nordström has withdrawn from the world. Her health, which has not been all that good since the arduous years spent in Kamchatka, has forced her to move with more haste, less speed, and in a rural environment [. . .] "I am much fitter now and unimaginably, insanely happy about my little home," says Miss Nordström as she presents her house, with large, low rooms where the fires blaze [. . .] "Yes, I will be writing a book," Miss Nordström reveals once she has changed out of her overalls and wooden slippers and we settle before a giant fire.

From a report in *Vecko-Journalen*, no. 15 (1931).

As early as 1913, Bansai wrote in *Svenska Dagbladet* that women were fully capable of farming. It had been fifteen years since the hay-making in Värmland County with Elin Wägner, when she declared that she would become a farmer. Eleven years earlier, she'd received her diploma as proof of completed education at the country's largest agricultural school, where she was the only woman among 112 male students.

Since then, she had yearned and dreamed while applying her knowledge on farms in Sweden and America. In 1930, her dream became a reality—Sweden's most famous maid finally got her very own farm.

The land that belonged to the Bjursnäs estate that Ester Blenda rented was admittedly not included in the lease, but she had a large garden with several large plots to take care of, and her future plans for animals included at least one horse. A local girl, Klara, was employed as her maid.

The old red farm dating back to the seventeenth century was located on the narrow isthmus between two small lakes in Björnlunda, a town in mideast Sörmland. There was no telephone or electricity; the water had to be pumped up from a well. The nearest train station was roughly six miles away. The tiled ovens in almost every room were fired up as much as possible to keep the cold and moisture away. But the captivating beauty of the place, the palpable seclusion, and the house itself—equal parts farmhouse and mansion—made Ester Blenda feel

strangely at home right from the start. Her work overalls quickly got
dirty. Her hands filled with blisters that stung so much after hard work
with the crowbar, and with wounds from the ax that slipped while she
chopped wood.

Bjursnäs was Ester Blenda's first real home. She had turned forty
and had filled room after room with her life: exotic objects from all her
travels around the world; the old pine sewing table that belonged to her
mother, Lotten; paintings by her father, Daniel; all the instruments—
the violin, the accordion, and, of course, the lute with her grandfather's
old pearl-embroidered groom suit suspenders as a strap. There was a
portrait of Hjalmar Lundbohm painted by Albert Engström. In the
kitchen was the square coffee grinder that she'd received from Prince
Eugen in Lapland, and she'd hung up the photograph of her deceased
friend Anders Zorn on a wall.

The home became a motley mix of plain chairs and rag rugs, elegant furniture made of exclusive woods, and genuine Persian rugs that
Ester Blenda picked up when Ekefors was emptied before the sale. The
furniture pieces were heirlooms from both parents—the farmer's son
who managed to create a fortune, and the maid who found her way into
fancy salons without ever really seeming to thrive there.

She named each room: the Birch Room, the Book Room . . . In
the latter, light poured in from several directions over dark patterned
wallpaper; along the walls stood low bookshelves divided by one of the
windows where Ester Blenda had placed her heavy mahogany desk with
the typewriter on top. A gilded mirror atop a table rested against the
wall; a beautiful glass chandelier with four lights hung from the ceiling.
On a pedestal stood a bust of her made by her one-time close friend
Hjördis Tengbom when Ester was a young woman.

The salon had been decorated manor style with rosy wallpapers and
white-painted floorboards. Ester Blenda sat in there for a long, long
time and rocked slowly back and forth in her father's old rocking chair

while listening to Tchaikovsky on the gramophone, and the rain as it pattered against the window.

> By the way, it is fabulously beautiful and fabulously quiet and solitary here, with only a single tiny village road winding past, and on it are a few farmers with mill loads and milk bottles. I want it that way. I do not like people around me—when I want to meet people, I drive to town for a while; I get my fill and more. The whole time I'm there, I long to return anyway.

> From a letter from Ester Blenda Nordström to author
> and lawyer Henning von Melsted, July 7, 1931.

Ester would often lie naked to sunbathe on the cliffs between her lawn and one of the small nearby lakes. Trying to be happy. The German shepherds, Tiara and Rudolf, rarely left Ester Blenda's side; the cats, Noak and Chaplin, walked around her legs. She had a pig, too, named Jacob. He was as tame as the other animals, was taken for walks on a leash, bathed in the lake, and shared food bowls with the dogs and cats.

The reporter who had sought out the missing star asked whether it ever got lonely on a remote farm. What did she actually do all those long winter evenings?

> "Time is certainly passed with the book waiting to be written, and books waiting to be read, with Klara and the dogs. Furthermore, I go into town sometimes, and my relatives and friends come out for what we call scout camps."

> "[. . .] But do you not still long to go into the world, as you are used to traveling, seeing new countries, meeting new people, experiencing things?"

> "Nooo."

A more loaded response has never been given. It clearly comes from the depths of the heart of a person who is happy to be at home after all her fluttering around the globe.

For as long as it lasts. It would certainly be a great deal unlike Ester Blenda Nordström to stop, and I suppose we shall see what happens.

[. . .] It is unlikely that a lady, who by the age of forty has managed to be a maid among maids on two continents, a Lapp teacher, a tourist on donkey back over the Cordilleras, a bear hunter in Kamchatka, and many more things in many other places, will find herself spending the rest of her life sitting on a flowery manor sofa and playing the lute.

From a report in *Vecko-Journalen*, no. 15 (1931).

The *Vecko-Journalen* report took up a lot of print space and was published with several photos: Ester Blenda in overalls playing accordion on the front steps with a lit cigarette in her mouth. Sitting on her stairs in front of the entrance, with one of her German shepherds under one arm, the accordion under the other, and the still-burning cigarette sandwiched between her right index and middle fingers. All dressed up in the Book Room, leaning back among the cushions on the sofa with her lute in hand.

To the audience, she was much like herself in many ways. Slightly older, but the hair was still cut short into a youthful, curly pageboy. The confident, masculine body language. The mischievous baby-blue gaze. The cigarettes. But if you looked closely, you could see the deep furrow between the eyebrows. How the smile on her lips did not reach all the way up to her eyes. How her gaze had something hard about it.

At forty years old, Ester Blenda settled down on Bjursnäs farm in Sörmland with two dogs, two cats, and a pig.

The collection of empty bottles grew so large that she started to hide it on a separate part of the property, near the shore of the lake next door. It would take more than half a century before the bottles happened to be found by residents of the farm who started an excavation to build a sauna.

When the pain in her stomach became too severe, she took one more of the small brown opium cakes from the medicine cabinet, mixed it with water, and drank it in big gulps.

Leasing the Bjursnäs property was not cheap. The honoraria for the few freelance articles she could be bothered to write weren't enough. Frithiof opened his wallet as he'd done so many times before and wrote numbers in his black notebook.

Soon, it stole its way in. The loneliness. She was starting to have days when her voluntary isolation in the countryside turned into an unexpected source of torment. Ester Blenda tried to work herself to the point of exhaustion on the farm, turned up the volume on the radio, and darned socks. She wrote to Gerda about the anxiety and her tricks for numbing it. Apologized for being talkative and bravely tried to joke about how she had darned up to thirteen pairs of socks on some days.

It was at its very worst after all the visits. Her old friends Célie Brunius and Elin Brandell from the League had come and gone in turns. Also Elin Wägner, who read and gave her thoughts on the next part of the girls' book series that Ester Blenda was working on.

When Gerda and Frithiof's youngest child, Gunilla, went back home, the silence reverberated. The child, recently turned a teenager, periodically stayed with her godmother and wrote long letters home to her parents about the wonderful life at Bjursnäs with Essan. How she loved to spend time in her aunt's gnarled climbing tree where they'd attached ropes that you could balance on; how she rode Frigge, one of the farm's three horses; how she often sat with Klara, the maid, in the kitchen while Ester Blenda planted seedlings, cut hedges, sewed furniture fabrics, stained furniture, and patched up her work overalls.

The three of them went on little trips together. In the summers, they swam in the lakes and drank orange juice that Gerda sent along with her from Stockholm. When the ice settled in the winter, they skated and ate sandwiches. These were days when no socks were darned and the radio was completely silent.

Ester Blenda at Bjursnäs with one of her nieces and the tame pig, Jacob.

Ester Blenda was careful with bedtimes, encouraged her to do her homework so that Gunilla didn't fall behind at school, and guarded the girl with her life. If there was even the slightest sniffle, she forbade her to swim and pointed Gunilla to the iron bed with her whole hand. Insisted that everything on her plate must be eaten before playtime outside. When the child was on her own, the food often went untouched.

> There's a quiet, sad rustling in the trees tonight. They must be greeting you and mourning that you are so far away. I recently went out to the roses and placed my face against them to feel their wild tenderness—and my face became wet with tears. So I suppose they're crying too, because you're not here. A XX [illegible crossed-out content] rain is falling—so the sky is crying as well, because you were here

so it could see you, and then you left again. But everyone says hello—the rustling of the oaks and the dew of the roses and the little wet tears of heaven! And me! In whom it rustles, who is wet with dew and rain, and heavy with darkness. Who is sort of just alive because I love a dawn-gray pair of eyes and a gentle little voice. I, too, say hello among all the rest of the night's orchestra as it plays out here. But I suppose you can only hear my voice so faintly.

Was it a visit by Carin that made Ester Blenda write this infinitely sad poem in October 1930? It was written directly to someone, but the short name written at the top was illegible, crossed out with hard pencil lines. It was clearly never sent; it was still in the large suitcase with the sum of Ester Blenda's remaining belongings.

The fact that Carin had started visiting Ester Blenda at Bjursnäs was evident from Ester Blenda's remaining photographs from her time on the farm. Suddenly, Carin started to feature in the pictures, wearing a straw hat, casual cotton shirts, and carpenter-style trousers.

She sat on the porch steps, surrounded by all of Ester Blenda's animals, and on the cliffs overlooking the perfectly reflective lake. A bit fuller, with graying hair.

Ester Blenda and Carin. Together again. It had been more than five years since they separated in Japan. We know nothing about how the reunion took place. In the photographs, they sat close, holding each other—just like before—with that obviousness that exists between two people who belong together. They looked happy. But the wedding ring Carin received from Gustaf Hellström still shone on her right ring finger.

There was renewed applause from the reviewers when *Patron Ann-Mari* was published in 1931. The author's fictional alias had managed to graduate with very modest grades, just as she herself once did. After studying in Oxford, she bought a small croft with her inheritance money and started to fend for herself on a privately owned patch of land.

In the early 1930s, Ester Blenda and Carin were reunited. Here together at Bjursnäs.

Work on the next volume of the series began almost immediately. As a single woman, Ann-Mari managed to nab herself a place among 213 snuff-using farm boys in an agricultural training program. Because now she knew that she wanted to be a farmer. Ann-Mari rode a motorcycle, did a healthy amount of swearing, and lived an independent and modern country life in harmony with nature and her animals on the farm, all of which were individually named. She renovated the house herself and milked her cows. Once again, readers were fascinated by the independence, the courage, the perseverance.

Ester Blenda herself had traded her motorcycle for a sports car, a Willys-Knight.

Just like the previous parts, the fourth one—*Patron förlovar sig* (*Patron Gets Engaged*)—emerged in close collaboration with Elin Wägner, who turned fifty during that time. For Elin's birthday, the League put together a twenty-page tribute book with their collected memories of the Småland girl, newswoman, editor, author, peace fighter, and one of the Swedish women's movement's foremost figures.

Ellen Rydelius persuaded publisher Tor Bonnier to print five hundred copies for free. The now-iconic poet Karin Boye wrote a poem specifically for the tribute. She called it "Of Course It Hurts." Linnea, the housekeeper, also contributed and wrote about her everyday life with Elin. The text was added without the changing of so much as a punctuation mark.

Ester Blenda was given a whole page.

> I hardly know, Elin, which of all our shared experiences I remember most strongly [. . .] Now, when I sit and think back on all the years that have passed since I first met you—when I really think about it—I find that I no longer have to wonder which was the best part of our lives that we have shared together.
>
> Of course, it's Bön, the farm in Värmland.
>
> It is a beautiful summer to have among one's memories—don't you think, Elin? Thank you for this in particular, and thank you for everything else you have given me to remember of all that is beautiful and good and wise and real. I am so glad that you are only fifty

years old! We can still have many summers—and winters, too—before we become tired and worn, and decidedly start talking about memories. We can still gather many more, so that we will have a few more to talk about, when we meet in old age—I at your Little Björka and you at my Bjursnäs. In about twenty, thirty years, of course.

> From *Minns du?* [*Do You Remember?*] by Ester Blenda Nordström for Elin Wägner's fiftieth birthday celebration.

In the text, she looked to the future; in the present, she was tired and ill and severely alcoholic. In February 1933, Ester Blenda was admitted to a sanatorium. Her blood work was terrible; the main worry was her liver.

That same year, René Malaise remarried, this time choosing a teacher of biology and religion. He was planning a new expedition, to Burma, and was constructing an insect trap that would earn him a place in the history books: the so-called Malaise trap.

From the sanatorium bed, Ester Blenda wrote a long letter to one of her nieces who had met a man and was about to get married:

> My dear little friend—thank you for your sweet letter, which I would have replied to a long time ago, if not for the idiocy and apathy that grips one in this goddamn hospital, after a few weeks that have totally depleted all my energy; now, the writing of a letter is a far greater undertaking than a thousand-mile dogsled journey in Kamchatka ever was. But now I am to lie on my back for five days because of the albumin, and with that—the fact that I will be separated from the other idiots—I will become like a human being

again, able to say a sensible word to a human being. So to you right now.

[. . .] I sometimes feel that you and I are dangerously similar—dangerously so for you, that is [. . .] You have a bit of my devil-may-care attitude, which has done so much harm to me—and such an immense amount of good. More good, anyway, than harm, I think. For my carelessness with myself, you see, is more superficial than any of my highly valued siblings can appreciate—it is just that I get so tired of, and uninterested in, myself and could not give a damn about what I do [. . .] You have to be careful not to become like that [. . .] Now you have Georg, so I will not come to you with words of wisdom about men, of which rulers have passed through my life, and whom I have hurt the most. Because they do not understand—because they are little, little "tiny boys," whom you have to handle with care and who must be treated as if they were fully grown adults, which they never become, you see.

[. . .] I lie here, feeling like I am my own goddamn corpse. Because the people here make no sense; they are so lovely, you see, that the whole room is packed with flowers of all colors and shades, but not a single little stalk of what I long for most—violets.

[. . .] By the way, I have put a note on my door: "The patient is unconscious and doesn't come to until seven o'clock"—which had a magnificent effect [. . .] I have wonderful plans for summer work, but I haven't the energy to talk about it now. If anyone wants to rent Bjursnäs from me from June 1, they are welcome. As it stands. The damn maid got married and has gone. But that's probably good anyway. I dare not think about it, because then I get sentimental.

Yours, Essan

From a letter from Ester Blenda Nordström to Anne-Marie Nordström, February 28, 1933.

Once again, she put herself together. Spent a new spring back at Bjursnäs where April turned into an unusually warm May. The garden was buzzing with activity, and the head of the farm didn't miss a single detail. She watched the lilacs that were about to bud, noted when chestnut-blossom season was just days away, and how the scent of the lilies of the valley spread like a light cloud of perfume over the garden.

She solemnly plucked the last cowslips of spring, placed them in small vases in the house. It had gone too fast. She wrote to Gerda that she had been cheated out of spring, that she hadn't had time to enjoy every new flower that one was to enjoy. That she was so physically tender and fragile and couldn't bear to think about the nights.

That same year, the book *Patron förlovar sig* (*Patron Gets Engaged*) was published. The *Dagens Nyheter* reviewer, Gurli Linder, wrote that ever since Ester Blenda Nordström's "honest, knowledgeable, and intelligent" portrayal in *A Maid among Maids*, a number of books had been published about young upper-class ladies who had worn the overalls or uniforms of kitchen staff, babysitters, or waiters. She sarcastically pointed out that all the other girls' book heroines, despite their lack of any prior knowledge, had of course taken on their new roles with panache. But the stories had always ended in the same, traditional way: "Whether these ladies are lying on their fronts and cleaning up a garden plot or standing by the stove, a young man—usually of noble birth or great wealth—always walks by, discovers the disguised princess, and falls in love with her."

The writer seemed deeply tired of the mass-produced endings and paid tribute to Ester Blenda, who showed "a completely different level of respect and groundedness in reality" following her own time as a maid on a farm.

Over fifteen years after having the idea of dressing up as a maid and writing about her experiences, Ester Blenda was still the "maid" in the eyes of the Swedish people. And despite the fact that she also let her fictional character fall in love, the reviewer dared to call it "salubriously free from nonsensical talk, neuroses, and strange complexes."

Another *Dagens Nyheter* writer, Eva von Zweigbergk, stated that Ester Blenda's little rascal was about to become as immortal as the girls' book legend Anne of Green Gables by Lucy Maud Montgomery.

The Nordström family's sense of pride was immense. Ester Blenda said that she had an idea ready for the next book and was, for once, looking forward to starting the work of writing it. But there would be no new Ann-Mari book going forward. And despite the fact that one of Sweden's biggest publishing houses would reprint the beloved series almost twenty years later, and even though *Dagens Nyheter* subsequently concluded that "*A Little Rascal* should be on every Swedish girl's bookshelf" in connection with the publication, both Ester Blenda Nordström and her beloved character faded into obscurity.

Instead, a new children's book author would step into the arena and be celebrated for her inventive and innovative characters. The author Astrid Lindgren was clearly inspired by Ester Blenda Nordström. Or are the similarities between Ann-Mari and Pippi Longstocking, whose first tales were published twenty-eight years apart, a mere coincidence? Both girls are uniquely kindhearted, brave, energetic, rebellious, independent, and "boyish," and they challenge norms and conventions. They have no vanity, do not care for nice dresses or whether they'll get dirty, have no parents, and are seen by the public as uneducated and more wild than is deemed appropriate.

Many of their odd and startling feats are also remarkably similar. Ann-Mari, for example, jumps on horseback in a circus and does the most daring tricks that take the audience's breath away. Pippi also shocks a circus audience when she jumps up on horseback behind circus princess Miss Carmencita and outshines her.

There are many more overlaps, even when comparing Ester Blenda Nordström's Ann-Mari with Astrid Lindgren's other children's books. Inspired by the inventions and pioneers of the times, such as airplanes and pilots who were hailed as heroes, Ann-Mari takes to the roof with an umbrella in one of the books. She wants to try to fly and flings herself off. This also becomes one of the most famous scenes in Astrid Lindgren's book *Madicken på Junibacken* (*Meg of June Hill*). Both characters hurt themselves but aren't particularly scared afterward. In another one of her escapades, Ann-Mari takes her nasty and mean teacher's bike and hoists it up a flagpole. Emil of Lönneberga does the exact same thing but is helped by little sister Ida. Ann-Mari scares the snobbish and overbearing priest's wife with a rat. Mrs. Petrell in *Emil of Lönneberga* is subjected to the same treatment by Emil himself.

The remarkable similarities weren't publicly noted. It wasn't Ester Blenda's Ann-Mari who went on to enjoy immortality—it was Astrid Lindgren's Pippi. After the publication of *Pippi Longstocking* in 1945, Astrid Lindgren was the one who was given credit for having created what would be called "The first modern children's book."

A controversial dissertation calling for historical revision first appeared half a century later. Both Ester Blenda Nordström and the Danish author Karin Michaëlis, who published a similar girls' book series about the character Bibi between 1929 and 1939, are highlighted as clear predecessors of Astrid Lindgren. Especially Ester Blenda, who was the first of the two.

According to the dissertation, the similarities between the works of Astrid Lindgren and Ester Blenda Nordström texts are so striking that it was difficult to conclude anything other than that they represented "conscious loans." According to the author of the dissertation, Astrid Lindgren did not create a new girls' book tradition—she wrote her way into an already existing one.

In September 1934, Frithiof and Gerda received a phone call. A doctor introduced himself and informed them that Miss Ester Blenda Nordström, then residing at Bjursnäs farm, had taken an overdose of sleeping tablets and was under close supervision.

> Bjursnäs on 9/20/34
>
> Dear little Gerda [. . .] So sorry that the doctor scared you so, but it was probably mostly my own fault for scaring him. Because I thought the devil was going to take me then and there, and thought it best that you were informed. I could not possibly remember Agda's new number—and still couldn't—without a thinking apparatus that is intact, which I didn't have just then, so I gave your number because I knew it.
>
> [. . .] You yourself can appreciate that once you take too much barbital sodium, your reasoning faculties are not what they need to be. In any case, it wasn't so bad [. . .] On Thursday, I was completely clear upstairs again, and I ate something. On Friday morning, the nurse left; I lay alone as usual [. . .] One is alive. And it was neither alcohol nor opium that took it out of me, but simply a bit of calming medication, which I took too much of so that my stomach would not hurt so much [. . .] Now you know how I feel, and no wonder there is a worried look on my face. Bye!
>
> Yours, EBL.

In a handwritten postscript at the bottom of the typed sheet, it says:

> I do not mean to take my life—when I read through the letter, it almost seems so. God knows what I'm going to do, because I certainly don't know. But for goodness' sake, do not think that I am threatening to do anything like that—it's just my way of speaking in strong terms, as you know. Greet everyone for me.

From a letter from Ester Blenda Nordström to Gerda
Nordström, September 20, 1934.

She promised the family that she would give up on alcohol, or at least cut down, and take care of herself. Carin took Ester Blenda to her summerhouse on Utö, forced her to drink cream to gain weight, and took her out for splendid dinners at the inn where they were looked after by waiters in white.

After 1935, Ester Blenda was free to join Carin on the island. At the time, Gustaf Hellström was banned, even threatened with murder by the locals, after his latest novel *Storm över Tjurö* (*Storm over Tjurö*) was published. The outrage was sparked by the fact that he was said to have written about real people and events on Utö. Carin was also furious with him. Their marriage was exceptionally frosty at this time.

In 1936, Ester Blenda turned forty-five. While the family and Carin had prepared a surprise party with salmon, stuffed olives, and dancing, the celebrant had secretly increased her self-medicating with opium. She thought they couldn't see it.

Stockholm, Kungsholmstorg 3a
11.1.36
Mr. Professor H. C. Jacobeaus, Sthlm.

My sister, Miss Ester (Blenda) Nordström, has recently come into the professor's care; you have already admitted her into your care once, several years ago. The professor is thus aware that alcohol abuse has been present for many years, at times quite troublingly so.

I now consider it my duty to inform you that since we, her siblings, have prevented the use of spirits as far as we are able, she has resorted to opium in the form of opium cakes dissolved in water. This has probably been going on for a few years before we have come to make this finding and has been impossible to prevent in an effective way. It has probably contributed to her current poor condition with stomach aches and other ailments.

My poor ill sister is aware that I have made the professor aware of this [. . .]

With highest regard

Frithiof Nordström

Registered dentist

Tel 531 699

Frithiof's black book filled up. Still, he didn't write down all the costs and expenses—far from it. Carin acted as guarantor for bank loans and lent her own money for the Bjursnäs lease, and for food. Income was basically nonexistent for Ester, and her next book was still only in her head, assuming it was anywhere at all. She didn't have enough energy. The Zorn portrait was put up for sale.

The dream of a quiet, independent life on her own farm was about to go up in flames. One last hope remained: the Swedish Academy. They quietly distributed funds to writers in need. The letter that Ester Blenda wrote was a desperate cry for help. It was addressed to the person in chair no. 7, the Academy's only woman: Dr. Selma Lagerlöf, the first woman ever to have won the Nobel Prize in Literature. The answer that came back was handwritten, but concise.

> 1/25/1936
> Miss Ester Blenda Nordström:
> I have made a supplication on your behalf to the Academy and will notify you as soon as I receive an answer.
> > Your devoted
> > Selma Lagerlöf

Despite repeated appeals to Selma Lagerlöf, money from the Swedish Academy never came.

And then Ester Blenda had a stroke.

CHAPTER 15

The Catastrophe

Her legs could no longer carry her. Paralysis of the left arm and hand. According to records from the Seraphim Hospital in Stockholm, the mobility of her shoulder joint was also severely limited, probably after a fall from the stool back home in Bjursnäs when she had her stroke on January 4, 1937. The patient was very thin.

One of the things she asked for when she woke up for the first time was for someone to go to her place and fetch her favorite pink silk nightgown. The one she got from Carin. The family members took turns sitting by the hospital bed through the transition from winter to spring. They placed cool hands on her hot forehead, lifted her legs and arms every day so they didn't waste away.

It took months of trying before Ester Blenda took a few staggered steps without a wheelchair or crutches, and before she managed to lift her arm that had only hung limply between her knees since she collapsed.

She had tried to find her way back to herself, joked, and told her niece Birgitta, who would visit her at the hospital, that "she needs to run over some old lady in the corridor with the wheelchair, just to make something happen." But that was not enough. The fall into darkness couldn't be stopped. When she put the paper in the machine, she knew exactly what she wanted to say.

> I BURNED MY CANDLE FrOM BOTH ENDS
> I burned it nzght and day.
> I DON't REGRET ONE BIT OF IT:
> THOUGH IT's CEASED SHINING IN MY PIT
> For oh, my dear, my precious one
> withwhatmagnificence it shONE!
> YES: THIS IS NOT A LONBG DITTY: BUT IT IS
> FROM THE HEART. I
> Regret NOTRHING AND LIFE HAS BEEN GOOD
> TO LIVE ON THE WHOLE, AND GIVEN ME much
> more than it has taken.
> I would gladly have every moment again apart from the
> last three months.

> From an undated letter after the stroke—from Ester
> Blenda Nordström to Frithiof and Gerda Nordström.

Writing her own farewell speech took several hours. Her fingers no longer obeyed her; they slipped off the keys. Uppercase and lowercase letters were jumbled; punctuation floated freely within large spaces between words.

The letter was addressed to the Nordström family, Kungsholm Square. But when Frithiof read the fateful lines from his youngest sister, his first feeling didn't seem to be fear over what drastic measures she might take—he grew livid and wrote back on the same paper:

> *You burned your candle from both ends,*
> *you burned it day and night*

If given more, those too you'd end
with joy, glee, laughter and delight.

But did you ever stop to think
What grief you caused your mother dear
Or father and siblings whose hearts would sink
and suffer more than you could fear?

Maybe it was his painfully sincere lines that shook her; maybe it was Carin's decision after the stroke. Something stopped Ester Blenda from completely letting go of life.

The "catastrophe," as she called it, had deprived her of almost everything—but it returned her life partner to her. Carin was now divorced and hardly ever left Ester Blenda's side. She never would again.

Gustaf Hellström didn't appear to mourn his broken marriage for very long. The divorce was barely finalized before he remarried a doctor's daughter from Gothenburg.

Before the summer of 1937, Carin hired a private nurse so that they could be on Utö island together. They moved out there in May. In her large villa, Carin prepared Ester Blenda's favorite food and baked fresh bread to go with their breakfast coffee. Every other morning, she heated up water from the ocean with the nurse's help and filled a tub of bathwater that they then lifted Ester Blenda into. Afterward, Ester sat on a chair in the shade and practiced bending her fingers. She took slow walks along the island's trails, using a cane.

Some days, even her hoarse laughter returned.

Utö 8/4/37
Sweet little darling—thank you for a long wonderfully written machine letter. Yes, you certainly need common sense, and all your fingers, to construct something legible in this ganre [*sic*], and it goes so-so only a fist and an

excruciatingly painful back [. . .] I dare say better and better day by day, to some extent. I have taken a long lovely seawater bath, and managed to float a bit once Carin and the nurse could be persuaded to let go [. . .] I forgot to say, that my arm is strong too—I pulled the nurse up from time to time, and was as proud as a rooster [. . .] for next year, I've been thinking that C. could buy a car and we could go to Greece. It's about time for us to take a little look at that country, and this is always best done by car.

From a letter from Ester Blenda Nordström to Gerda
Nordström, August 4, 1937.

Frithiof and Gerda also received letters from Carin. They were written and sent in secret, when Ester Blenda wasn't looking. Carin knew that there would never be a trip to Greece. In the letters, she talked about the fainting spells, the epileptic seizures, and the long nights when she and the nurse had to hold on, calm her down, and stay awake.

Utö on September 26, 1937
Dearest Gerda—thank you for calling—it is always wonderful to hear your voice [. . .]
Last night there was a new attack [. . .] Thank God, Ester Blenda knows nothing about this; today she is only talking about how she woke up last night and stood up & fell over and that she has a severe headache. Yes, dear Gerda and Frithiof—what are we going to do? [. . .]
Goodbye for now—warmest regards, C. H.

From a letter from Carin Hellström to Gerda
Nordström, September 26, 1937.

Things got better. But not good enough.

Was the decision voluntary?

> To Stockholm City Hall Court.
> The undersigned, Ester Blenda Elisabeth Nordström, hereby requests, as I need someone else's assistance to handle my affairs due to illness, that I be declared incompetent and that my brother, dentist Frithiof Nordström, be appointed my guardian.
>   Stockholm, March 23, 1938.
>
>   Ester Blenda Nordström's petition to Stockholm City
>   Court to be declared incompetent.

They usually called it fun money. The type you could use for newspapers, cigarettes, and a good lunch in town. Ester Blenda didn't have to tell Carin what she did with it. It was handed to her only once a month and that was that.

Carin knew how much it frustrated Ester Blenda to constantly have to account for expenses, however small, to Frithiof. Saw how small all the apologetic explanations made her feel. About how she'd had more butter and cookies than usual, or how she had taken a taxi home again because she hadn't the strength to lift herself into the new trams that didn't have handrails at the doors, now that she had started walking again.

In the end, Carin took over the accounts so that Ester Blenda didn't have to. She went through receipt after receipt in the pile and wrote down the figures on the notepad that was always out on the desk.

Summer, late 1930s. The stairs at the rural Lilla Björka house were tarred and had an overpowering smell. Ria Wägner, Elin Wägner's niece, sat quietly close by, listening to the stories about South America, Kamchatka's harsh tundra, the car trips through Spain . . . Ester Blenda described dramatically, swearing and gesturing as best she could with her stiff arm.

Ria laughed, but the darkness that surrounded them was unmistakably palpable. Many years later, she would describe the moment as feeling like she was seated next to a legend whose wings had been clipped. Elin had said, with sadness in her voice, that Ester Blenda was merely a shadow of her former self.

> The times I sat next to her and we talked, she was very ironic about everything. Not cynical, I would not say that. But she looked upon life as if from a distance, with a certain somewhat absent feeling, I think. But to me, she was the funny, intelligent, slightly ironic person that I thought it fun to sit and talk to. Of course, I was also influenced by the fact that I had heard so much about her. Even then, in my mother's circle of friends, she was a legend. Everyone talked about how fun it had been, how quick she was, how she went for what she wanted. And I could sense that somehow in our time together. I was simply impressed with her. I think she was unusual.
>
> Ria Wägner speaks on the program *Historia att minnas* [*History to Remember*] on P1, September 8, 1995.

Her body had been severely affected by the blood clot. A fraction of the furniture from Bjursnäs, the most essential pieces, had been moved to a small two-room apartment with a kitchenette on Vikingagatan 34 E in Stockholm. The apartment, owned by a foundation, was rented out cheaply to old and sick people who couldn't afford any other accommodation.

Carin still lived with her now-elderly parents in the huge house on Karlavägen but spent almost as much time on Vikingagatan. She sorted out medication, forced Ester into a woolen jacket when it was cold, persuaded yet another private nurse who'd been yelled at by Ester to stay a bit longer. Knew exactly how the support cushion needed to lie on the left side of Ester's favorite armchair to relieve the pain in her arm. After the fainting spells, she mixed brandy with soda water on request. Ester Blenda said it stopped the postfaint symptoms.

But it wasn't all about the disease. In late spring, they moved to Utö and stayed for so long that they were able to pick mushrooms in the forest before returning to town.

Afterward, Carin would remember all the quiet dinners when the mosquitoes danced around Ester Blenda's freckled face and bare ankles. The endless hours spent in the garden where Ester Blenda knew the name of every single flower. How they laughed when the navy practiced shooting out by the fjards; the shots had such impact that Ester Blenda said it "shook her rear right where it was sitting." Or how her life partner sometimes surprised her by ordering her favorite cakes from the bakery next door.

They were almost always alone. Ester Blenda no longer wanted to meet old friends. Only close family could come by. In 1940, her sister Agda passed away, at only sixty. Her death took its toll. In a letter before Ester's fiftieth the following year, she pleaded with Gerda and Frithiof to cancel the planned dinner to which several of her acquaintances had been invited. She just wanted her own quiet evening at home and wrote that Carin "promised to pay for a nice little extra-lavish meal."

Years went by. Heat packs in bed. Sleeping pills. Nightmares. Sugary cookies and morning tea. Joint pain. Fainting spells. New beautiful summers on Utö.

Frithiof seemed relieved about the shared responsibility. At Christmas of 1944, he was effusive in the letter he sent (along with a hyacinth) to Carin's home address. She was able to compose herself enough to write back, after the hyacinth had grown so long and heavy that its crown fell right off, dropping next to the vase. Judging by the answer, she was frustrated that they didn't understand the obviousness of her actions.

> Dear Frithiof, your words were much too appreciative, and I feel almost embarrassed [. . .] And it is probably also the case that I feel indebted to Est.Bl—and in the same manner in which all of us who are close to her do—we only pay back what we owe—
>
> She gave of her abundance, and she did so with the utmost generosity. I have her to thank for the most carefree moments in my life, and I will never be able to repay my debt—so there!

> From a letter from Carin Hellström to Frithiof
> Nordström, January 6, 1944.

In the same year that Carin wrote the emotional lines, Elin Wägner was elected as a new member of the Swedish Academy. She would be the second woman ever to be admitted to the conservative coterie, after Selma Lagerlöf. Elin Wägner had just completed work on a lengthy novel, *Vinden vände bladen* (*The Wind Turned the Pages*), and was named one of Sweden's leading novelists of the first half of the century. But she was equally significant and influential as a feminist, pacifist, and cultural critic. At the Swedish Academy's weekly meetings in the Stock Exchange Building, she met Gustaf Hellström, who had been sitting in chair no. 18 for a couple of years now. His twentieth book had just been published. *Storm over Tjurö*, the book that had made him persona non grata among both Utö dwellers and his then-wife, was considered one of his foremost works.

Carin and Ester Blenda during a holiday in Norrland in the mid-1930s. Both are approaching their fifties.

Vecko-Journalen wrote a large photo report about Evert Taube, who had just published another song and poetry collection, consolidating his position as Sweden's national bard.

John Landquist was no longer just an outspoken literary critic and cultural director at *Aftonbladet*. He had also become a professor of pedagogy and psychology and would very soon become even more famous for completely bashing Astrid Lindgren's children's book character Pippi Longstocking, describing her behavior as "insane." On the other hand, he openly celebrated the policies of Hitler and the Nazis.

Alongside his long career as a dentist, Frithiof Nordström had published two books about the Swedish butterfly fauna. His single-minded collecting of large Swedish butterflies resulted in an atlas of roughly one thousand species. He was regarded as a central figure in butterfly research and was awarded an honorary doctorate of philosophy at Uppsala University for his contributions.

The year 1944 was also when the new housemaid law was introduced in Sweden. The country's maids were given regulated working hours, days off, and the right to take vacation. It had taken many years of long discussions to bring the new law into being. And it all started with a series of sensational reports in *Svenska Dagbladet* by a young female journalist who did something as groundbreaking as put on a headscarf and work her hands to shreds on a farm undercover, all so she could describe the maids' grueling work.

Thirty years later, the same journalist was sitting at home at the kitchen table, spreading thick layers of butter on her cookies to try to gain weight. With her idiosyncratic sense of humor, she wrote to her brother that she was "starting to get wide around the hips and expensive to run." *Dagens Nyheter*, where a new generation of reporters had taken over the columns, was always on the kitchen table.

The female journalists still had to fight hard to claim space with subjects that weren't housework, fashion, and family life. One of them was Barbro Alving, also known as Bang, who followed in the footsteps of the League and Ester Blenda. Several decades after the League's struggle for female journalists to become foreign correspondents, Bang reported from the Berlin Olympics and the Spanish Civil War. During the ongoing Second World War, she was in Norway, where she traveled on skis, for lack of other means of transport—just like Ester Blenda did during the Finnish Civil War.

Fifty million people around the world lost their lives as a result of the conflicts; about six million of them were European Jews murdered by the German Nazis. They were tortured to death in gas chambers, persecuted, and shot on open streets or in death marches during evacuations from concentration camps as Soviet and Allied troops approached.

But Ester Blenda's world seemed to have shrunk right down to the neighborhood around the apartment on Vikingagatan. She didn't, for instance, comment on how the places she once visited and lived in were being affected by the ongoing world war in a single letter sent to Frithiof and Gerda—and the letters were many in number at this time. Kamchatka, once her home for two years, had become a military zone. The area was used as a base for the recapture of the Kuril Islands chain, which runs from the southern tip of Kamchatka to the northeastern part of Hokkaido, Japan.

Impermeable border fences were being built between Finland and Russia, forcing the Sami people who were previously able to move freely across the border to choose whether they wanted to become Finnish citizens or to submit to Russia. The reindeer-herding Sami also went to war and fought. There were several reindeer battalions in the Soviet army.

Entire cities in Japan, which Ester Blenda and Carin explored together for five months, were bombed to smithereens. Soon, two more would be annihilated once US President Harry S. Truman ordered the dropping of the first nuclear weapons in war history, the atomic bombs over Hiroshima and Nagasaki.

But Ester Blenda was painfully aware of her own uneventful life in comparison with those of her former friends, as was clear from a few lines in a letter sent to her brother in 1947:

> Elin's new book is magnificent. I am as happy as a fiddler about it. She's sixty-five, as are you, so the academy was truly blooming. Gustav Hellström (sixty-five) has written his first play. Elin has written a great historical novel, which was solid as hell. And here I am, wanting to play the world's smallest violin, and everything aches, and it makes me furious.

That same year, Prince Eugen passed away. In another letter to her brother, Ester Blenda mournfully concluded that the last link that connected her to Hjalmar Lundbohm was gone and that the prince had always been a "good and solid friend."

Her isolation from the outside world was the beginning of the end. In the coming years, basically nothing worked. Not her body. Not her finances. Not the private care she received at home in the apartment. Not even the relationship with her family. In the end, it seemed only one person in this world understood her.

> The fact that she rages like a beast and sprays us with invectives does not mean that she hates us, but that she hates herself—her miserable, hopelessly destroyed, and maimed self. If she hungers for food or cigarettes at that, she sees even more red, of course. And no wonder! I still cannot help but admire her for continuing to rage and fight against this terrible fate—it would be so easy to open the gas valve or to resort to some other desperate measure. But she perseveres and tries to cope with life, despite being in constant pain—and in a way I think it was good of her to have done so.

> From a letter from Carin Hellström to Gerda
> Nordström, August 30, 1948.

The voice. It had become so deep, hoarse, and dark that it almost frightened the youngest members of the Nordström family, who politely took her limp hand and bowed and curtsied deeply at family gatherings. The last few times she bothered to join in, she didn't say much. The adventure in her eyes had gone. But the respect for her was immense—everyone knew, even the small children knew, that Ester Blenda was Sweden's bravest journalist only a few decades ago.

She knew she didn't have much time left. To her niece Birgitta, she said, just before her death, "Now, I will die." She simultaneously announced that she wouldn't be needing any hymns at the funeral as this would be "too fancy" for her. On the other hand, she wanted a broadside written by a Swedish maid in Chicago and the old sailor shanty *"Adjö, farväl! För sista gång"* (Adieu, Goodbye! For the Last Time), which she'd once asked Evert Taube to send her before the trip to Argentina.

On October 15, 1948, Ester Blenda Nordström died from complications of pneumonia, aged fifty-seven. She passed away peacefully at the Seraphim Hospital in Stockholm. In a letter to Elin Wägner, Gerda wrote, "She just stopped breathing, so quiet and strange."

Stockholm, November 1948

She walks around the tiny apartment. Her legs know where to go, even though the objects and the furniture are not her own. But it is, in a way, her home too. She knows exactly how things are organized in the kitchen cabinets and drawers; she personally sorted the pile of receipts lying on the desk, held together with a large clip. She knows exactly where the favorite nightgown hangs, the pink silk one. She would know at once if the armchair were at a different angle or if someone had moved the two black antique chairs by so much as an inch. Then the scent, *that* scent that every home has, unique to itself. It's also in her own clothes.

Only the silence is new. The Swedish state-run telecommunications agency has terminated the subscription for number 31 93 93. The name on the door will soon be replaced by a new one. The owners of the building have a long list of people desperate for an apartment.

She looks at everything for the last time. The typewriter on the solid mahogany desk, the rows of books, the accordion, the violin, and the lute with the pearl-embroidered strap, the vanity that's been passed down, the beautiful glass chandelier with four lights . . . Soon, it will all be scattered among Ester Blenda's relatives.

The gold cigarette case with an engraved Lapland motif will apparently be going to a nephew. She thinks of the number of times she's seen Ester Blenda open it, place a cigarette between her lips, light it up, and hungrily take the first puff. Then let it hang there, softly, in the corner of her mouth, while digging in the dirt or reading a book. The walls and furniture still smell strongly of smoke.

She looks for the letters before she leaves. She takes back her own words and puts them in her bag. Then Carin shuts the door to Vikingagatan 34 E.

Can you believe that there is something like this place? With blue lakes, which the sun shines on and sparkles on and dances on, and out over the water stand fiery trees reflecting themselves—aspens and birches like flames, and reeds that swish. That stand and swish all by themselves and pretend that there is wind. But there is no wind. The smoke rises straight up from the chimney and only vibrates in small, small bends next to the chimney, before it heads straight toward the sky. I should like to be a column of smoke rising to the sky today—rising and rising, until it is suddenly gone, until it is dissolved in all the blue and gold up there. Or I should like to be a reed, a golden straw among the others, and swish with them. Or a red aspen leaf trembling above the water. Or a rock, or a bit of moss, or anything at all—as long as I belonged.

From *Patron förlovar sig* [*Patron Gets Engaged*].

EPILOGUE

Carin and Ester Blenda were in each other's lives until the end.

They lived apart during periods of marriage, but Carin was always the person Ester Blenda returned to. In time, she became part of the Nordström family. Everyone is said to have understood.

According to relatives of Ester Blenda, her homosexuality was not a secret within the family, even though it wasn't talked about out loud. There seems to have been a quiet acceptance, as long as things were handled discreetly. Carin got to be Ester Blenda's "special friend," as Frithiof referred to her in a final letter to John Landquist several years after his sister's death.

Apart from the short poem that Carin wrote about Ester Blenda in a joint travel journal from 1919, there are no love letters to be found, in the traditional sense of that term. It has been speculated that a disapproving member of the family "cleaned up" that kind of "evidence" after Ester Blenda's death. But my research shows that it was Carin herself who, after Ester Blenda's death, went to the apartment on Vikingagatan and picked up the letters she had sent over the years. She wrote about it in a small card to Gerda Nordström, dated November 26, 1948, which was in a forgotten cardboard box in an attic at a relative's home.

It was the logical thing to do. Homosexuality was a punishable act in Sweden until 1944—almost all of Ester Blenda's life—and was medically defined as a mental disorder until 1979.

The villa on Karlavägen/Villagatan remained Carin Wærn Frisell's home for the rest of her life. She lived alone in the big house until her death in 1972. After her life partner passed away, she became, according to surviving relatives, a devoted Pentecostal and is said to have bequeathed a large part of her fortune to a free church congregation. Her house went to one of her nephews.

Almost four years passed between having the idea to write a book about Ester Blenda Nordström to completing the manuscript. I needed that amount of time to put the pieces of her life's puzzle together, and to understand her. Talking to relatives, plowing through archives, reading diaries and hundreds of private letters, and going through extensive photograph collections have provided increasing clarity with respect to the breadth of her complex and contradictory self. She was a social star with a luminosity that several people could attest to, while also being a child of nature who was drawn to the silence of the forest, the moody temperament of the sea, and the breathtaking views of the world of the fells.

She herself was like a whirling force of nature, in a constant war against order. Ester Blenda Nordström refused to live her life to please other people. She lived and loved uncompromisingly, on her own terms, and out of her own sense of curiosity—in violation of conventions, laws, and classifications.

To fit in and survive, she constantly switched between different identities, while never being allowed to live out her own in full. This seems to have created a sense of alienation, and to have driven a constant longing for genuine, unfalsified contexts. She grew to become a seeker and a loner looking to belong.

This lifestyle had a high price. She was slowly broken down by constantly challenging things, and by her lifelong struggle against the roles for women that she perceived to be claustrophobic. Her longing for children, which seems to have been very strong, was relentlessly pushed aside for a lifestyle in which children could not feature.

Sometimes, it got too difficult. Ester Blenda would break down many times. When that happened, the family, especially the siblings and her mother, Lotten, had to pick up the pieces and put her back together, to then helplessly watch as she would throw herself into the next mission, journey, or relationship.

They described her as "a goddamn ray of sunshine" in her youth, when she hadn't yet fully let the darkness and anxiety come through. Before alcoholism. Before the ailments. The "catastrophe" had not yet occurred.

Those close to her saw it early on. Almost everyone else seems to have considered Ester Blenda to be carefree and easy. This was also an image that she herself seems to have wanted to project. And then, in the beginning, the darkness was only present in the form of an internal restlessness, an anguish that could still be masked by a sly smile. Her need to self-combust hadn't yet taken over. The flame was there all her life, more or less under control. After the stroke, she herself used a candle burning at both ends as a metaphor for her lifestyle in her letter to Frithiof. In the end, she blazed so intensely that she burned up.

But the Ester Blenda Nordström we should remember and be inspired by is the pioneering reporter, the feminist role model, the brave world traveler. Untamed and with an almost insatiable curiosity about life.

FATIMA BREMMER
Stockholm, July 2017

ACKNOWLEDGMENTS

My first and biggest thanks to Forum, my publisher, and Adam Dahlin, the publishing director. Like me, he felt that this was an important life story to tell. No Adam, no book. To also have Adam as one's publisher is a blessing. He has lifted my narrative and has been able to identify what it would take to move forward and improve things throughout the work process.

Andreas Lundberg, my editor, has examined, questioned, and supported with an unfailingly professional perspective. He has also done a great job with all the pictures and handled all the external contacts needed to reach the finish line.

Pia Hylin and Mikael Sandberg, relatives of Ester Blenda Nordström, trusted me to examine the estate, letters, and other documents preserved within the family. Thanks to them, and other relatives of both Ester Blenda and Carin Wærn Frisell, some absolutely crucial pieces of the puzzle have fallen into place.

Anna Hylander, director of the film *Ester Blenda* and relative of Ester Blenda Nordström, has contributed with important research and manuscript reading. Our consensus and our conversations about Ester Blenda Nordström are things I valued highly right from the start of this process.

My husband, Magnus Bremmer, has spent many, many hours discussing narrative form, proofreading, and looking for logical gaps and incompleteness. He is the one who made me continue when I found reasons to give up. He has also conjured up time that doesn't really exist in our intense life as parents of toddlers, giving me the chance to write this book. My gratitude and love are infinite.

Ida Thunberg and Christina Larsson have read the manuscript with keen eyes and contributed with several wise viewpoints. Many thanks go also to Gloria Nneoma Onwuneme who translated the book into English, so Ester Blenda could reach the widest international audience.

I will carry the support received from family and good friends in my heart for the rest of my life. Completely biased, one hundred percent loyal, and constantly available to encourage and to cheer on. Love to you all.

The work has been financed with the help of generous contributions from the Stockholm Workers' Institute Association, the Helge Ax:son Johnson Foundation, and the Natur & Kultur Foundation.

SOURCES

All private letters without other reported sources belong to Pia Hylin or Mikael Sandberg, relatives of Ester Blenda Nordström.

Introductory and Final Sequence

- Stiftelsen Isaac Hirschs minne [Isaac Hirsch Memorial Foundation], www.sihm.se.
- Termination of telephone subscription, Miss Ester Blenda Nordström, Swedish state-run telecommunications agency.
- Inventory list, Vikingagatan 34 E; probably compiled by Frithiof or Gerda Nordström, 1948.
- Private letter to Gerda Nordström from Carin Frisell, dated November 26, 1948.
- Ester Blenda Nordström's private photographs from the years 1914 to 1948.
- *Målarmästare Daniel Johan Nordström och hans släkt* [*Master Painter Daniel Johan Nordström and His Family*]. Family chronicle compiled by Kjell Nordström between 1992 and 1995.
- Information about favorite pink nightgown taken from a private letter from Ester Blenda Nordström to Gerda Nordström.

Chapter 1

- All environmental descriptions and quotations taken from Ester Blenda Nordström, *En piga bland pigor* [*A Maid among Maids*] (Wahlström & Widstrand, 1914).

- "Massutvandring till Amerika hårt slag mot befolkningen" [Mass emigration to America hits the population hard], Historical Statistics, Statistics Sweden.

- Bansai, "Hemsköterskeidén väcker anklang" [The home-caregiver idea resonates], *Svenska Dagbladet*, September 4, 1912.

- Bansai, "Gott om platser—ondt om tjänarinnor" [Surfeit of vacancies—Shortage of maids], *Svenska Dagbladet*, October 14, 1913.

- Bansai, "En hemkonsulent om sitt arbete" [A home consultant about his work], *Svenska Dagbladet*, October 18, 1913.

- Private family photographs of Ester Blenda Nordström with family and friends.

- Ester Blenda Nordström's own photo album, 1914–1917, the National Archives' collections.

- Private photographs included in Ester Blenda Nordström's estate, belonging to Pia Hylin.

- Jogersta North Farm, "Slott & herresäten" [Castles & manors], 343.

- Anton Holtz, *Ett pennskaft som piga—svar av Bonn i Taninge* [*Newswoman for a Maid—Response by a Farmer in Taninge*] (Åhlén & Åkerlund, 1915).

- Information about Jogersta North Farm around the years 1914–1915 from its current owner, Anders Torgilsman.

- Ester Blenda Nordström, "Bilar som jag känt" [Cars I've known], *Vecko-Journalen*, no. 41 (1928).

- Information from the Car and Driving License Register, 1923 and 1924. Regarding driving license no. 4582, belonging to Ester Blenda Elisabeth Nordström, author. Belongs to Stockholm's city archives.

- Ester Blenda Nordström, "En långfärd på motorcykel med passagerare" [A long journey on a motorcycle with passengers], article series in *Svenska Dagbladet*, autumn 1914.
- Margareta Berger, *Pennskaft. Kvinnliga journalister under 300 år* [*Penholders. Female Journalists over 300 Years*] (Norstedts, 1977).
- Letter from Ingvar Holtz, son of Anton and Ida Holtz, Jogersta North Farm, 1993. From the autograph collection, manuscript collections at the National Library of Sweden.
- "En månad som tjänstflicka på en bondgård i Sörmland" [A month as a maid on a farm in Sörmland], *Svenska Dagbladet*, June 28, 1914.
- Letter from Ester Blenda Nordström to Ida Holtz, farmer's wife at Jogersta North Farm, dated July 17, 1914. From the autograph collection, manuscript collections at the National Library of Sweden.
- Letter from Ester Blenda Nordström to Sigrid Nilsson, maid at Jogersta North Farm, dated July 18, 1914. From the autograph collection, manuscript collections at the National Library of Sweden.
- Photographic portrait of Sigrid Nilsson; gift to Ester Blenda Nordström from Sigrid Nilsson, Jogersta, 1913.
- Eva Wahlström, "Fria flickor före Pippi—Ester Blenda Nordström och Karin Michaëlis: Astrid Lindgrens föregångare" [Free girls before Pippi—Ester Blenda Nordström and Karin Michaëlis: Astrid Lindgren's predecessors], dissertation for a doctorate in philosophy in the Department of Literature, History of Ideas and Religion, University of Gothenburg (Makadam, 2011).
- Margareta Stål, "Signaturen Bansai. Ester Blenda

Nordström—Pennskaft och reporter i det tidiga 1900-talet" [Bansai the pseudonym. Ester Blenda Nordström—Penholder and reporter in the early twentieth century] (Department of Journalism, Media, and Communication, University of Gothenburg, 2002).

- Eva Bäckstedt, "Bansai wallraffade i den lantliga lorten" [Bansai wallraffed in the bucolic muck], *Svenska Dagbladet*, May 10, 2002.

- Review of *En piga bland pigor* [*A Maid among Maids*], *Borås Dagblad*, December 2, 1914.

- Review of *En piga bland pigor* [*A Maid among Maids*], *Borås Tidning*, December 2, 1914.

- John Landquist, *In Youth. Scenes from the Lost Time* (Bonniers, 1957).

- Anton Holtz, *Ett pennskaft som piga—svar av Bonn i Taninge* [*A Newswoman for a Maid—Response by a Farmer in Taninge*] (Åhlén & Åkerlund, 1915).

- Bajsan (pseudonym), reader's letter in *Svenska Dagbladet*, September 1, 1914.

- "Bansais boksuccés" [Bansai's book success], *Svenska Dagbladet*, December 6, 1914.

- "Femte upplagan!" [Fifth edition!], *Svenska Dagbladet*, December 20, 1914.

- Anna Larsdotter, "Pigornas slit" [The toil of the maids], *Populär Historia*, May 22, 2009.

- "En piga bland pigor slår svenskt rekord" [A maid among maids breaks Swedish record], Museum of Gothenburg, Places with Stories.

- Henrik Agren, "När arbetet fick bestämma tiden" [When work began to determine the time], *Populär Historia*, March 13, 2002.

- "Ett socialdemokratiskt dilemma—Från hembiträdesfrågan till pigdebatt" [A social democratic dilemma—From the house help issue to the maid debate]. Text by Lisa Öberg in the anthology *Kvinnor mot kvinnor: Om systerskapets svårigheter* [*Women against Women: On the Difficulties of Sisterhood*] (Norstedts Förlag, 1999).
- Marco Smedberg, "Skyttegravskriget" [The trench war], *Militär Historia*, no. 2 (2013).
- "En piga bland pigor får premiär på Gävle teater" [*A Maid among Maids* premieres at Gävle Theater], *Dagens Nyheter*, September 8, 1917.
- "En piga bland pigor på scenen" [*A Maid among Maids* on stage], *Dagens Nyheter*, September 16, 1917.
- Various articles in Swedish newspapers in 1917 about dramatizations of Ester Blenda Nordström's book *En piga bland pigor* [*A Maid among Maids*].
- *The Motorcycle*, 100innovationer.com, exhibition at the Swedish National Museum of Science and Technology, 2012–2017.
- Bansai, "Med bilcertifikat på fickan. Litet om hur ett sådant eröfras" [With a car certificate in one's pocket. A bit about how to acquire such a thing], *Svenska Dagbladet*, March 16, 1913.
- "Ester Blenda Nordström 50 år" [Ester Blenda Nordström 50 years], *Svenska Dagbladet*, March 31, 1941.
- Royalenfield.com, "Royal Enfield" en.wikipedia.org, my royalenfields.blogspot.se.
- John Landquist, *In Youth. Scenes from the Lost Time* (Bonniers, 1957).
- Ester Blenda Nordström, "En historia från Montmartre" [A story from Montmartre], *Svenska Dagbladet*, June 1913.

Chapter 2

- Ester Blenda Nordström, autobiographical manuscript submitted to Märta Lindquist at *Svenska Dagbladet*, 1918.
- *Målarmästare Daniel Johan Nordström och hans släkt* [*Master Painter Daniel Johan Nordström and His Family*]. Family chronicle compiled by Kjell Nordström between 1992 and 1995.
- Information shared verbally by Ränte local heritage foundation, and written information from local sources about Daniel Nordström to Siw Svensson, Ljungby.
- Personal visit to the farm Åbyfors, Lagan, and conversation with the current owner, Gun Skoglund, October 2014.
- Personal visit to Villstad, October 2014.
- History of Lagan, Lagan.se.
- Photographs and documents about the Nordström family from Ljungby municipal archives.
- Information about Daniel Nordström with family and household from the National Archives, Censuses (Swedish population) 1880, 1900, 1910.
- Private family photographs of Ester Blenda Nordström with family and friends 1890s–1948. Some are included in the estate, and some are owned by relative Mikael Sandberg.
- Personal information and housing information about Ester Blenda Nordström from the Stockholm Population Archives, Stockholm City Archives.
- Private correspondence within the Nordström family, 1880–1960, various letters belonging to Mikael Sandberg.
- Interview with Ester Blenda Nordström in *Aftonbladet*, February 16, 1925.
- Private letter from Lotten Nordström to Agda Nordström, Ryafors, dated November 28, 18XX (year unspecified).

- Private letter from Frithiof Nordström to Hildur Nordström, Åbyfors, dated June 1903.
- Margareta Stål, "Signaturen Bansai. Ester Blenda Nordström—Pennskaft och reporter i det tidiga 1900-talet" [Bansai the pseudonym. Ester Blenda Nordström—Penholder and reporter in the early twentieth century] (Department of Journalism, Media, and Communication, University of Gothenburg, 2002).
- Ester Blenda Nordström, *En rackarunge* [*A Little Rascal*] (Wahlström & Widstrand, 1919).
- Ester Blenda Nordström, *15 år. Några blad ur en rackarunges liv* [*15 Years—A Few Pages from the Life of a Little Rascal*] (Wahlström & Widstrand, 1921).
- Daniel Nordström's patent for an electric rock-drilling machine for the Royal Patent and Registration Office, signed by S. A. Andrée.
- Deaths and life expectancy, Statistics Sweden.
- Kungsholmen Västra, Building Inventory, Stockholm City Museum, 1991.
- Private letter from Ester Blenda Nordström to Frithiof and Gerda Nordström, dated December 6, 1917.
- Ester Blenda Nordström's medical records, Karolinska Hospital.
- Seraphim Hospital, journal 447, December 1928, medical clinic 2.
- "Automobilen i Stockholm" [The automobile in Stockholm], *Svenska Dagbladet*, June 2, 1904.
- LO's salary report 2014.
- About the first motorcycle Hildebrand & Wolfmüller, tekniskamuseet.se.
- "En piga bland pigor skrev ej själv genmälet" [A maid among maids did not write the retort herself], interview with Ester

Blenda Nordström, *Aftonbladet*, February 16, 1925.

- Speech in connection with Sofi Nordström's funeral, written by Agda Nordström.
- "Elektricitet i Hakarps socken" [Electricity in Hakarp parish], wikipedia.org.
- Håkan Nordström. Portrait gallery from Småland, Project Runeberg.
- "Prosten Håkan Nordström avliden" [Provost Håkan Nordström deceased], *Smålandsstenar Nytt*, years 1932–1933.
- "Han var stadens första fartdåre—år 1900 . . ." [He was the city's first speed junkie—In 1900 . . .], *Svenska Dagbladet*, October 22, 2013.
- "Allt om DeDion" [All about DeDion]. Arvika car museum, www.bjorns-story.se.
- Otto von Friesen, Christer Hellmark, and Jan Stolpe, ed. *Tio reportage som förändrade världen–från Strindberg till Hemingway* [*Ten Reports That Changed the World—From Strindberg to Hemingway*] (Ordfront, 1982).
- Private letter from Agda Nordström to Frithiof Nordström, dated June 24, 1906.
- School grades of Ester Blenda Nordström, Wallinska skolan 1907, Palmgrenska Samskolan 1908–1909.
- Letter from Ester Blenda Nordström to Ida Holtz, dated July 17, 1914.
- Letter from Ester Blenda Nordström to Sigrid Nilsson, dated July 17, 1914.
- John Landquist, *In Youth. Scenes from the Lost Time* (Bonniers, 1957).
- Family anecdotes narrated by relatives Staffan Nordström and Mikael Sandberg, among others.
- Private letter from Lotten Nordström to Ester Blenda Nordström, undated.

- Private letter from Ester Blenda Nordström to Gerda Nordström, dated July 8, 1910.
- The information that the family often described Ester Blenda Nordström as "a goddamn ray of sunshine" comes from the author Otto von Friesen. He was told this during an interview with Birgitta Hylin, Frithiof Nordström's daughter, in the 1980s.

Chapter 3

- "De kvinnliga journalisternas soaré!" [The female journalists' soiree], *Dagens Nyheter*, February 9, 1911.
- "Kvinnliga journalister" [Female journalist], *Dagens Nyheter*, February 10, 1911.
- Program from the Newswomen's Soiree, February 17, 1911.
- "Filmen som försvann" [The film that disappeared], *Svenska Dagbladet*, January 5, 1960.
- "När pennskaften repetera" [When the newswomen rehearse], *Aftonbladet*, February 1911.
- *Svenska kvinnor från skilda verksamhetsområden: Biografisk uppslagsbok* [*Swedish Women from Different Areas of Activity: Biographical Reference Book*]. Project Runeberg.
- The Publicist Club's portrait roll 1936.
- John Landquist, "Ester Blenda Nordström," *Aftonbladet*, January 13, 1952.
- "Våra kvinnliga journalister i dagspressen" [Our female journalists in the daily press], *Idun*, no. 48 (1916).
- "Gatubelysning i Stockholm" [Street lighting in Stockholm], wikipedia.org.
- Per Anders Fogelström, *Minns du den stad* [*Do You Remember That City*] (Albert Bonniers Förlag, 1964).

- Margareta Berger, *Pennskaft. Kvinnliga journalister under 300 år* [*Penholders. Female Journalists over 300 Years*] (Norstedts, 1977).
- Margareta Stål, "Signaturen Bansai. Ester Blenda Nordström—Pennskaft och reporter i det tidiga 1900-talet" [Bansai the pseudonym. Ester Blenda Nordström—Penholder and reporter in the early twentieth century] (Department of Journalism, Media, and Communication, University of Gothenburg, 2002).
- Interview with Ester Blenda Nordström in *Aftonbladet*, February 16, 1925.
- "Journalistminnen" [Journalist Memories], a series of articles in the magazine *Idun*, 1952.
- Ester Blenda Nordström's private scrapbooks containing signed articles from the years 1911–1914.
- Ellen Rydelius, *Leva randigt* [*Living in Stripes*] (Albert Bonniers Förlag, 1951).
- "Elin Brandell död" [Elin Brandell dead], *Dagens Nyheter*, June 28, 1963.
- Ulla Isaksson and Erik Hjalmar Linder, *Elin Wägner—en biograf* [*Elin Wägner—A Biography*] (Albert Bonniers Förlag, 1977, 1980).
- Elin Wägner, "Från kvinnokongressen i London, bref från Iduns speciella korrespondent" [From the Women's Congress in London, letter from *Idun*'s special correspondent], *Idun*, no. 21 (Sunday, May 23, 1909).
- "Volontär i kvarnhjulshatt med rönnbär: sex pennskafts-damer om Wägnerminnen" [Volunteer wearing wide-brimmed hat with rowan berries: Six newswomen about Wägner memories], *Dagens Nyheter*, November 21, 1951.
- Newspaper clips and commemorative texts about the League, from Agnes Lindhagen's archive, the National Archives.

- *Stockholms Dagblad*'s house and home, Stockholmskällan, film and moving picture.
- "Mordet på d:r Olsson-Seffer" [The murder of Dr. Olsson-Seffer], *Stockholms Dagblad*, May 24, 1911.
- "En intervju med den 13-åriga mästerskytten" [An interview with the thirteen-year-old master shooter], *Stockholms Dagblad*, June 27, 1911.
- "Bär- och fruktpriser i syltningstiden" [Berry and fruit prices in jam-making season], *Stockholms Dagblad*, August 29, 1911.
- John Landquist, *In Youth. Scenes from the Lost Time* (Bonniers, 1957).
- Margareta Stål, *Tre pennskaft i "Ligan." Elisabeth Krey, Célie Brunius och Gerda Marcus* [*Three Penholders in "the League." Elisabeth Krey, Célie Brunius and Gerda Marcus*], Studentlitteratur.
- "Elsa Kinell, Sveriges äldsta fäktare 100 år" [Elsa Kinell, Sweden's oldest fencer, 100 years old], *Fäktning* 6–7, volume 16, 1985.
- "Hem och stat" [Home and state], Selma Lagerlöf's speech at the International Voting Rights Congress in Stockholm, 1911, Project Runeberg.
- Ester Blenda Nordström in a fictional interview, written by herself. *Barnens dagblad*, September 18, 1913.
- Britt Marie Svedberg, "En piga bland pigor" [A maid among maids], *Dagens Nyheter*, August 1, 1971.
- Marianne Enge Swartz, "Ett glödande pennskaft" [A glowing penholder], elinwagner.se.
- Margareta Lundahl, "Ester Blenda Nordström, Ett författarporträtt" [Ester Blenda Nordström, an author portrait]. Special thesis, Borås Library Academy, spring term 1977.
- "Gustaf Hellström som krigskorrespondent: 1,5 mil härifrån står världens största slag!" [Gustaf Hellström as a war

correspondent: the world's greatest battle is one mile from here!], literature magazine *Parnass*, no. 3 (2014).

- Interview with Célie Brunius, member of the League, *Idun*, no. 10 (1952).
- Private family photographs of Ester Blenda Nordström with family and friends.
- Song about suffrage and civil rights for women. Undated. Part of Ester Blenda Nordström's estate, which is owned by relative Pia Hylin.
- "Första fotot i DN: Mannen på den historiska bilden är direktör Axel Manner" [First photo in *Dagens Nyheter*: The man in the historical picture is director Axel Manner], *Dagens Nyheter*, May 27, 2014.
- Information about the admirer Kalle Ahnfeldt taken from letters from Ester Blenda Nordström to Frithiof and Gerda Nordström, sent from Yamahuida in Chile on May 7, 1920. Gift to the manuscript department, the National Library of Sweden.
- Colomba (pseudonym), "Ett hus på Karlavägen" [A house on Karlavägen], article about the Wærn Frisell family's house on Villagatan, *Dagens Nyheter*, publication date unknown.
- Information about Carin Wærn Frisell comes from surviving relatives and an undated letter from Hjalmar Lundbohm to Ester Blenda Nordström in which Carin Frisell is mentioned and described as "careful that one doesn't forget to behave properly."
- "Rallarbusens villa blev polskt centrum" [The railway workers' villa became Polish center], *Metro*, August 29, 1998.
- Letter to director Anna Hylander from Eva Henning with a description of her aunt "Mosse," Carin Dahlbeck, née Wærn Frisell.
- Spex for FKPR by Ester Blenda Nordström. Undated. Part of

Ester Blenda Nordström's estate, owned by Pia Hylin.

- Verse on the Future and Women, by Ester Blenda Nordström. Undated. Part of Ester Blenda Nordström's estate, which is owned by relative Pia Hylin.

- Facts about the Association of Liberal Women taken from liberalakvinnor.se.

- Program sheet from the Publicist Club's annual party at Hasselbacken on March 23, 1912.

- Work certificate for Ester Blenda Nordström for the time she served at *Dagens Nyheter*, dated January 30, 1913, signed by editor Anton Karlgren.

Chapter 4

- "När kvinnan står vid rodret" [When the woman is at the helm], *Svenska Dagbladet*, 1913.

- Claës Lundin, "Nya Stockholm" [New Stockholm], 1890. From the anthology *Klara texter* [*Clear Texts*] (Carlsson, 2006).

- "Klarakvarteren från förr" [Klara of the past]. Slideshow on SvD.se, June 18, 2012.

- "Till hattnålarnas syndaregister" [To the hatpin's sin registry], *Svenska Dagbladet*, January 13, 1913.

- "Ny fart i striden mot hattspjuten behövlig" [New momentum needed in the fight against the hat spear], *Dagens Nyheter*, March 14, 1913.

- Private letters to and from Elin Wägner. Elin Wägner's collection, National Resource Library for Gender Studies, Gothenburg University Library.

- Self-advertisement to attract new subscribers, published in *Svenska Dagbladet*, 1913.

- Margareta Berger, *Pennskaft. Kvinnliga journalister under 300 år* [*Penholders. Female Journalists over 300 Years*] (Norstedts, 1977).
- Ellen Rydelius, *Leva randigt* [*Living in Stripes*] (Albert Bonniers Förlag, 1951).
- Ulla Isaksson and Erik Hjalmar Linder, *Elin Wägner—en biograf* [*Elin Wägner—A Biography*] (Albert Bonniers Förlag, 1977, 1980).
- *Pennskaftens spex* [The *Penholders' Spex*]. Part of Ester Blenda Nordström's estate and owned by relative Pia Hylin.
- Gunilla Lundström, Nordicom, *När tidningarna blev moderna. Om svensk journalistik 1898–1969* [*When Newspapers Became Modern. On Swedish Journalism 1898–1969*] (University of Gothenburg, 2004).
- Åke Jönsson, "Kvinnliga idrottare kämpade länge i motvind" [Female athletes fought uphill for a long time], *Populär Historia*, March 14, 2001.
- "Första dagen. Skarp opinion mot hattnålsdamerna" [The first day. Sharp words for the hatpin ladies], *Svenska Dagbladet*, January 21, 1913.
- About Gustaf Stridsberg, Swedish Biographical Lexicon, sok .riksarkivet.se.
- *Målarmästare Daniel Johan Nordström och hans släkt* [*Master Painter Daniel Johan Nordström and His Family*]. Family chronicle compiled by Kjell Nordström between 1992 and 1995.
- Ester Blenda Nordström, *En piga bland pigor* [*A Maid among Maids*] (Wahlström & Widstrand, 1914).
- Ester Blenda Nordström, *Minns du?* [*Do You Remember?*] gift to Elin Wägner in connection with her fiftieth birthday in 1932, published by the magazine *Bergsluft*.
- "Absinthe," wikipedia.org.

- Margareta Berger, *Pennskaft. Kvinnliga journalister under 300 år* [*Penholders. Female Journalists over 300 Years*] (Norstedts, 1977).

- *Det var en tjusande idyll . . .* [*It Was an Enchanting Utopia . . .*] Gustaf Hellström (Albert Bonnier, 1938).

- Private photographs of Ester Blenda Nordström and Carin Frisell.

- Facts about the Association of Liberal Women taken from liberalakvinnor.se.

- Colomba (pseudonym), "Ett hus på Karlavägen" [A house on Karlavägen], article about the Wærn Frisell family's house on Villagatan, *Dagens Nyheter*, publication date unknown.

- Information about Carin Wærn Frisell from surviving relatives.

- "Rallarbusens villa blev polskt centrum" [The railway workers' villa became Polish center], *Metro*, August 29, 1998.

- "Wærn nr 2326" [Wærn no. 2326], adelsvapen.com.

- "Släkten Wærn" [The Wærn family], gamlagoteborg.se.

- About Erik Frisell in *Nordisk familjebok, Uggleupplagan*, 35 (1923).

- "Erik Frisell," *Hvar 8 dag*, vol. 10 (1908/1909), runeberg.org.

- Facts about Sven Frisell taken from sv.wikipedia.org.

- Facts about Sven Frisell, "Vem är vem? Stor-Stockholm 1962" [Who's who? Greater Stockholm 1962], runeberg.org.

- "Sven Frisell," *Hvar 8 dag*, vol. 10 (1908/1909), runeberg.org.

- Private photographs from Ester Blenda Nordström's estate.

- EB Nordström and Carin Wærn Frisell, verse in rhyme, undated, "Metropolitain: Montparnasse," Paris, 1913.

- "I Agnes Frumeries ateljé" [In Agnes Frumerie's studio], *Svenska Dagbladet*, July 31, 1913.

- "Stockholmskan och parisiskan—en jämförelse som bara kan glädja oss" [The Stockholm woman and the Parisienne—A comparison that could only thrill us], Causerie in *Svenska Dagbladet*, May 30, 1913.

- Interior from Victoria Palace taken from www.victoriapalace .com.
- Letter from Ester Blenda Nordström to Hjördis Tengbom, dated May 29, 1913.
- Letter mentioning Erik's sailor pants, from Ester Blenda Nordström to Frithiof Nordström, June 14, 1936.
- "Bryggarkärran" [The brewery cart], neumuller.org.
- "Aircraft," tekniskamuseet.se.
- "100 år av Sveriges militära flyg" [100 years of Sweden's military aircraft], speech by Amela Rudebark in connection with the celebration of the one hundredth anniversary of Swedish military aviation.

Chapter 5

- Ellen Rydelius, *Leva randigt* [*Living in Stripes*] (Albert Bonniers Förlag, 1951).
- John Landquist, *In Youth. Scenes from the Lost Time* (Bonniers, 1957).
- Letter to Ester Blenda Nordström from John Landquist, dated March 22, 1913. Belongs to Pia Hylin and is included in Ester Blenda Nordström's estate.
- *Målarmästare Daniel Johan Nordström och hans släkt* [*Master Painter Daniel Johan Nordström and His Family*]. Family chronicle compiled by Kjell Nordström between 1992 and 1995.
- "Igår damernas dag vid Åre" [Yesterday was women's day at Åre], *Svenska Dagbladet*, March 8, 1913.
- "Åreveckan som fingo en så tragisk avslutning" [The Åre

Week that had such a tragic end], *Svenska Dagbladet*, March 15, 1913.

- Ulla Isaksson and Erik Hjalmar Linder, *Elin Wägner—en biograf* [*Elin Wägner—A Biography*] (Albert Bonniers Förlag, 1977, 1980).
- Hans Högman, "Uniformer vid landstormen" [Uniforms during the mobilization of militia], algonet.se.
- About John Landquist, sok.riksarkivet.se.
- "Elin Wägner—stadsbud i fredens tjänst" [Elin Wägner— City messenger in service of peace], *Parnass*, no. 3 (2014).
- Florian Illies, *Århundradets sommar* [*Summer of the Century*] (Norstedts, 2013).
- "Bondetåget 1914" [Peasant Armament Support March of 1914], filmarkivet.se.
- Karl-Olof Andersson, "Bondetåget 1914. Kungens tal fällde Staaf" [Peasant Armament Support March of 1914. The king's speech condemned Staaf], *Populär Historia*, January 20, 2014.
- Private family photographs of Ester Blenda Nordström with family and friends.
- *Målarmästare Daniel Johan Nordström och hans släkt* [*Master Painter Daniel Johan Nordström and His Family*]. Family chronicle compiled by Kjell Nordström between 1992 and 1995.
- Rotemännens arkiv [district registrars' archive], Rote 17, booklet 44182, Stockholm City Archives.
- "Febrilt arbete på bondetågets byrå" [Feverish activity at the peasants' office], *Svenska Dagbladet*, January 31, 1914.
- "På kommittébyrån i går" [At the committee's office yesterday], *Svenska Dagbladet*, February 6, 1914.
- "På bondetågsbyrån dagen före uppmarschen" [At the peasants' office the day before the march], *Svenska Dagbladet*, February 4, 1914.

- "Hallänningarna till mötes" [Meeting the people from Halland], *Svenska Dagbladet,* February 4, 1914.
- "Kronprinsen på Slottsbacken" [The crown prince at Slottsbacken], *Svenska Dagbladet,* February 6, 1914.
- Private family photographs of Ester Blenda Nordström with family and friends.
- "Grand Hotel Royal," sv.m.wikipedia.org.
- "Grand Royal väcker allmän beundran" [Grand Royal arouses general admiration], *Svenska Dagbladet,* 1914, date of publication unknown.
- Ellen Rydelius, *Leva randigt [Living in Stripes]* (Albert Bonniers Förlag, 1951).

Chapter 6

- Ulla Isaksson and Erik Hjalmar Linder, *Elin Wägner—en biograf [Elin Wägner—A Biography]* (Albert Bonniers Förlag, 1977, 1980).
- Private letter to Ester Blenda Nordström from John Landquist, dated November 1, 1914.
- Marianne Enge Swartz, "Ett glödande pennskaft" [A glowing penholder], elinwagner.se.
- John Landquist, *In Youth. Scenes from the Lost Time* (Bonniers, 1957).
- Birgitta Holm, "Stora John, lilla Lankan" [Big John, little Lankan], review in *Dagens Nyheter,* October 28, 2009.
- Svante Nordin, "Intellektuell gigant i helfigur" [Intellectual giant in full profile], review in *Svenska Dagbladet,* November 2, 2009.
- Facts about Ludvig Nordström, litteraturbanken.se.
- Britt Marie Svedberg, "En piga bland pigor" [A maid among maids], *Dagens Nyheter,* August 1, 1971.

- "Tiotalets Wallraff nöje för överklassen" [The 1910s Wallraff entertainment for the upper class], *Aftonbladet*, March 12, 1975.
- Maria Sandel, *Virveln* [*The Whirl*] (Ordfront, 1977).
- Anton Holtz, *Ett pennskaft som piga—svar av Bonn i Taninge* [*A Newswoman for a Maid—Response by a Farmer in Taninge*] (Åhlén & Åkerlund, 1915).
- Britt Marie Svedberg, "En piga bland pigor" [A maid among maids], *Dagens Nyheter*, August 1, 1971.
- Ellen Rydelius, *Leva randigt* [*Living in Stripes*] (Albert Bonniers Förlag, 1951).
- Margareta Stål, "Signaturen Bansai. Ester Blenda Nordström—Pennskaft och reporter i det tidiga 1900-talet" [Bansai the pseudonym. Ester Blenda Nordström—Penholder and reporter in the early twentieth century] (Department of Journalism, Media, and Communication, University of Gothenburg, 2002).
- Letter from Ingvar Holtz, son of Anton and Ida Holtz, Jogersta North Farm, 1993. From the autograph collection, manuscript collections at the National Library of Sweden.
- "Ord mot ord" [He said, she said], notice in *Dagens Nyheter*, published June 11, 1915.
- Letter from Ester Blenda Nordström to Ida Holtz, dated July 17, 1914.
- Letter from Ester Blenda Nordström to Sigrid Nilsson, dated July 18, 1914.
- Anna Jörngården, "Sommaren 1914—idyllen före kriget" [The summer of 1914—The idyll before the war], *Under strecket, Svenska Dagbladet*, July 18, 2014.
- Interview with Erik Karlsson, employed at Jogersta North Farm around the years 1910–1914, *Dagens Nyheter*, August 1, 1971.

- John Pohlman, "Våra värmerekord i Norden" [Our heat records in the Nordic countries], martinhedberg.se, September 8, 2009.

- Notice about Anton Holtz's attack book, *Dagens Nyheter*, September 17, 1915.

- Notice about Anton Holtz's attack book, *Stockholms Dagblad*, September 18, 1915.

- "Ett pennskaft som piga—Bonn i Tarringe går illa åt Ester Nordström" [A newswoman for a maid—Farmer in Tarringe (*sic*) mercilessly attacks Ester Nordström], *Dagens Nyheter*, September 14, 1915.

- Article on auction of Jogersta, *Dagens Nyheter*, February 7, 1916.

- Notice of "Bonn i Taninges förtjänster" [Farmer in Taninge's merits], *Dagens Nyheter*, October 18, 1915.

- "En piga bland pigor jubilerar" [A maid among maids celebrates], *Stockholms Dagblad*, November 17, 1915.

- "Bok mot bok" [Book against book], *Dagens Nyheter*, June 11, 1915.

- Anton Holtz, *Ett pennskaft som piga—svar av Bonn i Taninge* [*A Newswoman for a Maid—Response by a Farmer in Taninge*] (Åhlén & Åkerlunds förlag, 1915).

- Ester Blenda Nordström, *En piga bland pigor* [*A Maid among Maids*]. Tenth print run (Åhlén & Åkerlund).

- Letter to Ester Blenda Nordström from her mother, Lotten Nordström, undated.

- "Hjördis Nordin-Tengbom," signaturer.se.

- "Hjördis Tengbom-Nordin," lexikonettamanda.se.

- Ernst Manker, *På Tredje botten. Minnesbilder* [*On the Third Floor, Vivid Memories*] (LT, 1967).

- Göran Brunius in *Komiska konturer tecknade ur minnet* [*Comic Contours Drawn from Memory*] (Norstedts, 1975).

- Notice about Ester Blenda Nordström's application to become a nomadic teacher, *Stockholms-Tidningen*, January 16, 1915.
- Notice in *Dagens Nyheter*, April 16, 1915.
- Personal and address information about Carin Frisell from the Stockholm City Archives.
- Information from Carin Frisell's surviving relatives.
- Private photographs from Ester Blenda Nordström's album.
- Series of photos from a motorcycle picnic with Carin, from Ester Blenda's own private photography collections.
- Letter to Anna Hylander from Eva Henning with a description of her aunt "Mosse," Carin Dahlbeck, née Wærn Frisell, and other information about Carin from surviving relatives.
- "Bryggarkärran" [The brewery cart], neumuller.org.
- "Broderade märken" [Embroidered insignia], silvervingar.se.
- "Aircraft," tekniskamuseet.se.
- Astrid Lindgren, *Samuel August från Sevedstorp och Hanna I Hult* [*Samuel August from Sevedstorp and Hanna in Hult*] (Raben & Sjögren, 2007).
- Private photographs by Carin Dahlbeck, née Wærn Frisell.
- "100 år av Sveriges militära flyg" [100 years of Sweden's military aircraft], speech by Amela Rudebark in connection with the celebration of the one hundredth anniversary of Swedish military aviation.
- Private letter from Ester Blenda Nordström to Hjördis Tengbom, in Lagan, dated January 28, 1915.
- John Landquist, "Ester Blenda Nordström," *Aftonbladet*, January 13, 1952.
- Curt V. Persson, *På disponentens tid. Hjalmar Lundbohm och hans syn på samer och Tornedalingar* [*In the Time of the Manager. Hjalmar Lundbohm and His View of the Sami and Tornedalians*] (Tornedalica, 2013).

- About Hjalmar Lundbohm, sok.riksarkivet.se.
- "Angående Zorn-kvinna" [Regarding the Zorn woman], translation of "Gustafsson med mustacherna" [Gustafsson with the mustaches] (the journalist's chosen pseudonym), *Dagens Nyheter*, December 18, 1974.
- Letter from Karin Högberg to Anna Hylander, Zorn Museum, regarding the painting *Luta*, painted in 1915 by Anders Zorn.
- About Anders Zorn, zornmuseet.se.
- "Dekadensens långa historia. Adorée Villany och svenska moraliteter" [The long history of decadence. Adorée Villany and Swedish moralities], *Axcess magasin*, October 20, 2014.
- Letter from Ester Blenda Nordström to her friend Hjördis Tengbom, dated January 7, 1915.
- Per Wästberg, *Alice och Hjördis, Två systrar, Dagböcker och brev 1885–1964 i urval* [*Alice and Hjördis, Two Sisters, Selected Diaries and Letters 1885–1964*] (Wahlström & Widstrand, 1994).
- About Adorée Villany's visit to Stockholm in 1915, "Naturistens handbok" [The naturist's handbook], naturisten.se.
- Letter to Ester Blenda from Hjalmar Lundbohm, dated April 2, 1917.
- Private letter to Frithiof and Gerda Nordström from Ester Blenda Nordström, Kiruna, dated December 3, 1914.
- "Bansai och Bonn i Taninge" [Bansai and farmer in Taninge], published couplet, *Norlander* revue, undated.
- "Hr Carl Svensson är icke Bonn i Taninge" [Mr. Carl Svensson is no farmer in Taninge]. Debate printed under the heading *Kort och godt*, undated.
- "Banzais julsång. Solo med körer" [Banzai's (*sic*) Christmas carol. Solo with choirs] by Per Skrivare. Performed at

Christmas party, December 23, 1914.
- Letter from John Landquist to Ester Blenda Nordström, dated November 1, 1914.

Chapter 7

- Ester Blenda Nordström, "Bland kyrkfolket vid lappmässan i Juckasjärvi" [Among the church people at the Lapp mass in Juckasjärvi], *Svenska Dagbladet*, December 1914.
- Ester Blenda Nordström, "I pulka öfver öde snövidder" [In a sled across deserted snowfields], *Svenska Dagbladet*, December 24, 1914.
- Ester Blenda Nordström, "Kring den sprakande riselden i kåtan" [Around the crackling fire in the goahti], *Svenska Dagbladet*, December 1914.
- Ester Blenda Nordström, "En äfventyrlig hemfärd i pulka" [An adventurous journey home in a sled], *Svenska Dagbladet*, January 12, 1915.
- Private letter from Ester Blenda Nordström to Hjördis Tengbom, from Kiruna, dated March 27, 1913.
- Article about Ester Blenda's application to become a nomadic teacher in Lapland, *Stockholms-Tidningen*.
- "Samiska ärr" [Sami scars], *Vi*, March 2017.
- Maja Hagerman, *Käraste Herman. Rasbiologen Herman Lundborgs gåta* [*Dearest Herman. The Race Biologist Herman Lundborg's Riddle*] (Norstedts, 2015).
- Facts about Herman B. Lundborg from sok.riksarkivet.se, sv.wikipedia.org.
- Per Wirtén, "Raskrigaren som levde ett dubbelliv" [The race warrior who lived a double life], *Expressen*, October 7, 2015.
- Articles about Ester Blenda's application to become a

nomadic teacher in Lapland, *Dagens Nyheter*, April 16 and
August 25 (no year specified).

- Curt V. Persson, *På disponentens tid. Hjalmar Lundbohm
  och hans syn på samer och Tornedalingar* [*In the Time of the
  Manager. Hjalmar Lundbohm and His View of the Sami and
  Tornedalians*] (Tornedalica, 2013).

- Otto von Friesen, "I andras kläder . . . Ester Blenda var
  1910-talets Wallraff" [In other people's clothes . . . Ester
  Blenda was the Wallraff of the 1910s], *Journalisten*, no. 17
  (July 4–15, 1982).

- Private letter from Ester Blenda Nordström to Gerda
  Nordström, dated December 3, 1914.

- "Till nomadlivet som lappkateket—Bansai styr åter kosan
  mot norden" [To the nomadic life as a Lapp catechist—
  Bansai turns northward again], *Svenska Dagbladet*, February
  27, 1915.

- Private letter from Ester Blenda Nordström to Hjördis
  Tengbom, dated January 28, 1915.

- Private letter from Ester Blenda Nordström to Frithiof and
  Gerda Nordström, Kiruna, dated on April 8, 1915.

- John Landquist, *In Youth. Scenes from the Lost Time*
  (Bonniers, 1957).

- Margareta Stål, "Signaturen Bansai. Ester Blenda
  Nordström—Pennskaft och reporter i det tidiga 1900-
  talet" [Bansai the pseudonym. Ester Blenda Nordström—
  Penholder and reporter in the early twentieth century]
  (Department of Journalism, Media, and Communication,
  University of Gothenburg, 2002).

- Ester Blenda Nordström's private photo albums from her
  time in Lapland, 1915–1916, one of which belongs to the
  National Archives' collections. The rest are part of her estate

and belong to Pia Hylin.

- Ester Blenda Nordström, *Kåtornas folk* [*Tent Folk of the Far North*] (New edition published by Bakhåll, 2013).

Chapter 8

- Ester Blenda Nordström, *Kåtornas folk* [*Tent Folk of the Far North*] (New edition published by Bakhåll, 2013).
- Margareta Stål, "Signaturen Bansai. Ester Blenda Nordström—Pennskaft och reporter i det tidiga 1900-talet" [Bansai the pseudonym. Ester Blenda Nordström—Penholder and reporter in the early twentieth century] (Department of Journalism, Media, and Communication, University of Gothenburg, 2002).
- Maja Hagerman, *Käraste Herman. Rasbiologen Herman Lundborgs gåta* [*Dearest Herman. The Race Biologist Herman Lundborg's Riddle*] (Norstedts, 2015).
- Sara Ranta-Rönnlund, *Nådevalpar. Berättelser om nomader och nybyggare I norr* [*Grace Puppies. Stories about Nomads and Settlers in the North*] (Askild & Kärnekull, 1971).
- John Landquist, *In Youth. Scenes from the Lost Time* (Bonniers, 1957).
- Ester Blenda Nordström's private photo albums from her time in Lapland, 1915–1916, one of which belongs to the National Archives' collections. The rest are part of her estate and belong to Pia Hylin.
- About Hjalmar Lundbohm, sok.riksarkivet.se.
- Private letter from Ester Blenda Nordström to Hjördis Tengbom, dated June 8, 1915.
- Private letter from Ester Blenda Nordström to Hjördis Tengbom, dated July 20, 1915.

- Ester Blenda Nordström's private photographs from an excursion to Puoltsa with Carin Wærn Frisell, Hjalmar Lundbohm, Prince Eugen, and Baron Leuhusen.
- Facts about Puoltsa, Kiruna municipality, lansstyrelsen.se /norrbotten.
- Private photographs of Ester Blenda Nordström and Carin Dahlbeck (formerly Wærn Frisell) during the years 1914–1948.
- "Prinsens 'värdelösa' konst visas" [The prince's 'useless' art is exhibited], *Svenska Dagbladet*, August 24, 2007.
- Ester Blenda Nordström, *Minns du?* [*Do You Remember?*], gift to Elin Wägner in connection with her fiftieth birthday in 1932, published by the magazine *Bergsluft*.
- Letter from John Landquist to Ester Blenda Nordström, dated August 7, 1915.
- Private letter from Ester Blenda Nordström to Frithiof Nordström, dated August 23, 1915.
- Private letter from Hjalmar Lundbohm to Ester Blenda Nordström, dated May 26, 1915.
- Private letter from Hjalmar Lundbohm to Ester Blenda Nordström, dated August 7, 1915.
- *Målarmästare Daniel Johan Nordström och hans släkt* [*Master Painter Daniel Johan Nordström and His Family*]. Family chronicle compiled by Kjell Nordström between 1992 and 1995.
- Curt V. Persson, *På disponentens tid. Hjalmar Lundbohm och hans syn på samer och Tornedalingar* [*In the Time of the Manager. Hjalmar Lundbohm and His View of the Sami and Tornedalians*] (Tornedalica, 2013).
- Per Wirtén, "Raskrigaren som levde ett dubbelliv" [The race warrior who lived a double life], *Expressen*, October 7, 2015.

- Letter from Hjalmar Lundbohm to Ester Blenda Nordström, dated December 15, 1915. Belongs to Mikael Sandberg.
- "Samerna och religionen" [The Sami and religion], samer.se.
- Birgitta Rubin, "Katarina Pirak Sikku: Det väckte en oerhörd sorg" [Katarina Pirak Sikku: It caused immense grief], *Dagens Nyheter*, February 8, 2015.
- Anna Kågström, "Min mormor och rasbiologerna" [My grandmother and the race biologists], *Vi*, no. 1 (2016).
- "'Samer utmålas som obildade och barnsliga'—debattören: Obegripligt att kritiserad bok ges ut igen" ["Sami people are portrayed as uneducated and childish"—The debater: The republishing of a criticized book is incomprehensible], debate article in *Aftonbladet*, January 9, 2014.
- Ester Blenda Nordström's period of illness and bloodletting is described in a private letter from Ester Blenda Nordström to Frithiof Nordström, dated August 23, 1915.
- Private letter from Ester Blenda Nordström to Gerda Nordström, dated December 8, 1915.

Chapter 9

- Per Wästberg, *Alice och Hjördis, Två systrar, Dagböcker och brev 1885–1964 i urval* [*Alice and Hjördis, Two Sisters, Selected Diaries and Letters 1885–1964*] (Wahlström & Widstrand, 1994).
- Ellen Rydelius, *Leva randigt* [*Living in Stripes*] (Albert Bonniers Förlag, 1951).
- Ulla Isaksson and Erik Hjalmar Linder, *Elin Wägner—en biograf* [*Elin Wägner—A Biography*] (Albert Bonniers Förlag, 1977, 1980).

- Texts and articles about the League from Agnes Lindhagen's collection, the National Archives.
- Personal and address information about Carin Frisell from Stockholm City Archives.
- Facts about Anders Zorn from zorn.se.
- *Målarmästare Daniel Johan Nordström och hans släkt* [*Master Painter Daniel Johan Nordström and His Family*]. Family chronicle compiled by Kjell Nordström between 1992 and 1995.
- Private photos from Ester Blenda Nordström's estate.
- Personal and address information about Carin Frisell from Stockholm City Archives.
- Information from Carin Frisell's surviving relatives.
- Private photographs from Ester Blenda Nordström's album.
- Letter to Anna Hylander from Eva Henning with a description of her aunt "Mosse," Carin Dahlbeck née Wærn Frisell, and other information about Carin from surviving relatives.
- Curt V. Persson, *På disponentens tid. Hjalmar Lundbohm och hans syn på samer och Tornedalingar* [*In the Time of the Manager. Hjalmar Lundbohm and His View of the Sami and Tornedalians*] (Tornedalica, 2013).
- Private letter from Hjalmar Lundbohm to Ester Blenda Nordström, dated December 28, 1915.
- Private letter from Hjalmar Lundbohm to Ester Blenda Nordström, dated January 8, 2016.
- Private letter from Ester Blenda Nordström to Gerda Nordström, dated January 15, 1916.
- Private letter to Gerda Nordström from Ester Blenda Nordström, dated February 4, 1916.
- Private letter from Ester Blenda Nordström to Frithiof Nordström, dated February 17, 1916.
- Birthday greetings from Carin Wærn Frisell Dahlbeck to

various members of the Nordström family.
- Ester Blenda Nordström's own photographs from her time in Bäcka.
- Margareta Stål, "Signaturen Bansai. Ester Blenda Nordström—Pennskaft och reporter i det tidiga 1900-talet" [Bansai the pseudonym. Ester Blenda Nordström—Penholder and reporter in the early twentieth century] (Department of Journalism, Media, and Communication, University of Gothenburg, 2002).
- Private letter from Ingvar Holtz to Carl Olof Josephson, dated September 25, 1993. Belongs to the manuscript collections of the National Library of Sweden.
- Author's interview with Anton and Ida Holtz's grandchildren Sören Holtz, Åsa Magnusson, and Linda Holtz, January 12, 2016.
- Article about auction in Jogersta North Farm, *Dagens Nyheter*, February 7, 1916.
- Marianne Enge Swartz, "Elin Wägner—stadsbud i fredens tjänst" [Elin Wägner—City messenger in service of peace], *Parnass*, no. 3 (2014).
- Håkan Arenius, "Kvinnorna som tog strid för freden" [The women who fought for peace], www.dagen.se.
- Letter from Elin Wägner to Ellen "Murre" Landquist, dated July 7, 1916.
- Letter from Elin Wägner to Ellen "Murre" Landquist, dated July 20, 1916.
- Letter from Ester Blenda Nordström to Ellen "Murre" Landquist, dated July 22, 1916.
- Letter from Ester Blenda Nordström to the Nordström siblings, dated July 24, 1916.
- John Landquist, *In Youth. Scenes from the Lost Time* (Bonniers, 1957).

- Ester Blenda Nordström's own photographs from the sum-
  mer in Bön, both in her estate and in letters preserved at the
  National Library of Sweden.
- Ester Blenda Nordström, *Kåtornas folk* [*Tent Folk of the Far
  North*] (New edition published by Bakhåll, 2013).
- Letter from Ester Blenda Nordström to Hjalmar Lundbohm,
  dated July 5, 2016.
- Letter from Ester Blenda Nordström to the Nordström sib-
  lings, dated July 24, 1916.
- Letter from Lotten Nordström to Ester Blenda Nordström,
  dated August 15,1916.
- Private letter from Hjalmar Lundbohm to Ester Blenda
  Nordström, dated August 21, 1916.
- Private letter from Ester Blenda Nordström to Gerda
  Nordström, dated August 24, 1916.
- Private letter from Ester Blenda Nordström to Frithiof
  Nordström, dated August 28, 1916.
- Letter from Hjalmar Lundbohm to Ester Blenda Nordström,
  dated September 21, 1916.
- Private letter from Hjalmar Lundbohm to Ester Blenda
  Nordström, dated January 8, 1916.
- Private letter from Hjalmar Lundbohm to Ester Blenda
  Nordström, dated August 5, 1917.
- "'Samer utmålas som obildade och barnsliga'—debattören:
  Obegripligt att kritiserad bok ges ut igen" ["Sami people are
  portrayed as uneducated and childish"—The debater: The
  republishing of a criticized book is incomprehensible], debate
  article in *Aftonbladet*, January 9, 2014.
- Valdemar Lindholm and Karin Stenberg, *Dat läh mijen situd:
  En vädjan till Svenska Nationen från samefolket* [*It Is Our Will:
  An Appeal to the Swedish Nation from the Sami People*] (AB

Svenska Förlaget, 1920).

- Private letter from Hjalmar Lundbohm to Ester Blenda
  Nordström, dated March 29, 1917.

- Private letter from Hjalmar Lundbohm to Ester Blenda
  Nordström, dated April 2, 2017.

- Private letter from Hjalmar Lundbohm to Ester Blenda
  Nordström, dated May 5, 1917.

- Private letter from Hjalmar Lundbohm to Ester Blenda
  Nordström, illegible date, 1918.

- Private letter from Hjalmar Lundbohm to Ester Blenda
  Nordström, Norrbotten, illegible date, 1918.

- "Våra kvinnliga journalister i dagspressen" [Our female journalists in the daily press], *Idun*, no. 48 (1916).

- "*Svarta Katten* (cinema)," *wikipedia.org*.

- "Debut på Svarta Katten" [Debut at *Svarta Katten*], *Svenska
  Dagbladet*, December 20, 1916.

- Curt V. Persson, *På disponentens tid. Hjalmar Lundbohm
  och hans syn på samer och Tornedalingar* [*In the Time of the
  Manager. Hjalmar Lundbohm and His View of the Sami and
  Tornedalians*] (Tornedalica, 2013).

Chapter 10

- Article on Bansai being accepted as an extra student at
  Ultuna Agricultural Institute, *Dagens Nyheter*, October 19,
  1917.

- Certificate of summer internship at Adelswärd Barony,
  Åtvidaberg, issued September 3, 1917.

- "Sveriges roll under första världskriget—ett neutralt men
  påverkat land" [Sweden's role during the First World War—A

neutral but affected country], *Dagens Nyheter*, June 2014.

- "Hungersnöd och kravaller tema: första världskriget" [Famine and riots, theme: World War I], www.stockholmskallan.se.

- *Målarmästare Daniel Johan Nordström och hans släkt* [*Master Painter Daniel Johan Nordström and His Family*]. Family chronicle compiled by Kjell Nordström between 1992 and 1995.

- Letter from Hjalmar Lundbohm to Ester Blenda Nordström, dated January 21, 1918. Belongs to Mikael Sandberg.

- "Kaffehistoria" [History of coffee], hasseandersson .dinstudio.se.

- "Ransoneringen—när maten inte räcker" [Rationing—When the food is not enough], www.stockholmskallan.se.

- "Kålodling i Karlaplans blomsterrabatter under första världskriget" [Cabbage cultivation in Karlaplan's flower beds during the First World War], www.stockholmskallan.se.

- Bengt Lindroth, "Finska inbördeskriget: Ett nedtystat trauma" [Finnish Civil War: A suppressed trauma], Fokus.se, no. 3 (2008).

- Herman Lindquist, "Röda mot vita dödade 40 000" [Reds against Whites killed 40,000], *Aftonbladet*, January 8, 2012.

- "Finska inbördeskriget" [The Finnish Civil War], ne.se.

- "Finland's independence," wikipedia.org.

- John Landquist, *In Youth. Scenes from the Lost Time* (Bonniers, 1957).

- Letter from Hjalmar Lundbohm to Ester Blenda Nordström, dated January 21, 1918.

- Curt V. Persson, *På disponentens tid. Hjalmar Lundbohm och hans syn på samer och Tornedalingar* [*In the Time of the Manager. Hjalmar Lundbohm and His View of the Sami and Tornedalians*] (Tornedalica, 2013).

- Letter from Ester Blenda Nordström to Gerda and Frithiof

Nordström, dated June 30, 1917.

- "Bjarne Stenquist: De vita tog svart hämnd på de röda" [Bjarne Stenquist: The Whites took dark revenge on the Reds], *Under strecket, Svenska Dagbladet*, January 26, 2008.
- Private letter to Ester Blenda Nordström from Hjalmar Lundbohm, dated January 26, 1918.
- Visa for travel to Övertorneå for "investigation regarding the food shortage in Finnish Lapland, from March 3, 1918, to June 1, 1918." Issued to Ester Blenda Nordström on behalf of the government of Finland, March 3, 1918.
- Letter from Frithiof Nordström to Ester Blenda Nordström, dated March 19, 1918.
- Letter from Ester Blenda Nordström to Frithiof Nordström, dated March 15, 1918.
- Report to national archivist Sam Clason, sent by Ester Blenda Nordström in connection with the completed mission in Finnish Kolari, dated May 4, 1918.
- "Kyrkklätt har fallit i de rödas våld" [Those dressed for church have fallen into the hands of the Reds], *Svenska Dagbladet*, March 2, 1918.
- "Banan söder om Vilppula sprängd av de vita" [Railway track south of Vilppula blown up by the Whites], *Svenska Dagbladet*, March 3, 1918.
- "De rödas våldsdåd fortsättas" [The Reds continue their acts of violence], *Svenska Dagbladet*, March 3, 1918.
- "Björneborg intaget av skyddskårerna" [Björneborg seized by the protection corps], *Svenska Dagbladet*, March 5, 1918.
- "Alla partier i Finland mot en medling" [All parties in Finland against a mediation], *Svenska Dagbladet*, March 5, 1918.
- "Det röda skräckväldet i Helsingfors kulminerar—blott en liten del av alla ohyggligheter hittills kända i Sverige" [The

Red Terror in Helsinki culminates—Merely a fraction of all
the horrors hitherto known in Sweden], *Svenska Dagbladet*,
March 6, 1918.

- "Hungernöden i Finland. Förvärrad genom bristande organ-
  isation och disciplin" [The famine in Finland. Exacerbated
  by lack of organization and discipline], *Svenska Dagbladet*,
  March 7, 1918.
- "5 000 ton livsmedel från England" [Five thousand tons of
  food from England], *Svenska Dagbladet*, March 7, 1918.
- "Hjälpen till Finlandsflyktingarna" [Aid to the Finnish refu-
  gees], *Svenska Dagbladet*, March 10, 1918.
- "Svenskar!" [Swedes!], appeal urging Swedes to participate in
  battles in the Finnish Civil War. *Svenska Dagbladet*, March 11,
  1918.
- Telegram from Ester Blenda Nordström to Elin Wägner on
  March 9, sent from Pajala.
- Elin Wägner, "Ha vi inte en kaka bröd åt Finland?" [Don't
  we have a loaf of bread for Finland?], reader's letter/debate
  article, *Svenska Dagbladet*, March 11, 1918.
- "Hjälp till det svältande Kolari" [Help for the starving
  Kolari], *Svenska Dagbladet*, March 12, 1918.
- "Finland och hjälporganisationerna—Nödhjälpskommitténs
  bistånd önskat och välbehövligt" [Finland and the aid
  organizations—Famine Relief Committee assistance wanted
  and much needed], *Svenska Dagbladet*, March 14, 1918.
- Ester Blenda Nordström, "Svensk hjälp till det hungrande
  Nordfinland! Kolariborna vänta ängsligt på hjälp från Sverige
  för att ej dö hungersdöden" [Swedish help to the hungry
  Northern Finland! The people of Kolari anxiously wait for
  help from Sweden so as not to die of starvation], *Svenska
  Dagbladet*, March 15, 1918.

- "En vädjan från Finska legationen" [An appeal from the Finnish legation], *Svenska Dagbladet*, March 15, 1918.
- Ester Blenda Nordström, "Den första hjälpen till Kolari. Två tusen kilogram mat mottagna med rörande tacksamhet" [First aid to Kolari. Four thousand pounds of food received with touching amount of gratitude], *Svenska Dagbladet*, March 25, 1918.
- Letter from Ester Blenda Nordström to Frithiof Nordström, dated March 28, 1918.
- Poem written by Frithiof Nordström to Ester Blenda Nordström in connection with fell walking in Lapland in 1918 during a skiing holiday in Torne Marsh, Pajala, along with René Malaise.
- Ester Blenda Nordström's diary entry from fell walking in Lapland with Carin Wærn Frisell, July 1918.
- Facts about Hurtigruten, sv.wikipedia.org.
- Autobiographical manuscript written by Ester Blenda Nordström, manuscript collections, National Library of Sweden.
- Letter from Ester Blenda Nordström to Gerda Nordström, dated February 1, 1920.
- "Rösiö startade landets största skola i Vätterbygden" [Rösiö started the country's biggest school in Vätterbygden], jnytt.se, April 13, 2013.
- "Jordbrukets apostel i Jönköping" [The apostle of agriculture in Jönköping], jmini.se, April 27, 2015.
- Facts about Per J. Rösiö, sok.riksarkivet.se.
- "Första världskriget i bilder" [First World War in pictures], varldenshistoria.se.
- "Första världskriget i bilder" [First World War in pictures], ne.se.

- Private letter from Ester Blenda Nordström to Frithiof and Gerda Nordström, dated November 21, 1918. Manuscript collections, the National Library of Sweden.
- Private letter from Ester Blenda Nordström to Gerda Nordström, dated November 30, 1918. Manuscript collections, the National Library of Sweden.
- Private letter from Ester Blenda Nordström to John Landquist, dated December 1, 1918.
- Private letter from Ester Blenda Nordström to Gerda Nordström, dated February 7, 1919. Manuscript collections, the National Library of Sweden.
- Ester Blenda Nordström, *En rackarunge* [*A Little Rascal*] (Wahlström & Widstrand, 1919).
- Private letter from Agda Nordström to Frithiof Nordström, spring 1919.
- "Svensk upptäcktsfärd till Kamtschatka" [Swedish voyage of discovery to Kamchatka], *Svenska Dagbladet*, February 23, 1919.
- Private letter from Ester Blenda Nordström to Frithiof Nordström, dated February 24, 1919.
- Fredrik Sjöberg, *Flugfällan* [*The Fly Trap*] (Bokförlaget Nya Doxa, 2004).
- Evert Taube about Klarakvarteren, *Klara texter* [*Clear Texts*], compiled by Jenny Westerström (Carlsson, 2006).
- Edvard Matz, "Med Taube på Pampas" [With Taube on the Pampas], *Populär Historia*, March 16, 2001.
- Biography of Evert Taube, www.taubesallskapet.se.
- About Evert Taube, wikipedia.com.
- Card with handwritten invitation to dinner, from Ester Blenda Nordström to Evert Taube, undated.
- Private letter from Ester Blenda Nordström to Evert Taube,

dated January 5, 1920. From Evert Taube's collection, manuscript collections, Gothenburg University Library.

- Carin Wærn Frisell and Ester Blenda Nordström's shared journal from a motorcycle holiday in the summer of 1919. Included in Ester Blenda Nordström's estate.

- Eva Wahlström, "Fria flickor före Pippi—Ester Blenda Nordström och Karin Michaëlis: Astrid Lindgrens föregångare" [Free girls before Pippi—Ester Blenda Nordström and Karin Michaëlis: Astrid Lindgren's predecessors], dissertation for a doctorate in philosophy in the Department of Literature, History of Ideas and Religion, University of Gothenburg (Makadam, 2011).

- Private photographs of Ester Blenda Nordström with family and friends. From Ester Blenda Nordström's estate.

- Letter from Ester Blenda Nordström to Frithiof Nordström regarding butterfly catching, among other things, dated August 23, 1915.

- Letter from Ester Blenda Nordström to Gerda and Frithiof Nordström, dated June 25, 1919, belonging to the relative Mikael Sandberg.

- Ulla Isaksson and Erik Hjalmar Linder, *Elin Wägner—en biograf* [*Elin Wägner—A Biography*] (Albert Bonniers Förlag, 1977, 1980).

- "MS *Balboa*," faktaomfartyg.se.

- Letter from Ester Blenda Nordström to Gerda Nordström, dated February 1, 1920. Gift to the manuscript collections of the National Library of Sweden.

- Letter from Ester Blenda Nordström to Frithiof and Gerda Nordström, dated April 15, 1921. Gift to the manuscript collections at the National Library of Sweden.

- Two postcards from the port of Hamburg, from Ester

Blenda Nordström to Evert Taube, dated January 28, 1920.
From Evert Taube's collection, manuscript collections at
Gothenburg University Library.

- Private letter from Hjalmar Lundbohm to Ester Blenda
  Nordström, dated January 4, 1920. Belongs to Mikael
  Sandberg.
- Private letter from Hjalmar Lundbohm, addressed to "Ester
  Blenda Nordström, South American expedition SS *Balboa*,"
  dated January 26, 1920.
- "Homosexualitet blir lagligt i Sverige. Om normer och makt
  1944" [Homosexuality becomes legal in Sweden. On norms
  and power 1944], levandehistoria.se.

Chapter 11

- Ester Blenda Nordström's private photographs from the jour-
  ney with MS *Balboa* and the time spent in South America.
  Part of her estate and belonging to Pia Hylin.
- "MS *Balboa*," faktaomfartyg.se.
- Letter from Ester Blenda Nordström to Gerda Nordström,
  dated February 1, 1920.
- Bris (pseudonym of unknown journalist), "Se Sydamerika
  och skriva om Sverige. En avskedsintervju av signaturen
  Bris med Ester Blenda Nordström" [See South America and
  write about Sweden. A farewell interview of Ester Blenda
  Nordström, by Bris], *Svenska Dagbladet*, January 18, 1920.
- Ester Blenda Nordström, "En piga bland pigor hos senioritor
  och caballeros" [A maid among maids with señoritas and
  caballeros], travel letter/article, *Svenska Dagbladet*, May 30,
  1920.
- Mixed clips from Brazilian newspapers about visit to

the country by "the journalist and author Ester Blenda Nordström." Included in Ester Blenda Nordström's estate.

- Ester Blenda Nordström, "Över Cordilleras på åsnerygg. En riskfylld, men härlig färd utmed gamla Inkas stigar" [Over Cordilleras on donkey back. A risky but wonderful journey along the old Inca paths], travel letter/article, *Svenska Dagbladet*, July 11, 1920.

- Verbally shared information about Ester Blenda Nordström's time in South America from relative Staffan Nordström, and to Otto von Friesen, author of the book *Tio reportage som förändrade världen* [*Ten Reports That Changed the World*] (Ordfront).

- Letter from Ester Blenda Nordström to Frithiof and Gerda Nordström, dated March 15, 1920. Included in her estate and belonging to Pia Hylin.

- Travel permit for Ester Blenda Nordström issued by the governor of Mendoza and visa from the Chilean legation. Included in the estate.

- Letter and drawings from Ester Blenda Nordström to Frithiof and Gerda Nordström, dated April 21, 1920. Part of the estate and belonging to Pia Hylin.

- Letter from Ester Blenda Nordström to Frithiof and Gerda Nordström, dated May 7, 1920. Gift to the manuscript collections at the National Library of Sweden.

- "Vidare över Cordilleras. Hur man blir förplägnad i en argentinsk bondgård" [Onward across the Cordilleras. How to be nourished on an Argentine farm], travel letter/article, *Svenska Dagbladet*, July 18, 1920.

- "Värre än vilda västern. Bansais fortsatta färd på åsnerygg över Cordilleras" [Worse than the Wild West. Bansai's continued journey on donkey back across the Cordilleras], travel letter/article, *Svenska Dagbladet*, August 29, 1920.

- About the Mendoza district, pampastravel.se.
- Information about the letter from A. R. Hvoslef to Ester Blenda Nordström, dated July 23, 1920, taken from a list of documents on Ester Blenda Nordström's estate belonging to Pia Hylin.
- "Skygga gäster" [Shy guests], article about Ester Blenda Nordström's pets from South America. *Vecko-Journalen*, February 6, 1921.
- Letter of thanks from Anders Zorn to Hildur and Ester Blenda Nordström in connection with his sixtieth birthday in 1920. Included in Ester Blenda Nordström's estate and belonging to Pia Hylin.
- Letter of thanks from Emma Zorn to Hildur and Ester Blenda Nordström in connection with Anders Zorn's death in 1920. Included in Ester Blenda Nordström's estate and belonging to Pia Hylin.
- Verbally shared information about annual Christmas celebrations at the home of Frithiof and Gerda Nordström, from their grandson Mikael Sandberg.
- Letter from Ester Blenda Nordström to Frithiof and Gerda Nordström, dated December 26, 1920. Gift to the manuscript collections at the National Library of Sweden.
- Letter from Ester Blenda Nordström to Gerda Nordström, dated February 9, 1921. Gift to the manuscript collections at the National Library of Sweden.
- Letter from Ester Blenda Nordström to Gerda and Frithiof Nordström, dated April 15, 1921. Gift to the manuscript collections at the National Library of Sweden.
- Ester Blenda Nordström. *15 år. Några blad ur en rackarunges liv* [*15 Years—A Few Pages from the Life of a Little Rascal*] (Bonnier's junior series, 1951).
- Eva Wahlström, "Fria flickor före Pippi—Ester Blenda

Nordström och Karin Michaëlis: Astrid Lindgrens föregångare" [Free girls before Pippi—Ester Blenda Nordström and Karin Michaëlis: Astrid Lindgren's predecessors], dissertation for a doctorate in philosophy in the Department of Literature, History of Ideas and Religion, University of Gothenburg (Makadam, 2011).
- John Landquist, *In Youth. Scenes from the Lost Time* (Bonniers, 1957).

Chapter 12

- Ester Blenda Nordström, *Amerikanskt* [*American*] (Åhlén & Åkerlund, 1923).
- Information on fees for travel items from America taken from the afterword by Anna Hylander for the new edition of Ester Blenda Nordström's book *Amerikanskt* [*American*] (Bakhåll, 2015).
- Ester Blenda Nordström's inspection card for travel on SS *Hellig Olav*, May 18, 1922.
- Ester Blenda Nordström's own photographs from the trip to America and her time there. Part of the estate owned by Pia Hylin.
- Byron J. Nordström, "Svenskarna i Amerika" [The Swedes in America], *Populär Historia*, July 5, 2010.
- "Emigrantråd" [Emigrant advice], kb.se.
- Ester Blenda Nordström's private photographs from the trip to America in 1922. Included in her estate and belonging to Pia Hylin.
- Johan Deurell, "F. Scott & Zelda Fitzgerald, 20-talets hetaste par" [F. Scott & Zelda Fitzgerald, the hottest couple of the 20s], *Populär Historia*, no. 5 (2013).

- Private letter from Ester Blenda Nordström to Alma Hedin, dated August 8, 1922.

- "Julförfattare rånad i juli" [Christmas writer robbed in July], *Dagens Nyheter*, July 10, 1922.

- Katrin Andersson and Christina Ekeblad, "Högsommardagar i Sverige 1917–2003" [High summer days in Sweden 1917–2003], Department of Earth Sciences, University of Gothenburg, essay from 2004.

- Facts about Fredrik Andersson and the film *En rackarunge* [*A Little Rascal*], Swedish Film Database, sfi.se.

- Information about Ester Blenda Nordström's weapon comes from relative Staffan Nordström.

- Agreement between Ester Blenda Nordström and the film director Fredrik Andersson regarding the film adaptation of the book *En rackarunge* [*A Little Rascal*]. Dated August 28, 1922. Part of Ester Blenda Nordström's estate, belonging to Pia Hylin.

- Facts about Elsa Wallin. Swedish Film Database, sfi.se, www.wikipedia.org.

- "Elinor Glyn—den modemedvetna urmodern till dagens skildringar av sex och snusk" [Elinor Glyn—The fashionable mother of today's depictions of sex and filth], sr.se.

- Facts about Elinor Glyn, wikipedia.org.

- Ester Blenda Nordström, "En svensk platsbyrå i Chicago" [A Swedish job agency in Chicago], *Vecko-Journalen*, no. 26 (1923).

- Ester Blenda Nordström, America articles from issues 1, 8, 10, 15, and 19 of *Vecko-Journalen*, 1923.

- "Swedish American Line (1915–1975)," ellisisland.se.

- Ester Blenda Nordström, *En piga bland pigor* [*A Maid among Maids*] (Wahlström & Widstrand, 1914).

- Photographs with accompanying envelopes from Ester

Blenda Nordström and Carin Wærn Frisell's trip to Storlien in 1923. Included in the estate owned by Pia Hylin.

- Private letter from Ester Blenda Nordström to Frithiof Nordström, dated February 10, 1923. Belongs to Mikael Sandberg.
- Biography and facts about Albert Engström, albertengstrom .se and wikipedia.org.
- Drinks list after night of partying with Albert Engström, May 6, 1923. Included in Ester Blenda Nordström's estate and belongs to Pia Hylin.
- The party episode at the home of Frithiof and Gerda Nordström retold to author Otto von Friesen, author of the book *Tio reportage som förändrade världen* [*Ten Reports That Changed the World*] (Ordfront). Reproduced by Birgitta Nordström, daughter of Frithiof and Gerda, who was present when Ester Blenda Nordström dropped the tray on the floor.
- Private letter from Agda Nordström to Gerda Nordström, dated summer of 1923. Belongs to Mikael Sandberg.
- Article in unknown newspaper with photograph depicting Ester Blenda Nordström lying under a car. From Bonniers Photo Archive. Dated 1923.
- *Målarmästare Daniel Johan Nordström och hans släkt* [*Master Painter Daniel Johan Nordström and His Family*]. Family chronicle compiled by Kjell Nordström between 1992 and 1995.
- Private family photos of Ester Blenda Nordström with family & friends.
- "Björnjakt i Sibirien" [Bear hunting in Siberia], jakt-resor.se.
- Letter from Lotten Nordström to Ester Blenda Nordström, dated July 10, 1924. Included in Ester Blenda Nordström's estate and belonging to Pia Hylin.
- John Landquist, *In Youth. Scenes from the Lost Time* (Bonniers, 1957).

Chapter 13

- Self-advertisement, *Vecko-Journalen*, no. 51 (Sunday, December 21, 1924).

- "J. P. Åhlén: Grundaren av Åhléns" [J. P. Åhlén: The founder of Åhléns], Handelnshistoria.se.

- Ester Blenda Nordström's own photographs from her trip in Asia and time in Siberia. Partly from the estate owned by Pia Hylin. Several Kamchatka photographs are owned by relative Mikael Sandberg.

- Information about the countries Ester Blenda Nordström and Carin Wærn Frisell visited before the trip to Japan comes from Anna Hylander, director of the film *Ester Blenda*.

- Ester Blenda Nordström, "Byn som sopades bort" [The village that was swept away], report in *Vecko-Journalen*, no. 28 (1925).

- "Taifun och kackerlackor—ett Kamtchtkabrev från Ester Blenda Nordström" [Typhoon and cockroaches—A Kamchatka letter from Ester Blenda Nordström], report in *Vecko-Journalen*, no. 35 (1926).

- Private letter from Ester Blenda Nordström to Gerda Nordström, dated July 19, 1925.

- Letter from René Malaise to Frithiof Nordström, dated September 8, 1925. Belongs to Mikael Sandberg.

- Ester Blenda Nordström's own diary from Kamchatka, 1925–27. Part of the estate and owned by Pia Hylin.

- "Åter en falubo till Kamtschatka" [Another Falu resident to Kamtschatka], *Falu Courier*, April 1924.

- Tomas Hoffman, "Den nya Kamtjschatkaexpeditionen" [The new Kamchatka expedition], August 11, 2014, samlingar .varldskulturmuseerna.se.

- Fredrik Sjöberg, *Flugfällan* [*The Fly Trap*] (Bokförlaget Nya Doxa, 2012).
- Ester Blenda Nordström, *Byn i vulkanens skugga* [*The Village in the Shadow of the Volcano*] (Albert Bonniers Förlag, 1930).
- "Sven Hedin's travels and expeditions," sv.m.wikipedia.org.
- Poem by Ester Blenda Nordström, Klyuchi, dated October 23, 1925.
- Letter from Elin Wägner to Ester Blenda Nordström, dated September 2, 1925.
- Ulla Isaksson and Erik Hjalmar Linder, *Elin Wägner—en biograf* [*Elin Wägner—A Biography*] (Albert Bonniers Förlag, 1977, 1980).
- "Homosexualitet blir lagligt i Sverige. Om normer och makt 1944." [Homosexuality becomes legal in Sweden. On norms and power 1944], levandehistoria.se.
- "Hjalmar Lundbohm," sv.m.wikipedia.org.
- Information from Yvonne Malaise, niece of René Malaise, provided to director Anna Hylander.
- Letter from Elin Wägner to Ester Blenda Nordström in Kamchatka, undated. From the National Resource Library for Gender Studies at the University of Gothenburg.
- Letter from Elin Wägner to Ester Blenda Nordström, dated September 2, 1925. From the National Resource Library for Gender Studies at Gothenburg University Library.
- Letter from Elin Wägner to Ester Blenda Nordström, dated November 10, 1925. From the National Resource Library for Gender Studies at Gothenburg University Library.
- Colomba (pseudonym), "Ett hus på Karlavägen" [A house on Karlavägen], article about the Wærn Frisell family's house on Villagatan, *Dagens Nyheter*, publication date unknown.
- Speech about Gustaf Hellström by Kurt Mälarstedt, Jolo's garden, June 10, 2014.

- Facts about Gustaf Hellström, gustafhellstrom.se.
- Johan Svedjedal, "Det var ingen tjusande idyll. Gustaf Hellström och hans tid" [It was no enchanting idyll. Gustaf Hellström and the times he lived in], review in *Dagens Nyheter*, November 2, 2009.
- Private letter from Ester Blenda Nordström to Frithiof Nordström, October 22, 1926.
- Private letter from Elin Wägner to Ester Blenda Nordström, dated December 11, 1926.

Chapter 14

- Information about the Nordström family, family documents lent by Mikael Sandberg.
- *Målarmästare Daniel Johan Nordström och hans släkt* [*Master Painter Daniel Johan Nordström and His Family*]. Family chronicle compiled by Kjell Nordström between 1992 and 1995.
- Private letter from Ester Blenda Nordström to Frithiof Nordström, dated October 22, 1926. Belongs to Mikael Sandberg.
- Private letter from René Malaise to Frithiof Nordström, dated October 22, 1926.
- Ester Blenda Nordström, *Byn i vulkanens skugga* [*The Village in the Shadow of the Volcano*] (Albert Bonniers Förlag, 1930).
- Cover with a picture of Ester Blenda Nordström's arrival back in Sweden, *Vecko-Journalen*, no. 31 (1927).
- Ester Blenda Nordström's diary from Kamchatka, included in the estate and belonging to Pia Hylin.
- Afterword written by Anna Hylander in a new edition of the book *Byn i vulkanens skugga* [*The Village in the Shadow of the Volcano*] (Bakhåll, 2016).

- "Ester Blenda hemma igen" [Ester Blenda at home again], *Vecko-Journalen*, no. 31 (1927).
- Fredrik Sjöberg, *Flugfällan* [*The Fly Trap*] (Bokförlaget Nya Doxa, 2012).
- Private letter from Agda Nordström to Frithiof Nordström about the sale of Bjursnäs, dated December 1, 1928.
- "Middagarna med morbror Gustaf" [The dinners with uncle Gustaf]; *Kristianstadsbladet*, February 22, 2005.
- Carina Burman, "Hellströms klassresa kom för sent" [Hellström's class trip came too late], *Under strecket, Svenska Dagbladet*, November 2, 2009.
- "Det var ingen tjusande idyll. Gustaf Hellström och hans tid" [It was no enchanting idyll. Gustaf Hellström and the times he lived in], review in *Dagens Nyheter*, November 2, 2009.
- Letter to director Anna Hylander from Eva Henning with a description of her aunt "Mosse," Carin Dahlbeck née Wærn Frisell, and her marriage to Gustaf Hellström.
- Information about Gustaf Hellström's environs and literary environments, www.gustafhellström.se.
- Facts about Sven Frisell, sv.wikipedia.org.
- Facts about Sven Frisell, "Vem är vem? Stor-Stockholm 1962" [Who's who? Greater Stockholm 1962], runeberg.org.
- Portrait of Sven Frisell, *Hvar 8 dag*, vol. 10 (1908/1909), runeberg.org.
- Ester Blenda Nordström, "Mitt livs boxningsmatch" [The boxing match of my life], *Vecko-Journalen*, no. 39 (1927).
- Ester Blenda Nordström, "Ester Blenda köper julklappar" [Ester Blenda buys Christmas presents], *Vecko-Journalen*, no. 51 (1927).
- "En piga bland pigor skrev ej själv genmälet" [A maid among maids did not write the retort herself], interview with Ester Blenda Nordström, *Aftonbladet*, February 16, 1925.

- The manorial court's ruling on divorce between René Malaise and Ester Blenda Nordström, Södra Roslags domsaga, December 30, 1929.
- Signed EB, review of the book *Byn I vulkanens skugga* [*The Village in the Shadow of the Volcano*], *Dagens Nyheter*, December 15, 1930.
- Ester Blenda Nordström's summarized medical record from Karolinska Hospital, undated.
- Seraphim Hospital, Journal 447, December 1928.
- Private letter from Hildur Nordström to Gerda Nordström, dated Epiphany Day 1929.
- "En piga bland pigor återfunnen" [A maid among maids found], report in *Vecko-Journalen*, no. 15 (1931).
- Ester Blenda Nordström's private photographs from the time at Bjursnäs farm, Björnlunda.
- Inventory of Ester Blenda Nordström's belongings, written in July 1938, prior to moving out of Bjursnäs.
- Letter from Ester Blenda Nordström to the author and lawyer Henning von Melsted, dated July 7, 1931.
- Letter from Ester Blenda Nordström to the author and lawyer Henning von Melsted, dated July 12, 1931.
- Letter from Frithiof Nordström to Professor H. C. Jacobeaus, regarding alcohol and opium abuse, dated January 11, 1936. Belongs to the Swedish National Archives.
- "Opium som medicin" [Opium as medicine], opium.nu.
- Letter from Frithiof Nordström to John Landquist, dated November 2, 1948. From the manuscript collections of the National Library of Sweden.
- Letter from Frithiof Nordström to John Landquist, dated January 17, 1952. From the manuscript collections of the National Library of Sweden.
- Letter from Ester Blenda Nordström to Frithiof Nordström,

dated February 21, 1930. Belongs to Mikael Sandberg.

- Letter from Gunilla Nordström to Gerda Nordström, dated May 6, 1930. Belongs to Mikael Sandberg, son of Gunilla Nordström.
- Letter from Ester Blenda Nordström to the Nordström siblings, dated December 29, 1930.
- Handwritten love letter/poem by Ester Blenda Nordström, dated October 20, 1930.
- "Flickböcker" [Girls' books], a review by the writer Gurli Linder of new and recently published girls' books, *Dagens Nyheter*, December 10, 1931.
- "Rackarungen igen" [The little rascal again], review of Ester Blenda Nordström's book *Patron förlovar sig* [*Patron Gets Engaged*], *Dagens Nyheter*, December 11, 1933.
- Notice about republishing of Ester Blenda Nordström's book *En rackarunge* [*A Little Rascal*], *Dagens Nyheter*, November 22, 1950.
- Eva Wahlström, "Fria flickor före Pippi—Ester Blenda Nordström och Karin Michaëlis: Astrid Lindgrens föregångare" [Free girls before Pippi—Ester Blenda Nordström and Karin Michaëlis: Astrid Lindgren's predecessors], dissertation for a doctorate in philosophy in the Department of Literature, History of Ideas and Religion, University of Gothenburg (Makadam, 2011).
- Ester Blenda Nordström, *15 år. Några blad ur en rackarunges liv* [*15 Years—A Few Pages from the Life of a Little Rascal*] (Bonnier's junior series, 1951).
- *Patron förlovar sig* [*Patron Gets Engaged*]. (Wahlström & Widstrand, 1933).
- Various letters between family members in the Nordström family, in the years 1927–1948. Belong to Gerda and Frithiof's grandson Mikael Sandberg.

- "Lindgrens dialog med litteraturen ingen nyhet" [Nothing new about Lindgren's dialogue with literature], about Eva Wahlström's dissertation "Free girls before Pippi," *Under strecket, Svenska Dagbladet,* July 3, 2011.
- "Bergsluft" [Mountain air], tribute for Elin Wägner's fiftieth birthday on May 16, 1932.
- Ellen Rydelius, *Leva randigt* [*Living in Stripes*] (Albert Bonniers Förlag, 1951).
- Private letter from Ester Blenda Nordström to Anne-Marie Nordström, dated February 28, 1933. Belongs to Mikael Sandberg.
- Private letter from Ester Blenda Nordström to Gerda Nordström, dated April 10, 1934.
- Private letter from Ester Blenda Nordström to Gerda Nordström, dated May 13, 1934.
- Mixed reviews of *Patron Gets Engaged* by Ester Blenda Nordström (Wahlström & Widstrand, 1933).
- Private letter from Ester Blenda Nordström to Gerda Nordström, dated September 20, 1934.
- Reply from Dr. Selma Lagerlöf regarding Ester Blenda Nordström's appeal to the Swedish Academy for financial assistance, dated January 25, 1936. Included in Ester Blenda Nordström's estate and owned by Pia Hylin.
- Information from the current owner of Bjursnäs, Björnlunda, Gunnar Eliasson.
- Private letter from Ester Blenda Nordström to her "precious siblings," dated December 29, 1930.
- Private letter from Ester Blenda Nordström to Gerda Nordström, dated October 30, 1934.
- Private letter from Ester Blenda Nordström to Gerda Nordström, dated December 3, 1934.

- Letter from Ester Blenda Nordström to Gerda and Frithiof Nordström, dated April 2, 1936.

Chapter 15

- Ester Blenda Nordström's summarized medical record from Karolinska Hospital, 1937.
- Private letter from Birgitta Nordström to Frithiof and Gerda Nordström, dated April 1, 1937.
- Undated letter and poem about the time after the stroke from Ester Blenda Nordström to Frithiof and Gerda Nordström.
- Private letter from Ester Blenda Nordström to Frithiof Nordström, dated February 1, 1937.
- Letter from Ester Blenda Nordström to Frithiof Nordström, dated August 25, 1947.
- Letter from Ester Blenda Nordström to Frithiof Nordström, dated April 17, 1937. Belongs to Mikael Sandberg, grandson of Frithiof.
- Letter from Ester Blenda Nordström to Gerda Nordström, dated August 4, 1937.
- Private letter from Carin Hellström to Gerda Nordström, dated September 26, 1937.
- Ester Blenda Nordström's petition to the Stockholm City Hall Court to be declared incompetent.
- Letter from Ester Blenda Nordström to Frithiof and Gerda Nordström, dated July 20, 1939.
- Ria Wägner about Ester Blenda Nordström in the program *Historia att minnas* [*History to Remember*], aired on P1, September 8, 1995.
- Facts about Stiftelsen Isaac Hirschs minne [Isaac Hirsch

Memorial Foundation], sihm.se.

- Information about Carin Frisell, including personal information and address cards, from the Stockholm City Archives, the Rotemannen [district registrar] database, and the National Archives in Gothenburg.

- Colomba (pseudonym), "Ett hus på Karlavägen" [A house on Karlavägen], article about the Wærn Frisell family's house on Villagatan, *Dagens Nyheter*, publication date unknown.

- Information about Carin Wærn Frisell in old age comes from relatives.

- Letter from Stockholms Enskilda Bank to Ester Blenda Nordström, regarding promissory note, June 12, 1936.

- Letter from Ester Blenda Nordström to Frithiof Nordström, Utö, dated June 14, 1936.

- Letter from Carin Hellström to Frithiof Nordström, dated January 6, 1944.

- Letter from Ester Blenda Nordström to Frithiof Nordström, dated March 18, 1947.

- Letter from Ester Blenda Nordström to Frithiof Nordström, dated November 9, 1947.

- Letter from Ester Blenda Nordström to Frithiof Nordström, dated November 15, 1947.

- Letter from Ester Blenda Nordström to Frithiof Nordström, dated November 12, 1947.

- Letter from Ester Blenda Nordström to Frithiof Nordström, dated December 16, 1947.

- Letter from Ester Blenda Nordström to Frithiof Nordström, undated 1947.

- Letter from Ester Blenda Nordström to Frithiof Nordström, dated February 26, 1948.

- Collections of letters belonging to relatives of Ester Blenda Nordström.

- Sketch list of equipment, Vikingagatan 34 E. Probably compiled by Frithiof or Gerda Nordström, 1948.
- About Gustaf Hellström, sok.riksarkivet.se.
- Letter from Ester Blenda Nordström to Gerda and Frithiof Nordström, dated March 10, 1941.
- Svenskaakademien.se.
- Facts about Evert Taube from taubevannerna.org.
- "Tog avstånd från såväl nazism som kommunism" [Distanced self from both Nazism and Communism], elinwagner.blogspot .com, published November 5, 2006.
- Ulf Boëthius, "Pippi var ett vanartigt barn av sin tid" [Pippi was a deranged child of her time], *Under strecket, Svenska Dagbladet*, December 8, 2007.
- List of Gustaf Hellström's books, gustafhellstrom.se.
- Facts about Frithiof Nordström from, among others, wikipedia.org.
- Facts about Barbro Alving, from www.ub.gu.se/kvinn /portaler/fred/biografier/alving.xml.
- Kamchatka—Nordic Philately, www.filateli.se.
- Facts about the Holocaust and death marches from www .levandehistoria.se/fak-ta-om-forintelsen/forintelsen /koncentrationslager.
- "Abe och Putin vill avsluta kriget" [Abe and Putin want to end the war], *Aftonbladet*, September 3, 2016.
- "Stängda gränser och okända marker" [Closed borders and unknown grounds], samer.se.
- "Samiskt krigsmonument dröjer" [Sami war monument still awaiting], sverigesradio.se, September 20, 2015.
- "Ett socialdemokratiskt dilemma—Från hembiträdesfrågan till pigdebatt" [A social democratic dilemma—From the house help issue to the maid debate]. Text by Lisa Öberg

in the anthology *Kvinnor mot kvinnor: Om systerskapets svårigheter* [*Women against Women: On the Difficulties of Sisterhood*] (Norstedts Förlag, 1999).

- Memories of Ester Blenda Nordström in old age, retold by relatives.
- Otto von Friesen, Christer Hellmark, and Jan Stolpe, ed. *Tio reportage som förändrade världen–från Strindberg till Hemingway* [*Ten Reports That Changed the World—From Strindberg to Hemingway*] (Ordfront, 1982).
- "*Adjö, farväl! För sista gång*" [Adieu, Goodbye! For the Last Time]. Sailor shanty published in *August Bondeson's Songbook*, 1909. Unknown author.

Photos

Unless otherwise noted below, all images are courtesy of Pia Hylin's collection.

Chapter 1: Milkmaid photographs (both) courtesy Ester Blenda Nordström's photo album/The National Archives Sweden. Chapter 2: Ester as a child images courtesy Mikael Sandberg's collection. Chapter 3: John Landquist and Elin Wägner by photographer Axel Malmström (1872–1945)/Stockholm City Museum; Carin Wærn Frisell photograph courtesy Carin Wærn Frisell's relatives. Chapter 6: Covers (both) courtesy Bonnierförlagen. Chapter 11: Ester's portrait of Carin courtesy Mikael Sandberg's collection. Chapter 13: Ester and Carin in Korea and Malaise couple in Siberia (both) courtesy Mikael Sandberg's collection.

More about Ester Blenda

- Otto von Friesen, Christer Hellmark, and Jan Stolpe, ed. *Tio reportage som förändrade världen–från Strindberg till Hemingway* [*Ten Reports That Changed the World—From Strindberg to Hemingway*] (Ordfront, 1982).
- Margareta Stål, "Signaturen Bansai. Ester Blenda Nordström—Pennskaft och reporter i det tidiga 1900-talet" [Bansai the pseudonym. Ester Blenda Nordström—Penholder and reporter in the early twentieth century] (Department of Journalism, Media, and Communication, University of Gothenburg, 2002).
- Eva Wahlström, "Fria flickor före Pippi—Ester Blenda Nordström och Karin Michaëlis: Astrid Lindgrens föregångare" [Free girls before Pippi—Ester Blenda Nordström and Karin Michaëlis: Astrid Lindgren's predecessors], dissertation for a doctorate in philosophy in the Department of Literature, History of Ideas and Religion, University of Gothenburg (Makadam, 2011).
- *Ett djefla solsken* [*A Goddamn Ray of Sunshine*]. A play by Yvonne Gröning with a premiere at Tornedalsteatern 2015. Directed by Markus Forsberg. Starring Lisa Hennix Raukola and Gun Olofsson.
- *Ester Blenda*. A film by Anna Hylander with voices by, among others, Rakel Wärmländer and Sara Sommerfeld. Premiered 2016 with screenings at festivals, cinemas and on SVT.

ABOUT THE AUTHOR

Photo © Helén Karlsson

Fatima Bremmer is a Swedish journalist and author. In 2017, *Life in Every Breath* was awarded the August Prize. Upon the book's success in Sweden, she curated a follow-up exhibition on Nordström at Skarhults Castle in Skåne. She is currently working on a new biography.

ABOUT THE TRANSLATOR

Gloria Nneoma Onwuneme is Nigerian born and was raised in Scandinavia. She is a freelance translator of Swedish, Danish, and German; a United Kingdom–trained medical doctor; and a bit of a bookworm. She currently lives and works in London.

21982320519477